PROSE OF THE WORLD

Prose of the World

Denis Diderot and the Periphery of Enlightenment

HANS ULRICH GUMBRECHT

STANFORD UNIVERSITY PRESS
Stanford, California

STANFORD UNIVERSITY PRESS
Stanford, California

Printed in the United States of America on acid-free, archival-quality paper

Library of Congress Cataloging-in-Publication Data
Names: Gumbrecht, Hans Ulrich, author.
Title: Prose of the world : Denis Diderot and the periphery of Enlightenment /
    Hans Ulrich Gumbrecht.
Other titles: Prosa der Welt. English
Description: Stanford, California : Stanford University Press, 2021. |
    Originally published in German in 2020 under the title "Prosa der Welt":
    Denis Diderot und die Peripherie der Aufklärung. |
    Includes bibliographical references.
Identifiers: LCCN 2020038191 (print) | LCCN 2020038192 (ebook) |
    ISBN 9781503615250 (cloth) | ISBN 9781503627864 (epub)
Subjects: LCSH: Diderot, Denis, 1713-1784—Criticism and interpretation. |
    Enlightenment—France. | France—Intellectual life—18th century.
Classification: LCC PQ1979 .G86 2021 (print) | LCC PQ1979 (ebook) |
    DDC 848/.509—dc23
LC record available at https://lccn.loc.gov/2020038191
LC ebook record available at https://lccn.loc.gov/2020038192

Cover design: Rob Ehle

Cover art: *Denis Diderot*, Louis-Michel van Loo, 1767. Oil on canvas, via
Wikimedia Commons.

Typeset by Kevin Barrett Kane in 10/14.4 Minion Pro

Karl Heinz Bohrer gewidmet:
für wen sonst hätte ich nochmal ein Buch
mit Fußnoten geschrieben?

Contents

Enthusiasms and Two Diderot Questions

1967 HAS NEVER BECOME an emblematic year but its affective and intellectual climate sure felt incubational. Something major seemed on the horizon, we impatiently anticipated it becoming a "Revolution," and my generation then needed quite some time to admit that "May 1968 in Paris" had not really been one. Of course I joined the SDS (the German Socialist Students' Association) on the morning of the very same mid-October day (I don't remember the exact date) on the afternoon of which I enrolled for my first semester at the University of Munich. "German Literature" and "Romance Literatures" (in that order) were the two subject matters, curricula, departments that I chose, with much less conviction and enthusiasm for "literature" than I pretended. My father, with the ultimate mindset of a true surgeon, had convinced me that there was no place in medicine for the psychiatry I was dreaming of as a profession and, on the other hand, doing Romance literatures (which in those German years meant French literature with appendixes in Italian and Spanish) gave me the vague illusion of continuing to live in Paris, where I had spent part of my final year of secondary education at Lycée Henri IV, without any notion of the grand tradition that this name carried. What I knew and felt about my studies at the very beginning was quite vague, especially compared to the form that the SDS had me sign in order to confirm that, quite literally, I believed in

Marxism as "the only Scientific and True Worldview." And things turned really disappointing for me that fall. In all those many courses on "leftist" topics, I can say today, enthusiasm and inspiration stayed on the horizon, never to become present, whereas those classes that pretended to be politically neutral (almost a dying genre then) only recycled the same worn-out concepts of praise without contours that I was sufficiently familiar with from my Gymnasium. The one surprising exception was an introductory seminar on "Diderot's Aesthetic Writings," taught by Dr. Ursula Schick, that I took along with three or four other students and that I had probably chosen because, on my way to school every day in Paris, I had regularly walked by the Diderot statue on Boulevard Saint-Germain and liked the smile on the greenish-shimmering metal face of the eighteenth-century author. In January 1968, I gave an in-class presentation on "Eloge de Richardson," Diderot's heavily enthusiastic praise for the contemporary English novelist, and although its tone struck me as "typically bourgeois," as I critically stated, Denis Diderot had begun to grow on me. I could not have said why it happened, but Diderot must have been the one reason why, after my first semester, I ended up not changing from literature to law, as I had thought I should for all practical and spiritual purposes—and even made "Romance Literatures" my primary area of studies, instead of "German Literature." Ever since then, through fifty intellectual and altogether happy professional years, as I have progressively and self-deprecatingly left behind the ideals of the SDS, Diderot and his prose have been with me, in a sympathy that is both profound and peripheral, both unconditional and arbitrary. When about a decade ago, all of a sudden and in a tone that sounded like an order, my friend Karl Heinz Bohrer said that he expected at least one more serious academic (*wissenschaftliches*) book from me, instead of so much essay writing, I immediately knew that it had to be about Diderot, more precisely about the unknown reasons for that profound and yet peripheral sympathy. This was the first Diderot question I ever had. Soon it became clear that I shared an uncertainty about the grounds of my enthusiasm with the greatest (and also with some not so great) Diderot scholars. For Diderot's prose awakens sympathy in many readers—and yet seems to escape all attempts at a comprehensive description. Several times the problem had me on the verge of giving up on a book that I did not need and that nobody (except Bohrer) particularly wanted me to write. At one

such moment of hesitancy, the famous pianist Alfred Brendel, during a joint
fellowship in Berlin, remarked in passing and in public that I reminded him
of Diderot. This was too much, of course, but I also—and not only silently—
registered that Brendel had made explicit what I had not even dared to dream
over so many years. My subsequent embarrassment and pride turned into
the impulse for a second Diderot question, the question of whether my own
more-than-fifty-year-old sense of affinity with him had not just become one
intense case of his much wider—and growing—attraction for intellectuals
in the twenty-first century.

PROSE OF THE WORLD

1 | "ON FAIT DE MOI CE QU'ON VEUT"

A Happy Day in Diderot's Life

DENIS DIDEROT MAY HAVE BEEN precocious in some regards, as a student during his adolescence, for example, or, seen from our historical retrospective, in some of his ways of thinking and writing—but it seems that he never was rushed. The flow of time and the promises of the future did not distract him from the many objects, problems, and persons that he found interesting. Thus he appeared active, prolific, and generous to his contemporaries, and was hardly concerned with shaping the events and conditions of his life into thresholds or clearly circumscribed situations.

When exactly he left his native Langres in Champagne, a town of several thousand people where Diderot's father was a well-to-do master cutler and his uncle belonged to the higher clergy—on what date he departed from the provincial world of his upbringing, about which he continued to care without ambiguities, in order to continue his studies in Paris—is not clear. It must have happened in 1728 or 1729, when Diderot was fifteen or sixteen years old, and for the following decade and a half we only know about the names of some academic institutions, about frequent changes in intellectual interest and existential orientation that were wearing on his father's patience and, once the financial support from Langres had ceased for that reason, about multiple activities geared towards making ends meet, in a rhythm of life that his biographers have somehow anachronistically called "bohemian." In 1743 and without the legally required permission of his family that he had seriously tried to obtain, Denis Diderot secretly married the embroidery maker Anne-Toinette Champion, who was three years older than him, without fortune, of modest social status, firmly religious and, according to several sources, very beautiful. Angélique, their only surviving and much beloved daughter, was born in 1753, to a forty-three-year-old mother and a forty-year-old father. Her parents would end up living together for more than four decades, unhappily most of the time but without any visible separation or distance.

It was only around 1750, when he was already beyond the middle of an average lifetime for the eighteenth century, that Diderot began to establish himself in the intellectual world of Paris, as a source of energy and as an appealing presence within an emerging new form of sociability, rather than as a spiritual authority. Early on, the state censorship system had identified him as "*un garçon très dangereux*," and in 1749 he was held prisoner in the Fortress of Vincennes for three and a half months. The first volume of the *Encylopédie ou dictionnaire raisonné des arts, des sciences, et des métiers*, the all-embracing enterprise whose editor Diderot had become in 1747, together with the mathematician Jean le Rond d'Alembert, appeared three years later and found immediate resonance in Europe and even in North America; meanwhile, among his own writings, a treatise on epistemological problems in epistolary form, the 1749 *Lettre sur les aveugles*, was the reason for his imprisonment and stirred the most intense discussions.

During those years, Diderot became acquainted with some of the most renowned and influential figures in the Enlightenment circles of Paris, such as Voltaire and Rousseau, but also Friedrich Melchior, Baron de Grimm, and Paul-Henri Thiry, Baron d'Holbach, two wealthy immigrants from Germany, who were both ten years younger than him and provided, in multiple ways, the material framework for those conversations and encounters that were the fabric of an atmosphere in which he began to excel. It must have been in this context that Diderot first met, sometime after 1755, Louise-Henriette Volland, whom he would call "Sophie" and to whom he remained devoted until 1784, the year in which they both died, with a serenity and tenderness that he had found neither with his wife nor with Madeleine de Puisieux, a contentious writer and philosopher whose passionate lover he became in 1745. Sophie was the unmarried daughter of a respectable bourgeois family and almost forty years old when her relationship with Diderot began. She lived with her widowed mother and, during long stretches of time, also with her married sister, of whom Diderot was often jealous. The well-read Sophie shared her friend's intellectual inclinations; she must have been of precarious health and she wore glasses and had, as Diderot once mentioned in a letter, "dry hands." No portrait of Sophie has come down to us, nor any of the letters that she wrote to her friend. And yet she becomes a lively presence for us in the hundred eighty-seven (out of probably more than five hundred) letters to her from Diderot that have been preserved. More than a diary in epistolary form, they are best described as the trace of Diderot's lasting wish to share with Sophie the immediacy and the lively experience of his daily life, in all of its social, intellectual, and even sensual complexities. Whether an erotic relationship was part of their love we do not know for certain, but it is likely that soon the desire of Sophie Volland and Denis Diderot found its most appropriate and enjoyable form in the writing and reading of those letters, and even in just impatiently waiting for them—for although they did not keep their relationship strictly secret, and the Vollands' apartment in Paris was close to d'Holbach's mansion where Diderot spent much of his time, the opportunities for them to have time together in each other's physical presence were quite scarce. When Sophie Volland died in 1784, five months before Denis Diderot, she left him a ring and an edition of Montaigne's letters, bound in red Moroccan leather.

Diderot spent much of the summer of 1760 far from Sophie Volland, as was typical for them, at La Chevrette, on the periphery of Paris, in a castle owned by Louise d'Epinay, the wealthy and cultivated lover of Baron Grimm. A foreigner in Paris, Grimm had made a name for himself and gained a fortune since 1753 by editing the *Correspondance Littéraire*, a regular collection of reports, in epistolary form, about new publications, debates, theater plays, and exhibits in the French capital; the small number of European aristocrats who subscribed to the hand-copied newsletter included Catherine the Great of Russia, Leopold II, the Holy Roman Emperor, and Gustav III of Sweden. During Grimm's mostly business-driven travels, Madame d'Epinay secured the continuity of the *Correspondance*, while Diderot was also a regular contributor who depended on this activity as a source of income and yet does not seem to have cared much about his own financial interest.

Stays at La Chevrette and sometimes at Grandval, d'Holbach's estate, had thus become a stable part of Diderot's existence, which otherwise alternated in downtown Paris between a family apartment occupied with his wife and daughter and a working space rented for him as the editor of the *Encyclopédie*, so that he was able to frequent several salons, above all those of Grimm and d'Holbach. The letters that he wrote to Sophie Volland and many of his fellow "philosophes,"[1] often nervous about the precarious status of their delivery, covered several dimensions of Diderot's intellectual sociability. Besides rare visits to Langres, this man whose interests had quite literally no limits left behind the narrow spatial range of his life only once, when, by invitation of the Russian empress and after years of hesitation, he traveled to Saint Petersburg in June of 1773, returning to Paris in the fall of the following year.

Compared to that of friends like Voltaire, Rousseau, or Grimm, the horizon of Diderot's life was indeed particularly restrained but, as the even more extreme case of Immanuel Kant suggests, this probably did not appear unusual, let alone incompatible with the role of an intellectual in his time. What distinguished Diderot from Kant, by contrast, was the lack of a rigorous working schedule, which is truly astonishing given the number of texts he wrote and, even more so, given the truly heroic achievement of finishing by 1772, singlehandedly since the departure of d'Alembert in 1758, the entire seventeen-volume of the *Encyclopédie*, complete with eleven volumes of illustrations. Diderot's distinctive strength, a paradoxical strength as it depended on a disposition often criticized as detrimental to any kind of success, may have consisted in an openness to the world so radical that it constantly implied the risk of getting lost in details that fascinated him, together with a truly unusual intensity in his reactions to all kinds of experiences and perceptions ("enthusiasm" was the word for such intensity in the language of the eighteenth century). Instead of turning into a unique strength, his intersection of openness and intensity could well have become a problem for a life less restrained in its spatial dimension.

Although Diderot's friends and admirers were always eager to have him as a lively presence in their circles, he did not think of himself as a socialite but believed himself to be naturally shy. Thus, as he wrote to Sophie Volland on Monday, September 15, 1760, from Madame d'Epinay's castle at La Chevrette,[2] he had decided to return to Paris for the weekend because

Sunday was the holiday of the village and he feared the usual crowd, composed of young peasant women decked out for the celebration and made-up ladies from Paris who were attracted by the supposed naiveté of the event: "I dislike crowds. I had decided to go into Paris for the day [. . .]. It was a motley crowd of young country girls all neatly dressed up and fine city ladies with rouge and beauty spots, reed canes in their hands, straw hats on their heads, and their squires on their arms."[3] But when Grimm and Madame d'Epinay saw him leave and expressed their disappointment, they were easily able to persuade Diderot to stay because, as he complained, he was simply unable to bear the feeling of having caused any sadness to his friends: "but Grimm and Madame d'Epinay wouldn't let me go. When I see my friends with sad looks and long faces, my reluctance gives way and they can do what they want with me."[4]

In a way, then, that mid-September Sunday of 1760 could not have begun any worse for Denis Diderot, the self-declared pushover. But instead of reacting with resentment or ill humor, he forgot both his original intention and his own disappointment as soon as he turned to focus on the group of people assembled in the castle: "We were all at that time in the gloomy and magnificent drawing room; at our various occupations, we made a very pretty picture" (55).[5] Even in the casual context of a letter to Sophie, Diderot's language is precise and does not shy away, in its precision, from apparently insignificant details or the contradictions that they seem to produce. He perceived the mood of the space where Madame d'Epinay, Melchior Grimm, and their guests were concentrated on their "different occupations" as both "magnificent" and "gloomy," and although the different groups made up a "very pretty picture," he depicted each of their interactions in its singularity, like a series of sketches drawn with simple and strong contours. The first of these drawings in Diderot's prose shows the hosts being portrayed by two artists:

> By the window which looks on to the gardens, Grimm was being painted and Madame d'Epinay was leaning on the back of the painter's chair.
>
> Someone was sitting on a stool lower down and drawing her profile in pencil. It is a charming profile. Any woman would be tempted to see if it is a good likeness. (55)[6]

While Madame d'Epinay contemplates Grimm being portrayed, she herself becomes the model for a drawing, at which Diderot, also present in the scene, is looking. What fascinates him about this is not, as a twenty-first-century reader may be inclined to imagine, the cascades of self-reflection but the complex form of a group of figures seen as if they were a sculpture (the "tableau très-agréable"). And then Diderot, both as a protagonist of the scene and as its observer, reacts to the drawing of Madame d'Epinay with intensity (*"il est charmant, ce profil"*) and lets himself get derailed by an association with the potential jealousy of other women who might find the portrait of the hostess all too flattering.

The next of the prose images, all of which are separated into different paragraphs, shows Monsieur de Saint-Lambert, an officer and poet, omnipresent in the upper-class circles of his time, reading "the most recent brochure which," as Diderot adds, now turning to Sophie Volland, "I had also sent to you" (could he be referring to the latest installment of the *Correspondance*?). Diderot himself is playing chess with Madame d'Houdetot, Saint-Lambert's mistress, who had become notorious, three years before, due to a strong attraction that she and Jean-Jacques Rousseau had felt for each other.[7] Five more scenes follow: Madame d'Epinay's mother with her grandchildren and their tutors; two sisters of the artist painting Grimm who are working on their embroidery; a third sister of the painter playing a piece by the Italian composer Scarlatti on the harpsichord; Monsieur de Villeneuve, a friend of Madame d'Epinay's, complimenting her and beginning a conversation with Diderot; and Monsieur de Villeneuve and Madame d'Houdetot recognizing each other, along with a comment about Diderot's intuition that there is no sympathy lost between them. The specific tone and grace of his prose emerges from an overlap between three different discursive levels: the compact, sometimes even aphoristic precision of the descriptions; the intensity of Diderot's reactions, associations, and intuitions while he both belongs to each scene evoked and watches it from outside; and the transitions from his concentrated openness towards the world that surrounds him to those moments in which he turns to Sophie Volland in his desire to let her participate.

How his openness to the world can turn into an opening towards Sophie becomes particularly clear when later on Diderot talks about the Sunday dinner:

Dinner time came, Madame d'Epinay was in the middle of the table on one side and Monsieur de Villeneuve on the other. They did all the honours and very agreeably too. We dined magnificently, gaily, and lengthily. Then there were ices. Oh my dears, what ices! You should have been there to taste them, you who like good ices. (55)[8]

Coming from Italy, recipes for ice cream had progressively conquered the royal and aristocratic cuisines of Europe since early modernity and were turning into a more popular gastronomic preference during the eighteenth century. Obviously aware that Sophie, together with her mother and sister, shared this taste, Diderot once again passes from the description of a social scene to his own sensual reaction, which then triggers the desire to let the three women be part of the perception. His concentration on a sensuous moment thus becomes generosity and a gesture of closeness.

The next step in Diderot's evocation of this increasingly enjoyable Sunday that so departed from his negative expectations has again to do with perception but then focuses on "grace" as a modality of aesthetic experience and as a concept that had already come up in his letter several times. After dinner, Emilie, a fifteen-year-old girl whom Diderot had apparently already mentioned to Sophie, plays the harpsichord and impresses the entire company: "The girl I mentioned, who has such a light and skilful touch on the harpsichord, astonished us all. The others were surprised by her unusual talent and I by the charms of her youth, her sweet manners, her modesty, her grace, and her innocence."[9] The description has an affinity with the famous essay on the "Marionettentheater" in which Heinrich von Kleist, a few decades later, would analyze grace as a specific aesthetic quality in human behavior that depended on the absence of any intention to please. But Diderot finds himself alone in his enthusiasm for Emilie's grace. His friends are more admiring of her technical "talent" than they are charmed by her innocence. Thus Diderot gets into a discussion about their different views with Monsieur de Villeneuve, who believes that unusual talent should always be developed by further practical and theoretical instruction:

I said to Monsieur de Villeneuve: "Who would dare to change anything in a work where everything is perfect?" But Monsieur de Villeneuve and

I do not share the same principles. When he encounters innocence, he rather likes to be its instructor. According to him it is a special kind of beauty. (56)[10]

Striking in this passage is not only Diderot's position on grace as a dimension of aesthetic experience, as it must still have been quite eccentric in a mid-eighteenth-century environment. He is also quite naturally willing to "agree to disagree" with Monsieur de Villeneuve on the issue, without any need to press for consensus—and without harboring any hard feelings. Monsieur de Villeneuve and he, writes Diderot, are simply separated by "different principles." This is why they can casually switch to a different topic in the further course of their conversation. The new focus happens to be the intellectual and social merits of Sophie Volland, her mother, and her sister, whom Monsieur de Villeneuve had gotten to know during a previous stay "in the countryside." And again Diderot's descriptive prose turns into an opening towards his beloved, this time in the form of a dialogue that begins by quoting a statement made by Monsieur de Villeneuve:

"Madame Volland . . . is an outstanding woman." "And the older daughter?" "She is fiendishly intelligent." "She is very intelligent, but it is her openness that I like best in her. I would wager that she hasn't told a deliberate lie since she reached the age of reason." (56)[11]

Where exactly Diderot's discourse turns from a self-quote into a compliment directly addressed to Sophie Volland is not fully clear. We can say, however, that the ongoing doubleness between the compact descriptions of his day in its different stages and the reiterated moments of opening towards his beloved ends up becoming a discursive form in its own right.

The evening ends with music and dancing:

The violins were brought in and there was dancing until ten. Supper was over by midnight and by two o'clock everyone was in bed; so we got through the day without the tedium I had expected. (56)[12]

Looking back from the end of this long day, Diderot is quite happy to admit that his earlier fear and anticipation had turned out wrong. The weakness that did not allow him to stick to his own plans when they conflicted with his friends' expectations had proven strength, the strength of simply allowing the world to happen. Unexpectedly for Denis Diderot but also typically for him, this strength had made Sunday, September 14, 1760, a happy day—as he was able to concentrate on the presence of persons, objects, perceptions, and feelings in their concreteness and singularity, without much direction or purpose. "The boredom that he feared" never arrived.

We may refer to this unconditional openness that refrains from idiosyncratic projections as "Diderot's generosity"—and the compact precision of his prose was this generosity's medium. Openness, generosity, and precision in relation to the world, however, constantly turned into another form of generosity that was the desire to share with his beloved whatever he enjoyed in and about the world. Letting the world happen finally explains why Diderot was never enslaved by the progression of time. Without any obsession or nervousness, he cared and was confident about being remembered by posterity. And yet he wanted to die without drama and rituals, all of a sudden, in the middle of his happy involvement with the happening of the world.[13]

2 | "PROSE OF THE WORLD"

Is There a Place for Diderot in Hegel's System?

READING DENIS DIDEROT often evokes feelings of empathy, and this is not only true for his letters. What I have begun to describe as his openness to the material and social world, together with a specific style of generosity, suggests the presence and sometimes even the closeness of a lively individual, an individual with whom we soon believe ourselves to be familiar, in his texts. This must be the reason why Diderot has long been a favorite author in the French literary canon, abundant with shining author profiles and their distinct tonalities, that so flawlessly spans the centuries since the Middle Ages. But to feel at ease and even in sympathy with such an author does not always translate into there being clear concepts that identify his intellectual and literary style. Diderot is an eminent case of this condition.

A strange but recurrent mixture of fluidity and stable structures makes it difficult for us to have a picture of the way he lived his life and to grasp the contours of his work. As if to tease us, Diderot attracts our interest, almost irresistibly, and then seems to withdraw. We have seen how his everyday life involved permanent, perhaps even restless movement within a particularly restrained space, interrupted by few incisive events and accompanied by long-term and yet, again, difficult-to-define relationships: with his daughter and his wife in Paris; with his sternly traditional parents; with his brother, a canon, and his two sisters, one of whom died as a nun, in Langres; and the correspondence with his beloved friend Sophie Volland. In similar fashion, Diderot's work lacks the one single text (or the small number of canonized books) that we could consider a center of gravity; thus, it also seems to lack a thematic core. While Diderot, though he was enthusiastic about ancient Roman poetry and about music, hardly used prosodic forms himself, his versatility in many different varieties of prose was astounding: he wrote novels and tales that were serious, funny, and "pornographic" (within the eighteenth-century genre conventions of taste), two dramas laden with domestic pathos and detailed stage instructions, aphorisms, philosophical fragments and a number of treatises in epistolary and dialogic structures, and of course a considerable number of entries for the *Encyclopédie*. Without any visible programmatic intentions, he also invented a new discourse for the presentation and discussion of contemporary art and, under the title *Le rêve d'Alembert*, a unique textual hybrid combining several of these prose tonalities.

For almost half of his life, from the mid-1740s until 1772, Diderot's work towards the publication and completion of the *Encyclopédie* gave him the grounding of a stable occupation and source of income—but his contributions to this enterprise and its daunting logistical challenges were multidimensional and irregular in their intensity, which makes even them hard to gauge and to appreciate. His coeditor d'Alembert wrote the prospectus and the preface for the *Encyclopédie*, while Diderot recruited many of the roughly four hundred authors (two hundred of whom we know, because they were happy to put their name to their articles), edited these texts (although we do not know exactly how far his "editing" went), and took care of navigating the project through complex contemporary constellations between changing strategies of censorship and fluctuating financial interests on the publishers' side. If Diderot's truly passionate intellectual initiative and long-term commitment within the *Encyclopédie* was, surprisingly perhaps, the presentation of contemporary crafts and technologies, both in a number of important entries and, above all, in eleven volumes with illustrations ("*Planches*"), the unique historical merit of this both most volatile and most faithful of all eighteenth-century "philosophes" may have been the stamina with which he secured the completion of the project's first edition.

But while his work for the *Encyclopédie* shows the same interpenetration of permanence with fluidity that runs through his style of living and his work, even an enterprise of that magnitude did not impose a stable identity upon Denis Diderot. In 1765, just one year before a prohibition was lifted that had held back the delivery of the final ten volumes with texts, and seven years before the completion of the *"Planches,"* his friend Grimm convinced Catherine II of Russia to buy Diderot's library (granting him permission to keep these books in Paris until his death) and to bestow upon him the title of Librarian, with an anticipated salary for fifty years and with an invitation to visit to Saint Petersburg—which he did not act on until 1773. The new financial situation allowed Diderot to indulge his manifold interests even more deeply and made their centrifugal nature even more obvious, as it relieved him of the need to pursue the publication of his texts, with all the risks and concessions that this had long involved. It also allowed him, thanks to a considerable dowry, to arrange a marriage for his daughter that he found socially advantageous.

Although it has been said that Diderot exchanged his dependency on French censorship and on the book market for a life at the mercy of a foreign monarch, there is no evidence, from the two final decades of his life, that Catherine ever used her potential power over him. For all practical purposes and with the exception of the journey to Saint Petersburg about which, in spite of his gratitude and genuine admiration for the empress, Diderot was never enthusiastic, he seems to have only gained intellectual and personal freedom. With, indeed, fewer institutional obligations and more independence, his life and his work reached a final stage in their paradoxical form—a form without stable contours or defining content.

This paradoxical form had a long-term impact on the reception of Diderot's texts and on the scholarship dedicated to them. Alongside a good number of often sophisticated editions of his individual texts, there have been since the late eighteenth century, largely due to the dispersion of his unpublished manuscripts between France and Russia, no fewer than six attempts to collect and publish Diderot's "complete works," the latest beginning in 1994. In the last forty years alone, more than ten full-volume biographies have appeared, most of them drowning in detail without providing any distinct profile of Diderot, let alone an impression of his life's driving energies. The number of critical essays dedicated to particular texts exceeds any scholar's reading capacity and has given bibliographical knowledge referring to

Diderot the status of an area of academic specialization of its own. Even Jean Starobinski, the most philosophically subtle of all the experts on eighteenth-century French intellectual history and the author of a masterful book titled *La Transparence et l'Obstacle* that provides a complex synthesis of Rousseau's work, refrained from a similar attempt when in 2012, a year before the three hundredth anniversary of Diderot's birth, he launched a collection of fifteen essays that, in an impressive convergence of philological rigor and historical intuition, focused on the complex horizon of key aspects of Diderot's thought and style of writing.[1]

In the preface to that collection, however, Starobinski draws a decisive hermeneutic consequence from the paradoxical status of Diderot's texts. Even more than with other classics, this work without any thematic center or stable contours has provoked dramatic shifts in its understanding and appreciation. While only a few decades ago Diderot's dialogue *Jacques le fataliste et son maître*, begun in 1765 and published in Grimm's *Correspondance* six years before the author's death, appeared to occupy the center of intellectual interest as a critique of any assumptions of "fate" or "necessity" in human existence, our twenty-first-century intellectual attention seems to be more attracted by *Le neveu de Rameau*, another dialogue that Diderot began working on even before he started *Jacques le fataliste*, but which was never printed during his lifetime and whose original manuscript was lost for most of the nineteenth century, thus making a retranslation into French of Goethe's early translation into German the only textual reference available in French. By confronting a first-person-singular protagonist who seems to fulfill all the expectations we have for an Enlightenment intellectual with "Him," the nephew of a famous composer, who as a historical person and an embodied provocation had spent his life on the margins of enlightened sociability, Diderot provided a both complex and unstable configuration of meaning that today we can use to play through and undercut some of the basic values and motifs that have come down to us from the Enlightenment. In the title of his book, *Diderot, un diable de ramage*, as well as in its opening essay, Starobinski highlights a feature of Diderot that Diderot himself, the author, had attributed to the Nephew, his protagonist: namely, and according to an arcane meaning of the phrase *un diable de ramage*, the Nephew's skill of spontaneously copying many different human voices, a capacity mainly associated with certain birds and often used metaphorically of humans. *Un diable de ramage*, we can say, is a person with multiple voices, in the literal sense of the word, and without the will to bend them back into a single, well-rounded profile.

Once we, in our identity-happy present, begin to use the formula of a "lack of conventional identity as a specific configuration of identity," some of the portraits of Denis Diderot painted during his lifetime may gain new relevance. Diderot himself was obsessed—and perhaps even concerned—with the impression that those images never converged and thus failed to project a specific character.[2] Holding them up against contemporary images of Voltaire and of Rousseau, we discover that, rather than being particularly different from each other, the portraits of Diderot all seem at a loss in their efforts to find and highlight specific physiognomic markers along the lines, for example, of the oblong shape of Voltaire's face and his always emaciated appearance or the both distant and benign smile with which most Rousseau portraits meet the observer's eye. In Diderot's case, even the aquiline nose that is salient in all paintings showing his profile fails to make an impression when we see him from a frontal perspective. It is precisely the frontal view, however, that is never fully developed in the Diderot portraits, whereas Voltaire and Rousseau face us directly in most cases.

The two probably most famous images of Diderot, by Jean-Honoré Fragonard and by Louis-Michel van Loo (the latter of which hung in the 1767 Salon) seem to catch him in movement, looking up, as if surprised, from reading (Fragonard) or from writing (van Loo). In another portrait, painted by Dmitry Levitsky during Diderot's visit to Russia between late 1773 and early 1774, and in a bust by Jean-Baptiste Pigalle from 1777, he seems to pause (and perhaps to breathe after having spoken and before beginning to speak again). These recurrent iconic gestures of movements seem to confirm multiple testimonies by contemporary witnesses who converge in insisting that Diderot never spoke without gesticulating and even without touching the bodies of the persons in his physical proximity (during the weeks of his visit to Saint Petersburg, Catherine II complained about it in apparently good humor). But above all, this ironic effect of movement must underlie all potential for enlightened monumentality, as it was obvious if not dominant in many depictions of Voltaire and Rousseau as well. Rather than relying on strong features that artists could pinpoint and then highlight in their portraits, the Diderot paintings seem to adjourn the identification of a specific personality from the two-dimensional canvas to his presence in real and therefore three-dimensional space, where movements could unfold.

If we transfer this comparison between Voltaire, Rousseau, and Diderot, who have long been jointly canonized as the three central protagonists of the French Enlightenment age, from art history to the history of ideas, we find a surprisingly similar relation. Voltaire and Rousseau are associated with certain key concepts from their works, with their first resonance in society—and even with the ultimate transsubstantiation of those meanings and their inherent values into social and political realities. By contrast, and perhaps because of a lack of concepts and values that could ever have become canonical, Diderot is mostly—if not exclusively—acknowledged for the logistical achievement of editing the *Encyclopédie*, whereas Voltaire stands for the public space to whose emergence he so decisively contributed (above all with his letters) and Rousseau has been seen, ever since the "radical" moments of the French Revolution, as the champion of equality.

These admittedly superficial and yet useful contrasts can help us explain why, from the point of view of reception and resonance, the nineteenth century—the time when political systems counting on the public sphere imposed themselves—was the time of Voltaire, as opposed to the twentieth century which, obsessed and enchanted as it was with achieving equality, belonged to Rousseau. Unlike the works of these two great French-language eighteenth-century thinkers, Diderot's texts have been permanently but peripherally present, rather on the horizon of intellectual attention than centrally connected to any specific historical moments or social movements. The main question that I want to pursue in this book is whether our twenty-first-century present could become the age of Diderot.

I propose this not by default, of course, nor by the logic of some banal concept of historical "justice" according to which Diderot "finally deserves to receive the attention he has always been denied"—but rather because some of his obsessions, fascinations, concerns, and intuitions, including, as their lively equivalent, the paradoxical personality structure that we have begun to discover, might well have a specific and specifically illuminating affinity with our time. I read the opening chapter of Starobinski's *Diderot, un diable de ramage* as an encouragement to go in this direction. Such a starting point, I am eager to insist, does not imply any assumptions about regularities or even "laws" of history that would make an affinity between our present and Diderot's specific place on the intellectual map of the eighteenth century appear "necessary." Should the claim of affinity turn out to be productive, we would have to consider this a random effect—which would by no means reduce its potential relevance to our present and to a new understanding of Diderot and his work.

Our paradoxical premise for the attempt at a comprehensive description of Diderot's intellectual style and his life, namely that his identity may have emerged from the lack of a stable identity, has helped us to come closer to an understanding of Diderot's status in his own environment and to develop a first question, that is the question of his work's specific relation to our present. But we are still missing appropriate and specific concepts with which to analyze Diderot's works. Georg Wilhelm Friedrich Hegel's remarks about him, a total of ten passages scattered through the German philosopher's *Complete Works*, may help us to take a step further in this direction, probably even a decisive step. These remarks are spread over the three decades of Hegel's writing, and where they become specific they do not mention Diderot's more abstract philosophical treatises but one of his reflections on painting, *Jacques le fataliste*, and *Le neveu de Rameau*, the two last texts having become part of the literary canon. What makes Hegel's reactions to Diderot so particularly interesting is that Diderot by no means seems to have had any obvious systematic place in Hegel's thinking. The status of these remarks, therefore, has to involve what Hegel liked to call "negativity," in other words, they were observations and forms of experience that offered resistance to Hegel's thought and whose sublation (whose integration into the systematic architecture of his philosophy) obliged Hegel to sharpen his own concepts and arguments. From precisely this perspective and, at first glance, surprisingly, given the fundamental contrast between their ways of thinking, Diderot turned out to be important for Hegel, and this importance has found its due scholarly attention.[3] But in order to sublate Diderot's ideas and views into his own system, Hegel needed to use (or at least tacitly presuppose) a number of concepts that will end up helping us to describe Diderot's work, even independently of Hegel's texts.

In only two of the ten instances where Diderot's name appears is the reference not textually specific, and both of these instances come up late in Hegel's work. His posthumously published "Vorlesungen zur Geschichte der Philosophie" mentions Diderot, together with Voltaire, Montesquieu, Rousseau, and d'Alembert, as representative of "what has been called French Philosophy to be subsequently rejected as atheist" (XX/294). Later within the same sequence of lectures, Diderot appears as one of a small number of intellectual authorities with whom Hegel's philosopher colleague Friedrich Heinrich Jacobi had been in contact during an early stage of his intellectual life, in Geneva and in Paris (XX/315). Already more interesting is a passage in Hegel's 1807 manuscript "Wer denkt abstrakt?", where he evokes *Jacques le fataliste* as an illustration of his proto-sociological impression that French servants, like servants everywhere, think of their masters on a highly abstract level (today we would probably call it pragmatic) whereas, unlike for example in Germany, French aristocrats have a habit of talking to their servants in a very "familiar" style:

> Der vornehme Mann ist familiär mit den Bedienten, der Franzose sogar gut Freund mit ihm; dieser führt, wenn sie allein sind, das grosse Wort, man sehe Diderot's Jacques et son maître, der Herr tut nichts als Prisen-Tabak nehmen und nach der Uhr sehen und lässt den Bedienten in allem Übrigen gewähren. [II/580]⁴

While in this passage Hegel is simply using a literary text as added evidence for one of his many theses about what is specific to French society, the function and status implicitly attributed to Diderot's words as a "typically French" description of everyday scenes becomes thematic, from a more general angle, in a passage from Hegel's lectures on "Aesthetics," delivered in 1826:

> In der Poesie ist das gemeine häusliche Leben, das die Rechtschaffenheit, Weltklugheit und Moral des Tages zu seiner Substanz hat, in gewöhnlichen bürgerlichen Verwicklungen, in Szenen und Figuren aus den mittleren und niederen Ständen dargestellt. Bei den Franzosen hat besonders Diderot in diesem Sinn auf Natürlichkeit und Nachahmung des Vorhandenen gedrängt. [XIV/224–25]⁵

Hegel goes on to mention that Goethe and Schiller, in some of their youthful writings, "had chosen a similar direction" but soon started to turn against this background of "naturalness and particularity," towards "more profound substance." Furthermore, he points to Kotzebue, a widely popular German author of his time, and to the actor Iffland, whose attempts at evoking the everyday world he describes as "superficial" and as producing "a philistine morality." But what exactly is supposed to make Diderot's descriptions of "common domestic life" different from Goethe's and Schiller's—and so much better than Kotzebue's and Iffland's—does not become explicit here. All we can say is that Hegel associates Diderot's depictions of the everyday with superficiality, with a superficiality, however, that seems to carry an as-yet-unexplained positive connotation.

Towards the end of "Aesthetics," Diderot's name appears again, this time in a context where Hegel focuses on "human flesh" as one of the greatest mimetic challenges for any painter. The "opaque flavor of the soul" (*glanzloser Seelenduft*) that human flesh shows, he says, cannot be captured in specific details, i.e. "in material color, strikes, dots" but only in an "integral liveliness" (*lebendiges Ganzes*). Then Hegel quotes Diderot, in Goethe's translation, as an authority capable of confirming his own point of view:

> Schon Diderot in dem von Goethe übersetzten Aufsatz über Malerei sagt in dieser Hinsicht: "Wer das Gefühl des Fleisches erreicht hat, ist schon weit gekommen, das übrige ist nichts dagegen. Tausend Maler sind gestorben, ohne das Fleisch gefühlt zu haben, tausend andere werden sterben, ohne es zu fühlen." [XV/79][6]

Not a single philosophical concept appears in all of these passages referring to Diderot that could—at least tentatively—assign to his thinking a place within Hegel's thought. The commentary on the depiction of human flesh, however, makes it possible to supplement the one notion invented by Hegel, that, while it remains implicit here, can explain his interest in Diderot. Earlier on in his "Aesthetics" Hegel mentions unambiguous ways of referring to the human body and to other non-spiritual phenomena and uses the expression "prose of human existence" for them, which he then proceeds to unfold quite profusely:

> Der menschliche Organismus in seinem leiblichen Dasein fällt [. . .] einer Abhängigkeit von den äußeren Naturmächten anheim, und ist der gleichen Zufälligkeit, unbefriedigten Naturbedürfnissen, zerstörenden Krankheiten wie jeder Art des Mangels und Elendes bloßgestellt.

Weiter herauf in der unmittelbaren Wirklichkeit der geistigen Interessen erscheint die Abhängigkeit erst recht in der vollständigsten Relativität. Hier tut sich die ganze Breite der Prosa im menschlichen Dasein
auf. Schon der Kontrast der bloß physischen Lebenszwecke gegen die
höheren des Geistes, indem sie sich wechselseitig hemmen, stören und
auslöschen können, ist dieser Art. Sodann muss der einzelne Mensch, um
sich in seiner Einzelheit zu erhalten, sich vielfach zum Mittel für andere
machen, ihren beschränkten Zwecken dienen, und setzt die anderen, um
seine eigenen engen Interessen zu befriedigen, ebenfalls zu blossen Mit-
teln herab. Das Individuum, wie es dieser Welt des Alltäglichen und der
Prosa erscheint, ist deshalb nicht aus seiner eigenen Totalität tätig und
nicht aus sich selbst, sondern aus anderem verständlich. [XIII/197][7]

Right from the beginning, I want to underline that "prose," the Hegelian
notion that I want to apply to Diderot's work and to his life at large, does
not of course relate exclusively to what we can easily identify as objects in
their "materiality" or in their pertinence to "nature." "Prose" refers in fact
to everything that cannot be assimilated into or subsumed under human
thought in its conceptual abstractness. This is why "prose" also stands for
randomness, dependency, unsatisfied desires, fragmentation (*Partikelchen
des Ganzen* [XIII/198]), and singularity, for everything indeed that "obstructs,
irritates, and destroys" the flights of the spirit, for everything finally that is
neither spiritual nor controlled by concepts or structures.

At the end of the complex passage from his "Aesthetics" whose first paragraph I have just quoted, Hegel again uses the notion of the "prose" of the
world and adds "finitude," "mutability," "entanglement with the relative," and
"liveliness" to its semantic components. It thus becomes a core dimension
for "negativity"; for those phenomena, as I said, that have no place in Hegel's
system and therefore turn into an inevitable and permanent impulse towards
sublation:

Dies ist die Prosa der Welt, wie dieselbe wohl dem eigenen als auch
dem Bewußtsein des anderen erscheint, eine Welt der Endlichkeit und
Veränderlichkeit, der Verflechtung in Relatives und des Drucks der Not-
wendigkeit, dem sich der Einzelne nicht zu entziehen imstande ist. Denn
jedes sich vereinzelte Lebendige bleibt in dem Widerspruche stehen, sich

für sich selbst als dieses abgeschlossene Eins zu sein, doch ebensosehr von anderem abzuhängen, und der Kampf um die Lösung des Widerspruchs kommt nicht über den Versuch und die Fortdauer des steten Krieges hinaus. [XIII/199][8]

In a later chapter of the "Aesthetics," Hegel returns to the concept of "prose" with a less metonymical meaning, as he distinguishes "poetic artwork" from its opposite, "prose." Hegel's self-assigned goal here is to develop a description of what he calls "poetic" by eliminating, as "prose," phenomena and ontological layers that cannot be reconciled with the spirit. If he states that acts of "perception, formation, and enunciation" are "purely theoretical" and thus belong to what he calls "poetic," everything "practical," by contrast, must fall to the side of prose (XV/241), which is above all true for nature and the human body as a basis and precondition:

> Was zunächst den Inhalt angeht, der sich für die poetische Konzeption eignet, so können wir [. . .] sogleich das Äußerliche als solches, die Naturdinge ausschließen; die Poesie hat nicht Sonne, Berge, Wald, Landschaften oder die äußere Menschengestalt, Blut, Nerven, Muskeln usf., sondern geistige Interessen zu ihrem eigentlichen Gegenstande. Denn so sehr wie sie auch das Element der Anschauung und Veranschaulichung in sich trägt, so bleibt sie doch auch in dieser Rücksicht geistige Tätigkeit und arbeitet nur für die innere Anschauung, der das Geistige nähersteht und gemäßer ist als die Außendinge in ihrer konkreten sinnlichen Erscheinung. [XV/239][9]

In exactly this sense, Diderot's prose, with its descriptions of "domestic matters" and its absence of "depth" or "profundity"—a prose whose quality Hegel had earlier acknowledged in comparison to similar attempts made by German authors and artists—focuses on "exterior phenomena in their concrete sensual appearance." In the context of his reflection on "poetic artwork," however, it becomes apparent how the word "prose," which Hegel here associates with "the common mind" (*gewöhnliches Bewußtsein*), not only points to phenomena that are incompatible with the "spirit" but includes specific patterns and configurations in which such concrete phenomena present themselves to the human senses. These are patterns and configurations that undercut more holistic or organic views:

Andererseits läßt das gewöhnliche Bewußtsein sich auf den inneren Zusammenhang, auf das Wesentliche der Dinge, auf Gründe, Ursachen, Zwecke usf. gar nicht ein, sondern begnügt sich damit, das, was ist und geschieht, als bloß Einzelnes, d.h. seiner bedeutungslosen Zufälligkeit nach, aufzunehmen. [. . .] Das Verstehen einer verständig zusammen-hängenden Welt und deren Relationen ist dann nur mit dem Blick in ein Neben- und Durcheinander von Gleichgültigem vertauscht, das wohl eine große Breite äußerlicher Lebendigkeit haben kann, aber das tiefere Bedürfnis schlechthin unbefriedigt läßt. [XV/243][10]

An ambiguity runs through these reflections, an ambiguity that Hegel is probably aware of. Whatever he alludes to as "prosaic" stands opposed to and is probably capable of obstructing the spirit's urge towards synthetic forms of experience and understanding—and yet he concedes to the "prosaic" in its concreteness, singularity, and juxtaposition the quality of an "exterior liveliness." This liveliness must have been the most important implicit—and perhaps even preconscious—ground that made him appreciate Diderot's texts about "domestic life."

Two decades before Hegel's lectures on aesthetics, a much more violent reaction to a structure that, from an epistemological perspective, resembled "prose of the world" had appeared in *Phenomenology of the Spirit*, his first book, published in 1807. Already then, Hegel referred to a text by Diderot, more precisely to *Neveu de Rameau* in Goethe's translation that had appeared in 1805. However, unlike the distance maintained in 1826 between the spirit and the poetic artwork on the one side and "prose of the world" on the other, the younger Hegel strongly opted for what he must have believed was Did-erot's side in the same semantic contrast, fictionally evoked in the *Neveu de Rameau* by the contrast between the philosopher ("I") and Rameau's nephew ("He") as a socially marginal existence. The passage I am referring to here from *Phenomenology of the Spirit* is dedicated to the analysis of *Bildung*.

Hegel understands *Bildung* as the existential process in which the mind ("spirit") has to abandon itself ("externalization") in order to become alien to itself ("alienation") and to finally return to itself with a greater degree of individuality, complexity, and reflection. No individual mind is supposed to exist without having gone through this movement:

Die Welt [des] Geistes zerfällt in die gedoppelte [Welt]: die erste ist die
Welt der Wirklichkeit oder seiner Entfremdung selbst; die andere aber
die, welche er, über die erste sich erhebend, im Äther des reinen Bewußt-
seins sich erbaut. Diese, jener Entfremdung entgegengesetzt, ist eben
darum nicht frei davon, sondern vielmehr nur die andere Form der Entfremdung, welche eben darin besteht, in zweierlei Welten das Bewußtsein zu haben, und beide umfaßt. [III/362–63][11]

If Hegel's lectures on aesthetics, as I have said, tend to keep the "poetic"
and the "prosaic" separate and, so to speak, in a hierarchical relationship
that leads to the sublation of the prosaic into a poetic frame of mind, *Phenomenology* highlights, by contrast and somehow surprisingly, the basic
tension between alienation and pure consciousness. It is described as "torn
consciousness" (*zerrissenes Bewußtsein*) and becomes the decisive positive
principle in the dynamics of *Bildung*, a principle of positive unrest, we may
perhaps say. Early on in this chapter, Hegel quotes some words from the
mouth (so to speak) of Rameau's nephew, Diderot's outrageous protagonist,
in a contemptuous remark about those contemporaries who, because they
are not "torn" and therefore "individual" enough, can be subsumed under
the concepts for different social types (*Arten*). "To be a type," he says, is "of
all nicknames the worst; for it both points to mediocrity and expresses the
highest degree of contempt" (III/354).

Only a few pages later in *Phenomenology of the Spirit*, Diderot's protagonist, whom Hegel understands as the illustration and fictional incarnation of
"torn consciousness," reappears as a truly surprising object of enthusiasm and
even identification. In a discourse that blends words quoted from Goethe's
translation of *Neveu de Rameau* with Hegel's own philosophical concepts, the
argument about *Bildung* turns into a diatribe against the flatness of the philosopher's (the "I"'s) pure and "quiet mind" and against his well-intentioned,
one-dimensional "honesty":

Der Inhalt der Rede des Geistes von und über sich selbst ist also die
Verkehrung aller Begriffe und Realitäten, der allgemeine Betrug seiner
selbst und der anderen; und die Schamlosigkeit, diesen Betrug zu sagen,
ist eben darum die größte Wahrheit. Diese Rede ist die Verrücktheit
des Musikers, der "dreißig Arien, italienische, französische, tragische,

komische von aller Art Charakter, häufte und vermischte, bald mit einem tiefen Baß stieg er bis in die Hölle, dann zog er die Kehle zusammen, und mit einem Fistelton zerriß er die Höhe der Lüfte . . . , wechselweise rasend, besänftigt, gebieterisch und spöttisch."—Dem ruhigen Bewußtsein, das ehrlicherweise die Melodie des Guten und Wahren in die Gleichheit der Töne, d.h. heißt in eine Note setzt, erscheint diese Rede als "eine Faselei von Weisheit und Tollheit, als ein Gemisch von ebenso viel Geschick, von ebenso richtigen als falschen Ideen, von einer so völligen Verkehrtheit der Empfindung, so vollkommener Schändlichkeit als gänzlicher Offenheit und Wahrheit." [III/387]¹²

It is both the presupposition and the conclusion of the chapter on *Bildung* in Hegel's *Phenomenology* that in order to reach a "higher level of consciousness" the spirit needs to return to itself from a state "of confusion as a spirit" (*Verwirrung als Geist* [III/389]). Not only does Diderot's protagonist appear as the champion of this productive and necessary confusion, we can even assume that here we have identified, from Hegel's perspective, why Diderot's "prose of the world" came as close as possible to the status of being a necessary dimension and stage on the way to *Bildung*, a dimension and stage to be worked through on the way towards individuality and its intellectual complexity.

––––––––––

And yet it would not be a viable conclusion to draw from our reading of this passage in *Phenomenology* a claim for a general affinity (or even for a similarity) between Hegel's philosophical system at large and Diderot's thinking, with its always moving positions. For Hegel's identification (as an author) with Rameau's nephew (as Diderot's protagonist) came at an early stage of his philosophical trajectory and in the very specific context of a chapter on *Bildung*. Instead of taking this single philosophical moment of closeness and convergence too seriously, I will now focus on the concepts that we have gained, in microscopic concentration on Hegel's texts, for a description of the fundamental difference between Diderot and Hegel, and I will do so in order to develop the outlines for a larger view of the historical situation to which Diderot belonged and in which he occupied an intellectual place that is not easy to identify. More precisely, I will try to show, on the one hand, that Hegel's philosophy was a part of and a driving force within the emergence of what we may call the "historical worldview" as the dominant epistemological structure of Western culture throughout the nineteenth and first half of the twentieth century and, on the other hand, that Diderot's work (and the work of some other contemporary authors and artists) can stand for an intellectual and epistemological position that remained institutionally peripheral during the same time, without ever being detached from the more central movement or even actively repressed. In making this point I will imply that the historical worldview had an inherent tendency to identify and canonize, retrospectively, the larger part of the intellectual eighteenth century as its prehistory under the concept of "Enlightenment," whereas Diderot's work and intellectual style do not find their adequate place in the same context.

I start my outline for a historical narrative with the thesis that we can pinpoint the habitualization of a second-order observer's position, i.e. the inevitability, for a small social group, of observing itself in the act of observing the world, as a decisive step towards the formation of the historical worldview since the third quarter of the eighteenth century.[13] The social group that I am referring to are the eighteenth-century "philosophes," and it is important to insist that we are talking about the habitualization of second-order observation as opposed to the general possibility of self-observation which, as one of the defining gestures and structures of the human mind, has always existed. Now, a second-order observer—unlike a purely spiritual ("first-order") outside observer of the material world, which had become an institution since early modernity (with Descartes's philosophy being its most visible condensation)—cannot help making at least two discoveries that were not accessible to the Cartesian observer.

She will discover, in the first place, that the result of each act of world observation (that is, the knowledge acquired through it and its potential representation) will depend on her specific point of view, and as she is aware of the potential infinity of such points of view, she will draw the conclusion that there is also a potential infinity of representations for each object of reference. Instead of celebrating the conceptual wealth of such "perspectivism" (as we tend to do in the twenty-first century, using the word "contingency"), many of our eighteenth-century predecessors felt confused by this experience and by the subsequent fear that self-identical objects of reference might after all not exist behind such a potential infinity of representations. The so-called "Kant Krise" in the life of Heinrich von Kleist, a young artillery officer—and author—from the Prussian aristocracy, is a case that illustrates how existentially real this fear had become. After reading but a few pages of Kant's critical writings, Kleist fell into a state of irritation, depression, and uncertainty about the palpable accessibility of the material world in which he lived and which, as an object of reference and precise description, was central to his work. The situation is all the more emblematic as Kleist, not unlike Diderot, would become one of those intellectuals of his time whose works do not find an obvious place within our vision of the Enlightenment.

The second discovery that a habitual second-order world observer cannot avoid, against the grain of the exclusively conceptual "Cartesian" world appropriation that we call "experience," is the tension, even incompatibility, between "perception" (a world appropriation barely affecting the bodily senses, without the necessary participation of consciousness) and "experience" (that is, objects of perception turned into "intentional objects" and interpreted in our consciousness). This tension marked the epistemological place of eighteenth-century "Materialism," to which Diderot dedicated a good number of reflections and treatises. The question of whether—and if so how—it might become possible to find a convergence or a compatibility between experience and perception has never found a definitive answer until the present day (with the one potential exception of Einsteinian relativity)— not only because of its complexity but also because it started to vanish from the central intellectual debates around 1800. If the two problems provoked by the emergence of second-order observation, that is, the problem of perspectivism (contingency) and the problem of Materialism, can be amply documented as part of the ongoing contemporary debates, what I will now refer to as their "solutions" were not the result of specific individual efforts and attempts but rather part of more general epistemological transformations at the basis of intellectual life around 1800—to which only from our own historical retrospective we can attribute the function and the status of being answers to open questions.[14]

The first of these non-intentional "answers" and "solutions" I have already mentioned. It was the vanishing, in the dominant intellectual debates around 1800, of the question of the compatibility between "experience" and "perception." We have also seen how, after *Phenomenology of the Spirit*, Hegel's concept of "sublation" turned into a process capable of absorbing this tension by integrating whatever we can refer to as "prose of the world" into the movement through which the spirit gains full self-awareness (this was probably more the case among readers of Hegel than in his own thought and writings). By contrast, the "solution" given for perspectivism is the transformation of the problem and its potential for irritation into a basis for the emerging historical worldview.

We can describe this solution as the progressive replacement of a mirrorlike form of world appropriation and world representation (one canonical description for each phenomenon, as for example the *Encyclopédie* had presupposed) with the form of narrative as an elementary epistemological pattern. From the early nineteenth century on (and different from the prevailing standards around 1750), questions about the identity of a place or a nation ("what is France?") thus became increasingly answered by way of narrative (by "historical" narratives, as we still call them today); likewise, questions regarding phenomena of nature ("what is a horse"?) would find "evolutionary" answers, using different but structurally similar forms of narration. Hegel's *Phenomenology of the Spirit* was part of this movement as it presented an analysis and definition of the "spirit" in narrative form, based on a long sequence of stages that the human mind was supposed to go through, both individually and collectively, on its way towards "absolute knowledge" (thus the title of the concluding chapter).

But how could such "narrativization" on multiple levels of knowledge take care of the challenge presented by perspectivism and contingency? It managed to do so because, as a form, narrations are capable of integrating different views of supposedly identical phenomena and of thereby neutralizing the specific intellectual provocation of perspectivism that is best captured by the German word *Kontingenz* (as I will explain in chapter 4). Through the solution that perspectivism found by way of narrativization, *Kontingenz*, above all in Hegel's philosophy, was transformed into "necessity." Therefore, historical, evolutionary, and philosophical narratives, starting in the early nineteenth century, not only neutralized the problems of perspectivism and *Kontingenz*, they also ended up suggesting that what had happened in the past could not have happened along different lines. As a consequence, they gave historical analysis the aura of possessing prognostic powers—or, more

precisely, of being able to identify regularities ("laws") of historical transformation that could be projected into the future.

As I said before, this emerging historical worldview was of course not exclusive to Hegel's philosophical system. It existed in many different, often less
complex versions and shapes. Clearly and on the one hand, its early stages had
been a frame condition for the development of Hegel's philosophy whereas,
not only in the specific form of Marxism, the much more explicitly defined
Hegelian concepts and arguments would become instrumental for a praxis-
oriented analysis of past and present. On the basis of the all-encompassing
movement towards narrativization (what Michel Foucault referred to as
historisation des êtres), the historical worldview turned into a specific, all-
compassing "social construction of temporality." It emerged as the form of
time, firstly, in which the past was supposed to recede into an ever-growing
distance from the ongoing present and to progressively lose its power of
orientation. At the same time, working through the past ("understanding
the past") was taken to be a condition of overcoming potentially traumatic
effects that it might have caused. The future within the historical worldview,
secondly and by contrast, appeared as an open horizon of possibilities to
choose from and with which to shape the world. Between this (open) future
and that (receding) past, thirdly, the present shrank to become an "imperceptibly short moment of transition," as Charles Baudelaire described it in
his 1863 treatise "Le peintre de la vie moderne." This minimal present, in the
fourth place, turned into the epistemological place for the Subject as a form
of human self-reference that was seen as pure consciousness (in the sense of
Descartes) and that, based on experience wrested from the past, was indeed
able to choose among the possibilities of the future. This was a behavior that
corresponded to the concept of "action" as it had been increasingly in the
center of forms of human self-reference since the Enlightenment. Finally,
there were no phenomena, according to the historical worldview, that could
resist modalities of—slower or faster—transformation in time.

Around 1830 (and until the end of the twentieth century), this worldview was so strongly institutionalized that it seemed to lose all connotations
of being "historically" specific itself and was rather regarded as part of an
apparently eternal "human condition." As such, it was, throughout more
than a century and a half, the basis of "evolutionism" and the "philosophy

of history" but also, based on the joint assumptions of an open future and of time as an inevitable agent of change, the matrix for both capitalism and socialism as opposite principles of economic and political behavior. It stood dominantly in the center of Western thought as it began to spread globally, in the process of colonization, during the nineteenth century.

If Hegel's philosophy, as I have suggested, can be understood as both an extremely condensed and a highly differentiated development of the conceptual and epistemological potential inherent in the historical worldview, then his reaction to a number of motifs in Diderot's thinking confirms the impression that Diderot's work cannot be easily subsumed under "Enlightenment," as the concept through which the historical worldview interpreted part of the eighteenth century's intellectual life as its own prehistory. Or, to put it more straightforwardly: Diderot's thinking and writing was fundamentally different from both the historical worldview and from what the historical worldview began to present as its own prehistory under the name of "Enlightenment." We can describe this difference from two perspectives: first, how the world must have presented itself to Diderot, and second, how he reacted to his (neither "Enlightened" nor "historical") world. Both perspectives can also be interpreted as Diderot's specific reaction (or as his lack of problem-searching reaction) to the two problems that had emerged from the role of second-order observation. Therefore, my first brief and of course preliminary outline of the basis of Diderot's thought—in its otherness vis-à-vis the Enlightenment—will have four parts (two reactions each to the two main problems), to which I will then add a remark about his relation to time and "history" as an epistemological premise. These five observations about Diderot do not, however, symmetrically (and by contract) correspond to the five elements through which I have previously tried to describe the historical worldview.

In Diderot's thought and writings, above all, the world tends to present itself as if the two problems stemming from the emergence of second-order observation—perspectivism and the tension between experience and perception—that so impressed many contemporary thinkers had never existed for him (which may well have been the case). Even less did he participate in the "solutions" that those problems would later find. Rather than being irritated by the multiplicity and potential infinity of perspectives under which supposedly self-identical phenomena could appear, it became the first and defining feature of Diderot's intellectual style to embrace that complexity. His world was a world of *Kontingenz*, a world whose phenomena always provoked multiple reactions and therefore demanded permanent openness. Each time that he returned to a phenomenon or to a question, both within individual texts and within his entire life's work, Diderot was able to come up with new reactions, interpretations, and further questions. No intellectual position was ever definitive for him, and no claims of historical or logical "necessity" were made. As we have seen, this particular presence of the world's complexity in Diderot's mind triggered the concepts of randomness, relativity, and mutability (*Zufälligkeit*, *Relativität*, and *Veränderlichkeit*) that Hegel used to negatively characterize "prose of the world." We can also associate Diderot's tendency to focus on the objects of the world in their individuality and even singularity with *Kontingenz* as an unreduced multiplicity of perspectives.

But individuality and singularity, as modes of attention under which the world presented itself and as premises for that presentation, also partly converged, secondly, with the substance of Diderot's world that could be both material (as object of perception) and spiritual (as object of experience). For, as we have seen, it did not belong to Diderot's intellectual gestures to subsume objects in their materiality under general concepts. Rather than worrying about the multiple relationships between matter and spirit (i.e. about the second problem emerging from second-order observation), Diderot indulged in the description of their concrete individual configurations, which made their singularity only more salient. A never-exploited epistemological affinity exists between Diderot's world, which presents itself as both material and spiritual (without including a formula that could make these two dimensions compatible), and the structural elements of *Abhängigkeit* (mutual "dependency" between spiritual and material phenomena) and internal *Lebendigkeit* ("liveliness") as dimensions within Hegel's concept of "prose of the world."

Crucial in terms of Diderot's reactions to the world was, thirdly, judgment, as the one operation that became so ubiquitous in his texts that we run the paradoxical risk of overlooking it. I mean "judgment" in the sense of a gesture through which we can react to worlds of *Kontingenz*—under the two premises that each situation in which we judge is individual and that there are no general principles or criteria able to promise or even to guarantee the judgment's quality and beneficial effects. Nothing was further away from Diderot's lifelong and lively practice of judging than abstract and internally coherent programs or "systems." If a world of *Kontingenz*, however, needed and triggered judgment as an intellectual life form, then Materialism, fourthly, as an obsessive frame of reflection, reacted to a worldview in which matter and spirit were not categorically separated. Diderot's Materialism became obsessive because it returned to the same type of problem, that is the entanglement and the mutual dependency between spirit and matter, in an infinity of individual cases. It was driven by a desire for monism as the possibility of seeing matter and spirit as one, a reflection therefore that tried to avoid clear-cut distinctions and indulged in nuances and smooth transitions instead. But Materialism also turned into a specific way of referring to oneself and of being in the world. For the world lived as matter and spirit appealed both (and never separately) to the mind and to the senses, and it did not allow for any experience that was not permeated by traces of perception. As such it also came across in Diderot's specific style of sociability.

What finally remained absent from Diderot's intellectual reactions to the world was temporality, more precisely time as economy, time as distance, and time as a flexible medium for claims of logical necessity (as Hegel so master- fully used it). Dedicated to so many different tasks and fascinations, Diderot, as I have already said, never appeared rushed. Perhaps this is the existential basis for the epistemological observation that there is no categorical differ- ence we can discover in his thinking and writing between the importance of ideas, phenomena, and events from the present and of those from the past; and there was even less of an interest in detecting regular structures under processes of transformation or in predicting the future on such a basis. It is therefore not accurate to state that Diderot did not have a conception of "time" or of "history" that was different from Hegel's—he simply seems never to have been interested in developing a similar conception.

To loudly polemicize, as a result of this still very abstract and unavoidably schematic description of Diderot's work and intellectual style, against his handbook identity as an "Enlightenment intellectual" would be nothing but a banal case of academic nominalism. After all, Diderot was comfortable and very active in the eighteenth-century Republic of Letters, and he shared many readings, topics, questions, and also enemies with other authors who better fit our standard image of their historical period. What seems at first glance to set Diderot apart from the center of the Enlightenment is his distance from "rationality" as a consistent tendency towards abstraction, argument, and goal-orientedness—and perhaps also his lack of passion for the liberation from "self-inflicted forms of dependency" (in the sense of Kant's canonical definition of Enlightenment). This double distance may explain why, in spite of his unusual (and probably even unique) popularity among intellectual readers, Diderot has never found a stable place in the literary and philosophical canon.

There is a standard tendency among cultural historians to present protagonists who, like Diderot, appear eccentric in their own present as "precursors" of their future. Some of Rousseau's writings, for example, have thus regularly been highlighted as representative of a pre-Romantic sensibility. Beside the problematic (but perhaps not always unintentional) effect of implicitly attributing "genius" to authors and artists who are supposed to have anticipated the topics and the style of their posterity, however, such a move normally turns out to be but an excuse for a lack of historical explanation—and it thus is a blessing indeed that Diderot has hardly ever been associated with Romanticism. After all, his texts lack the fascination with the inner realms of his individuality and with those precarious and ecstatic forms of their expression that we consider "typically romantic"—they were, rather, casual, sometimes distant and sometimes even ironic in this regard. Rather than being particularly self-centered, Diderot, as I have tried to show, must have been sensitive to the material world and open to the social world by which he was surrounded, which included being generous in sharing his reactions.

For all of these reasons, I propose to see his intellectual legacy as foundational for an epistemological configuration and an intellectual style that were different from the historical worldview, as the centrally institutionalized outcome of the Enlightenment—and that we can discover and appreciate in the work of some other authors and artists between the late eighteenth century and our present. Georg Christoph Lichtenberg, the natural philosopher from

Göttingen, was such a case, I believe, as were Francisco de Goya and Wolfgang Amadeus Mozart, among many others. In the following chapters I will occasionally refer to their works for illustration and variation—but I will also ask the question (normally considered to be in bad intellectual taste in academic circles) of whether affinities existed between their life situations and Diderot's.

Throughout the nineteenth and twentieth centuries, there have certainly been other cultural protagonists whose thoughts show an affinity with the non-Enlightened epistemology and its intellectual gestures that I have now begun to describe: Schelling, for example, may have been one of them, as well as Schopenhauer, Nietzsche and, closer to our present, Heidegger, Bataille, and probably Deleuze. There is no evidence for a tendency among them to refer to each other's works, and they certainly remained far from producing any continuity that we could label as a "tradition" or a "genealogy." Nor can we say that their works were ever repressed or programmatically marginalized. These authors and artists simply made up an ongoing and accumulative potential of alternative thinking at the periphery of the historical worldview as a stable mainstream institution of the past centuries.

Referring to the positions of these thinkers in their relation to Diderot as "a potential for alternative thinking" is not synonymous with pretending that their recurrent elements ever came together in a form that we can retrospectively label as a coherent "alternative" or even a "counterprogram" to the historical worldview. Diderot's thinking did not have enough of a stable structure for that; instead, its productivity unfolded in a fluid movement without any continuous direction. It was a movement capable of opening up surprising intellectual possibilities at any moment, instead of leading through logically connected arguments and to apparently necessary conclusions. In other words, the intellectual potential that fascinates me in Diderot's texts and in the works of some of his contemporaries might well have been the result of a mere absence of coherence or imposed institutional form, which could suggest that different moments and cases of such absence came together, throughout the nineteenth and twentieth centuries, in a loose juxtaposition of similarities.[15]

The question about the specific ways in which Diderot's legacy may have existed since the late eighteenth century brings us back to its potential affinity with our own intellectual and cultural present. For starters, I want to suggest that our present too might be in a state of entropy coming from a crisis or even from an implosion of the historical worldview (as a coherent form) rather than in possession of or under the dominance of a new, well-shaped worldview. To speak, however, about an affinity between Diderot and us by no means implies that our present can be seen as the product of a reception or of a continuity leading back to Diderot. Should such an affinity exist at all, we might better consider it as a random result of the intellectual transformations that have been taking place since the late eighteenth century.

But in the overall structure of this book, our present and its possible relation to Diderot's work will only play a secondary role. Rather, its four central chapters will try to unfold the complexity of his work in a concentration on four central texts, each of which can stand, albeit never exclusively, for one of the four particular dimensions in Diderot's thinking. I am thus aiming at a comprehensive description and an individual portrait without following the convention that is typical for author-centered monographs of taking into account the full range of their available texts. Chapter 3 is about the *Neveu de Rameau* and the particular modality in which it unfolds a self-reference including body and matter through the dialogue between the Nephew and the Philosopher. "Jacques le fataliste et son maître" occupies the center of chapter 4 as an illustration of the extreme degree of contingency and complexity in Diderot's experience and perception of the world. Chapter 5 tries to analyze *Le rêve de d'Alembert*, a strangely hybrid text whose forms and topics develop Materialism as a style of thinking and as a specific intellectual gesture, while chapter 6 is about Diderot's commentaries on the annual art exhibits in Paris (these texts are normally referred to as his *Salons*) in an ongoing practice of judgment and its discursive ramifications.

My key question connecting the chapters concerns how the different dimensions and practices of Diderot's thinking were connected in their never formalized overlapping and interaction. On this basis, I will return in the two concluding chapters to a further developed and more Diderot-specific version of the concept of "prose of the world." That should allow us to articulate some new perspectives for a description of the potential appeal that Diderot's texts and his personality may have for our present.

"JE SUIS DANS CE MONDE
ET J'Y RESTE"

Ontology of Existence in Le neveu de Rameau

HEGEL'S REACTION to *Le neveu de Rameau* and its main protagonist has found such unusual resonance, also in our present, because it
marks an exception from the decisive importance of sublation within the
form of his thinking as it emerged in *Phenomenology*. More than describing
"torn consciousness" just as a necessary step on the spirit's pathway towards
Bildung, a step whose otherness would soon become neutralized by sublation,
we have seen how Hegel highlighted, as "greatest truth," the shamelessness
with which Diderot's character exposes the self-sufficient harmony in the
constantly sublating "quiet consciousness" of the Philosopher with whom
he engages in a conversation. And while this surprising and indeed system-
breaking view of "torn consciousness" ended up remaining an episode in the
larger trajectory of Hegel's philosophy, he never revoked or even modified
his strong statement on the *Neveu de Rameau*.

Given that we have associated, on the one hand, the totality of Hegel's
work with the "historical worldview" that emerged from the eighteenth
century as an institutionally dominant form of thinking and, on the other
hand, his concept of the "prose of the world" with a different (and peripheral)
epistemological configuration that Diderot's work illustrates, not only does
Rameau's "torn consciousness," as a salient case of "prose of the world," provoke us to imagine a different development of Hegel's philosophy as it never

came to exist, but understood as part of a specific historical constellation of ideas, Hegel's reaction to Diderot's character might also provoke us to speculate about a form of *Bildung* and a way of existence resulting from it that we have not been able to envision until recently. This would have to be a way of existence in which torn consciousness (the one existential condition that mainstream Western culture has, since the late eighteenth century, consistently tried to overcome) assumes a positive function, no longer a function barely defined by negativity and finally neutralized by sublation. To make such an alternative view of *Bildung* and of human existence visible is the vanishing point for our reading of *Le neveu de Rameau* as a first major text by Diderot. More specifically, I want to focus on how the world presents itself in this text through the interaction and the development of its two characters. Obviously we cannot completely isolate these two dimensions, that is, the appearance of the world and the forms of human self-reference, from each other and from Diderot's larger epistemology, of which I have already provided a first tentative description. Due to this complexity, what may come into sight is an area within Diderot's thinking that I tentatively refer to as an unusual "ontology of existence"[1] or, in the words of the main protagonist, a conception of "being and remaining in the world," with particular implications regarding the degree of its reality claims (this is what the word "ontology" refers to).

———

The philological status of *Le neveu de Rameau* and its place in Diderot's life make up the most typical case of the fluidity permeating his work, above all during the later years. Most scholars suspect that Diderot worked on this text between 1761 and 1773, but even this vague assumption depends on the identification of the text-internal "Moi," i.e. the Philosopher, and some of his statements with the historical Diderot—which is far from unproblematic.[2] Also, there is no sign that Diderot ever tried to publish the text or at least wanted it to circulate among his friends, which, as I already mentioned before, was typical for his later years, especially from 1765 on, once Catherine II's financial support had begun. A manuscript of *Le neveu de Rameau*, probably hand-copied by the author, ultimately reached Johann Wolfgang von Goethe shortly after 1800 through the mediation of a German friend living in Russia, where Diderot's works were held (in Saint Petersburg) after his death in 1784. It is interesting but not surprising that of all German intellectuals, Goethe was fascinated enough by this book to undertake and publish a translation (while it must of course be considered a random circumstance that all copies in French from Diderot's lifetime were lost and that French readers were dependent on a retranslation of Goethe's text, until one manuscript resurfaced in 1890).

Finally, it also remains unclear what intentions, if any, Diderot pursued in the subsequent stages of his writing and reworking of *Le neveu de Rameau*. From a plethora of references to historical protagonists, facts, and often minor anecdotes in the text that make its full understanding difficult and its reading sometimes congested, the hypothesis seems plausible that, at first, he had a grotesque depiction in mind, a satire (in the present-day sense of the word) of the theologically conservative and intellectually aggressive "anti-philosophical" circles of Paris that made life difficult for the editors and authors of the *Encyclopédie* and whom the Nephew, as a literary condensation, was meant to represent. But if the text's final version, as it reached Goethe, does not exclude such an origin, its complexity and above all the complexity of the central character so clearly transcend the related genre conventions that some specialists have suggested reading Diderot's subtitle ("Satire Seconde") in the sense of classical antiquity, that is, as referring to an unlimited variety of contents from everyday life.

From a form-related perspective, the text is a monologue to be attributed to "Moi," rather than a true dialogue between "Moi" and "Lui," because only "Moi" addresses the reader and provides commentaries so that, strictly speaking, the much longer passages attributed to "Lui" have the status of quotes within "Moi's" narrative of their joint conversation. This primary structure may again be a remnant of the original purpose of criticizing Rameau and the "antiphilosophes" from the politically opposite viewpoint of "Moi," as standing for Diderot's thought and the orthodoxy of Enlightenment thought. Things are much more complicated, however, in the text that we have. Diderot was indeed familiar with a certain Jean-François Rameau, a man three years younger than him and the nephew of a composer who had been highly regarded in the early eighteenth century. This nephew of a famous uncle was a notorious presence in the world of Palais Royal, a square behind today's Comédie Française where, mainly due to its cafés, the core of Enlightenment sociability took place. Despite being a talented composer himself, the younger Rameau was not able to earn a living from his profession, so that he sought and obtained the protection of the anti-philosophical circles, to whose needs he adapted his lifestyle, probably serving as a spy. But unlike the textual character, the historical nephew was known, among contemporary intellectuals and artists, to be mellow, friendly, and, in all likelihood, far from possessing the brilliance and sharpness that make up Diderot's fictional character.

While the textual Rameau refers to "Moi" several times as "Diderot the contemporary philosopher," and while some biographical details mentioned seem to confirm this identification, the "Moi" is in fact too predictable, too much both an allegory and in the end a parody of how the *Encyclopédie* defines a "philosophe," to be convincing as Diderot's self-representation. Should the primary intention behind the text have been a satirical presentation of the "real" Nephew from the perspective of the "real" Denis Diderot, the version that we now have is, instead, a dynamic process in which two rather fictional characters produce views on human self-reference in its relationship to the world whose complexity cannot be reduced to the one or the other position from which the text starts out. What "Lui" and "Moi" visibly share is a fascination with the topic of self-reference and thus an urge to talk about themselves. "Moi," in this constellation, is a typical second-order observer, that is, a world observer quite deliberately observing himself in the act of world observation. The first sentences of the text thus feature him both as peripheral in relation to the energy center of the social world and as letting his thoughts reflect upon whatever he is experiencing. In conventional philosophical concepts, "Moi" wants to be a *subject* in relation to the world that he analyzes and to which he attributes meaning as an *object*:

> It is a habit of mine to go for a walk in the Palais Royal pleasure gardens every afternoon at five, whatever the weather. That's me you see there, always by myself, daydreaming on d'Argenson's bench. I have conversations with myself about politics, love, taste or philosophy. I give in to my mind's every fancy [. . .]. If it's too cold or too rainy, I like to take shelter in the Café de la Régence and watch chess being played. Paris is the place

in all the world, and the Café de la Régence the place in all of Paris, where
it is played the best. (15)[3]

"Lui" does not share with anybody this self-image so central to Enlightenment mentality, which makes him only more flexible, less prejudiced, and
more aggressive in the actual practice and language of self-observation. The
ultimate constellation that emerges, implicitly, in the course of the asymmetrical and productively unstable interaction between "Moi" and "Lui" is
thus the structural equivalent of the dialectic that Dieter Henrich, one of
the eminent contemporary specialists of European philosophy around 1800
and in particular of Hegel's work, has recently circumscribed as the core of
German Idealism, that is, a worldview locked into individuality: "In all of
their world-oriented behavior, humans inevitably refer to themselves. They
cannot develop any image of the world without inscribing themselves into
it. Whenever they are uncertain about themselves, their world orientation
will also become precarious. And whenever a new experience of the world
opens up for them, they will find themselves in a different life."[4]

In similar fashion, the dialogue making up Diderot's *Neveu de Rameau* is
neither exclusively about the world as it presents itself to "Moi" and "Lui" nor
exclusively about the two forms of self-reference through which they engage
with the world and that they project on to it (producing the very effect that
the twentieth century has labeled "constructivism"). Rather than emerging
from the predominance of either the subject or the world in the text, the
energy of the interaction between "Lui" and "Moi" seems to come from their
growing openness to the ever-unstable relation between the non-spiritual
traces of their self- and world-perception. "Prose of the world," as we have
seen, is the concept and the conception of life that refuses to eliminate these
reality components.

This is why I have proposed to link it to the motif of the spirit's self-
alienation as "torn consciousness" and why I follow Hegel in associating
"torn consciousness" with *Le neveu de Rameau*. Trying, as I promised, to
read the text as an impulse towards imagining a new "ontology of existence,"
I will highlight its motifs of externalization, alienation, and reality—which is
synonymous with the refusal to move on, via sublation, to a purely spiritual

conception of life and to human existence as part of it. This may be why, at a certain point, the Nephew states that he "is in the world and will stay there" (*je suis dans ce monde et j'y reste*). Diderot's character becomes an emblem of whichever elements of the world remain inaccessible to becoming spirit through sublation—and thus becomes a point of resistance from which an ontology of existence can emerge.

The unfolding of the text's philosophical topic, with its awe-inspiring complexity, finds its specific form in the double reversal of the relationship between "Moi" and "Lui," a form that, once again, Diderot may or may not have intended.[5] Its first paragraph is preceded by a motto taken from Horace's Second Satire, "*Vertumnis quotquot sunt natus iniquis*" ("To him who is born the victim of all kinds of changes in the weather"), and takes up its content by stating how changing weather will never break the Philosopher's habit of idly walking at Palais Royal in the late afternoon. In their convergence, the Latin and the French opening of "Le neveu" introduce and stage the Philosopher's half-amused, half-condescending description of Rameau (the Nephew) as a man whose life appears torn and unstable between all kinds of extreme attitudes and conditions in their mutual tension, which of course implicitly establishes a first contrast with the stability in the Philosopher's life:

> He's a mixture of the lofty and the sordid, of good sense and unreason. The notions of what's decent and what's indecent must be strangely mixed up in his head since he displays the good qualities that nature has given him unostentatiously and the bad ones shamelessly [. . .] you'd think he'd not eaten for days or that he'd just come out of a Trappist monastery. A month later, he is as fleshy and replete as if he'd been at a banker's dinner table the whole time or been comfortably cloistered with the Bernardins. Today, skulking in dirty linen, with torn breeches, his coat in tatters, his shoes hanging off his feet, and his head held low, you'd be tempted to call him over and slip him a coin. Tomorrow, hair powdered and curled, well shod and well dressed, he goes about in public, his head held high, and you would almost take him for a respectable man. He lives from one day to the next. (15–16)[6]

On the final page of Diderot's text, however, it is Rameau who, all of a sudden interrupting the flow of the conversation with the Philosopher, obliquely refers to his own stable daily habit of attending a performance at the Opéra at six o'clock and, as if in passing, says the following words of farewell: "Adieu, Mister Philosopher, is it not true that I'm still the same as I was before?" (97).[7] The Philosopher at this point seems to have forgotten his initial impression of Rameau as a human being full of changes and contradictions, and explicitly joins him in his casual claim for constancy, with a final regret, however, about the direction of Rameau's new position: "Hélas! Oui, malheureusement." Rameau moves on, keeping up his friendly distance, and ironically turns the word "malheur," which the Philosopher has used to articulate his disapproval, into a positive self-description: "Let's hope I only have that misfortune (*malheur*) for another forty years or so. He who laughs last laughs longest" (97).[8]

While the Philosopher's attitude vis-à-vis Rameau thus undergoes a profound change, Rameau himself never departs from a casual tone of irony. With a generosity that seems unaware of itself, he plays along, during the initial parts of the conversation, when "Moi" lectures him, with an attitude of superior authority and using pedagogical gestures, about the notion of *génie* ("But don't you see that with an argument of that sort, you overturn the general order of things?" [23]).[9] This condescension turns into open admiration, on the Philosopher's side, towards the end of the dialogue, an admiration that only accentuates his regret about what he interprets as an absolute lack of moral principles on Rameau's side: "How can it be that you have such insight, such a delicate sensibility when it comes to the beauties of musical art, and yet be so blind to things of beauty when it comes to morals, so indifferent to the charms of virtue?" (81).[10]

The most obvious change within this play of reversals between "Lui" and "Moi" comes in a double reference to Diogenes, in relation to the historical symbol of cynicism whose paradoxical attitude turns ethical minimalism into the one general ethical claim of not giving in to claims of morality. If at the beginning of the text it is Rameau who proudly speaks of an affinity between his own physiognomy and a cynical tradition of presenting Diogenes's way of life as unrestricted dedication to sensual pleasure, at the end the Philosopher refers to Diogenes as the champion and admirable predecessor of a monastic abstention from the joys of the world: "What used to be the cynic's habit is now the monk's habit, and it had the same virtues. The Cynics were the Carmelites and the Franciscans of Athens" (94).[11]

Whatever Diderot's agenda with this text may have been, there are more structural reasons for stating that the narrative takes place in a chiastic movement: while the Philosopher's solid identity is being progressively undermined, Rameau's initial lack of identity, mainly due to interior and exterior frictions and tension with the material world, becomes a both complex and coherent form of undeniable beauty. In describing this development of Rameau's form of existence from four different perspectives, I will no longer follow the text's narrative lines—for it functions according to a principle that belongs to the logical rather than the narrative order. It is revealed in Rameau's description of torn consciousness as a premise for his state of mind. When he speaks, for the first time and explicitly, about his necessity, born out of lack of success and poverty, to "kiss up" (*baiser le cul* [411]) to some of the anti-philosophes and their mistresses, Rameau admits—twice within less than two pages—that this easy way of surviving is not easy for his self-esteem to accept:

> It's hard to be a beggar when there are so many wealthy fools to live off. And then there's the self-hatred; it's unbearable. (29)[12]

> Be that as it may, this is exactly how I often address myself, and you can rearrange the words of my soliloquy however you fancy, so long as you always conclude from it that I am a man acquainted with self-hatred, that I know that tormented conscience which comes from not having been able to use the talents bestowed upon us by heaven above. It would almost have been better if such a man had never been born. (30)[13]

This self-contempt, emerging from Rameau's awareness of the contrast between his talent and his lack of success, is quite different from a number of moments where, early on in the conversation with the Philosopher, he admits to all kinds of vices and lacks of virtues: "You know that I am an ignoramus, a fool, a madman, an upstart, a hanger-on, what the Burgundians call a dirty scally, a cheat, a greedy pig . . ."(26).[14] As he will later on explain, Rameau believes that he has chosen to "give up his dignity"—and has no problem with such a deliberate loss of status: "I'm happy to be abject, but I don't want there to be any constraints on it. I'm happy to give up my dignity . . ." (49).[15] By contrast, the tension between the inner awareness of his talent (as a musician above all) and the need, imposed by the physical mechanisms of survival in the outer world, to adapt to wealthy people about whose quality he has no illusion, is a tension that tortures him.

On the premise of this suffering and its practical consequences, however, Rameau has developed a lifestyle that is coherent, without having any concept or program, and of which he is sharply aware but without luxurious loops of self-observation or self-reflection. Unlike his interlocutor, Rameau knows for example that, for him, bare life is a good enough motivation for living. The difference between not living and living, for him, is endlessly more relevant than that between a bare life and a perfect life:

> The important thing is that we should exist, you and me, and that we should exist as you and me. In any case, let everything find its way in the world. The best order of things, in my opinion, is the one that has me in it, and I couldn't care less about the best possible world, if I'm not in it. I'd rather be alive and offend everyone by speaking out of turn than not be alive at all. (23)[16]

Adapting his behavior and kissing up to those whom he despises while they make possible his survival (and may at any moment refrain from doing so) obliges Rameau to live under a mask in the role imposed upon him. This is exactly the technique, he tells the Philosopher, that he has learned from Molière, instead of drawing from his theater the banal—and moralistic—conclusion of simply wanting to be different from the monomaniacal characters: "When I read L'Avare [The Miser], I tell myself: be a miser if you like, but make sure you don't speak like one" (59).[17] No tension nor bad conscience results from this practice, because Rameau can say that, for very good and obvious practical reasons, he chooses to be greedy, hypocrital, or hypochondriac. He just has to hide it under a different discourse and visible behavior. As the only dimension he has to control and wants to think about is this visible behavior and its effects, we have the impression that Rameau, unlike the Philosopher's self-image, has no "depth" as a result of habitual self-observation or, with a different metonymy, that hollowness is part of his distinctive intelligence.

If the needs of bare living and survival determine Rameau's behavior (all the more so as at the moment of this conversation his anti-philosophical protectors are annoyed with him and he needs to regain their sympathy), it is only natural that he has developed and continues to maintain an active awareness of his physical constitution and of his senses, both from the angle of their minimal necessities and from that of their luxurious intensity, of which he speaks over and again. The highest goal in life, Rameau responds in answer to the Philosopher's question about a possible educational program for children, has to be enjoying "all sorts of things without getting into danger or difficulty" (86).[18]

At the same time, Rameau lives with an awareness of his body and its organs in their materiality that is both uncommon and relaxed. Not only is his loud voice a nuisance to anyone who gets close to him, he also scares the Philosopher by willfully producing a dry noise with the bones and joints of his hand:

> He had grabbed his left hand in his right and was pulling his fingers and wrist backwards and forwards so that he made the very tips of his fingers touch his arm; his joints cracked with the effort, and I was worried his bones would be permanently dislocated. (32)[19]

As for Rameau's intellectual capacities, the reader senses, after the first few pages, that his versatility and power will dominate the Philosopher at will. Part of this energy comes from Rameau's refusal to engage in any kind of abstraction, both on the level of general concepts and on that of universal procedures in his ways of world appropriation and thinking. Whenever he criticizes the Philosopher for his tendency towards abstraction, Rameau indirectly describes this habit:

> And method, where does that come from? Listen, my dear philosopher, in my head, physics will always be a poor science, a droplet of water lifted out of the vast ocean on the point of a needle, a speck of earth removed from the Alpine range. And the reasons behind natural phenomena? In truth, we might as well know nothing at all as know as little as we do, and know it so inadequately. (37)[20]

The refusal of method and abstraction, in its turn, explains one of the most salient features of Rameau's language. As soon as he describes parts of the social or of the material world, instead of general concepts, long lists of individual names and words will appear that refer to specific phenomena.[21] Regarding Rameau's long-term behavior, the same fundamental refusal of abstraction explains his unpredictability and the lack of "consequence" on which he insists several times. It is thus interesting to see that in one of these passages, Diderot lets his protagonist use almost the exact same words with which he had described himself in a letter to Sophie Volland from September 1760: "I am of no consequence. People can do to me, with me, and in front of me whatever they like without me taking offence" (26).[22] While there was most likely no intention behind this textual convergence, we see how, in both cases, Diderot associates what can be identified as a symptom of weakness with a particular degree of freedom and openness to the world.

Without any "consequence" in behavior and action, however, individual profiles cannot emerge. And without such profiles as an existential grounding, neither self-knowledge nor personal depth will be possible. But the consequence of such a lack of consequence is unlimited frankness:

> I'll be damned if I know what I am, deep down. In general, my mind is as straight as a rule, and my character as honest as the day; never false when it's in my interest to be true, never true when it's in my interest to be false. I say whatever comes into my head: if there's any sense in it, so much the better; if it's absurd, nobody takes any notice. I take every opportunity to speak my mind. Never in my life have I reflected, before, during or after speaking. (56–57)[23]

Frankness, as Rameau means and practices it, has nothing to do with either truth or lie. It is the absence of any control on the threshold between the individual mind in all its dimensions and the exteriority of the public sphere. Frankness as the mode of openness towards the world that depends on freedom from self-control converges with an openness in Rameau's world perception that the Philosopher greatly admires: "He attends to every detail" (92).[24] And all these traits of his character for which Rameau refuses to find an overarching concept end up coming together in the very liveliness (*Lebendigkeit*) that Hegel finds in the "prose of the world": "I never get tired" (33)[25] says Rameau in passing—and somehow proudly.

There is one final aspect worth mentioning in his paradoxical identity that is not aware of itself, and it stems precisely from its paradoxical structure. Rameau shows a sensibility for atrocity; in other words, he has a specific reaction to physical and psychic cruelty, a reaction that probably did not exist before the late eighteenth century. The relevant passage in the text comes, surprisingly somehow, towards the end of a story told about the "Renegade of Avignon." It describes a scheme of cruelty inflicted upon a well-meaning Jew by a renegade whose Machiavellian practical intelligence Rameau uses as a—deliberately shocking—example when he tries to show the Philosopher what type of behavior he admires. In claiming that he would like to be capable of practicing a similar cold-bloodedness, Rameau speaks of "the atrocity of his actions" (71),[26] which shows that he is not speaking from a one-sided perspective of identification that can bracket or suspend any potential critique of violence. Anti-Semitism, for example, would provide such a neutralizing perspective or, on the morally opposite side, a belief in the ultimate efficiency of divine justice. Only without such stable worldviews (that Rameau does not possess) can cruelty appear as naked cruelty, that is, as atrocity.

At the end of this attempt of mine to bring together some aspects of Rameau's both earthy and agile behavior, I want to emphasize again that they do not converge in any well-circumscribed self-image. Rather, Diderot's text presents a protagonist who can only claim to be "always the same" because there is a palpable recurrence in his forms of behavior and action. This is also why the transition from our image of Rameau to contingency, as a second dimension in his existence, seems to come quite naturally. Freely dealing with contingency is a premise of Rameau's behavior that is pertinent to the same level of conversation with the Philosopher on which his character has unfolded. It finds its clearest expression in a passage where the Philosopher wants to convince Rameau of the universal validity inherent to certain moral values, while Rameau questions the possibility of anything universal:

> You believe happiness is made the same for everyone. What a strange vision! Your happiness presupposes a certain romantic turn of mind that we do not have, a singular soul, a peculiar taste. You confer the title of virtue on this weirdness; you call it philosophy. But are virtue and philosophy made for everyone? Enjoy them if you can, hold onto them if you can. Imagine what a wise and philosophical universe would be like; you must agree it'd be miserable as hell. Come on, long live philosophy, long live the wisdom of Solomon: let's drink good wine, gorge ourselves silly on delicate morsels, roll around with pretty women, and go to sleep in lovely soft beds. What else is there? The rest is vanity. (43)[27]

Rameau's main point of resistance (rather than "argument") comes in the form of a paradox again. To assume that something like universal happiness could possibly exist presupposes a peculiar disposition and a particular moral taste. There is nothing real and uncontroversial, Rameau insists, except for sensual pleasures—in their singularity. And as he continues his conversation with the Philosopher, he applies this view to each of the specific values that "Moi" presents:

> MOI: What! What about defending one's country?
> LUI: Vanity! There is no country anymore; all I can see from one end of the earth to the other is tyrants and slaves.
> MOI: And serving one's friends?
> LUI: Vanity! Do any of us have any friends? And if we did, why would we want to make them ungrateful? Take a good look around and you'll see that's almost always what you get for doing anyone a service. Gratitude is a burden, and all burdens are made to be shaken off. (44)[28]

Of course it is not Rameau's claim that his own reactions are universally right. To make his point, it is enough simply not to share the Philosopher's appreciation of certain individual values and thus to show that they do not have universal validity. It is sufficient indeed to demonstrate that each "value" and each "virtue" is contingent upon specific ways of appreciating life and on individually specific premises. In this context, Rameau adds an existential dimension to his more logical critique of moral claims of universality. Not only does their epistemological status seem untenable, but transformed into horizons of ethical necessity and obligation they also turn out to be painful for those who do not spontaneously share them: "need is always a pain" (45).[29]

If in Rameau's world the perception, interpretation, and appreciation of things and people happen on the premise of contingency, if the fact that that nothing ever appears under the claim of being necessary makes up for the frankness and freedom of his life, then judgment has to be the central operation of behavior for him. As I said in the previous chapter, I understand by "judgment" a choice among a plurality of perspectives or options, a choice that cannot be based on any inductive or deductive logic and that must therefore be focused on phenomena or situations in their singularity.

After Rameau's profile and after contingency as a general presupposition, judgment is the third dimension through which we can describe Diderot's title protagonist. So ubiquitous are moments of judgment in Rameau's interventions and monologues indeed that they hardly need to become explicit. There is one passage, however, where "Lui" invokes judgment as a practice and social strategy at which he excels:

> But you mustn't always show your approval in the same way. It'd be monotonous. You'd seem false. You'd become insipid. That can only be avoided with good judgement and constant inventiveness; you have to know how to pave the way for the major chords so that you can suddenly bring them in, grasping the opportunity at the right moment; when, for instance, there is a difference of opinion, and the argument has reached its highest pitch, when you can't hear the sound of your own voice and everyone's talking at once, you've taken up a position on the side-lines, in the corner of the room the furthest away from the battlefield, you've kept quiet for a good long time so as to create maximum impact and suddenly you drop like a mortar bomb into the midst of the combatants. Nobody is more skilful at this than I am. But my most surprising skills are at the other end of the scale; I can produce tiny sounds which I accompany with a smile, an infinite variety of approving expressions. (51–52)[30]

Consensus, it seems, is neither expected nor particularly desirable in Rameau's view. Once a variety of opinions turns into the violence of a "dispute," however, it becomes important to capture such situations in their specific structures and circumstances. And what Rameau describes as the basis of his respective mastery is a strategy of subtlety and of "small" tones and gestures. Quite regularly, indeed, the premise of contingency and the practice of judgment go together with a behavioral register of nuances.

At the same time, judgment as a practice of nuances becomes the basis of Rameau's desire to be different from others: not better than others, more valuable, or of higher social respect, but just individually different (the word *singulier* appears quite frequently in these passages)—and thus irreplaceable: "MOI: However sublimely talented you might be, someone else can always take your place. LUI: Only with difficulty" (28).[31] This claim to singularity relies on the multiple registers of nuance in social behavior that Rameau can handle—and he insists more on their internal variety than on any claims of invention or innovation:

> I have over a hundred ways of setting up the seduction of a young girl, while in her mother's presence, without the latter realizing, and some-times even turning her into an accomplice. I'd hardly started out in this career when I realized that all the common ways of slipping someone a love-letter were beneath me. I have ten different ways of forcing people to snatch them from me, and among those ways, I flatter myself that some of them are novel. [. . .] If it were ever written down, I believe people would acknowledge I had some genius. (54)[32]

In the end, Rameau feels entitled to believe that he has indeed achieved singular distinction and that he is thus able to escape any predetermination inherent to social groups or situations: "I am uncommon in my species, yes, very uncommon" (63).[33] Even more confidently, with a hint of self-irony prob-ably intended by Diderot, he finally states: "And yet I'm well below average at music, whereas at morals, I'm near the top" (85).[34]

There is one final dimension left in our description of Rameau's nephew. "Lui" refers to it, several times in the text, by calling himself a *colporteur*, that is, a person who copies and spreads discourses, descriptions, and narratives without adding anything to them: "And moreover, all those awful stories, they're not mine, I don't make them up; I just hawk them around" (67).[35] This role is contiguous to Rameau's special capacity, highlighted by Jean Staro-binski, of imitating voices, of copying the body movements of other persons and, above all, of embodying whatever is on his own mind. We do not know whether it was the historical Rameau who inspired this single most salient feature in the fictional Rameau—but whenever it appears, the Philosopher remains deeply impressed. Rameau's "pantomine" occurs for the first time immediately after the scene where he produces a noise with the bones and joints of his hands:

> At this point, he is striking the pose of a violin-player; he is humming an allegro by Locatelli; his right arm is miming the action of the bow, his left hand and fingers look as though they are skipping all the way up the fingerboard; if the tuning goes out, he stops to tighten or lower the string; he plucks it with his nail to check it's right; he picks up the piece where he

left off; he beats time with his foot, he throws himself into it completely, head, feet, hands, arms, body. [. . .] In the midst of his writhing and howling, when there was a pause—one of those harmonious moments when the bow moves slowly across many strings at once—an expression of bliss would come across his face, his voice would soften, he would be in ecstasy just listening to himself. His ears could truly hear the chords resonating, and so could mine. Then tucking the instrument under his left arm with the hand he'd been holding it in, and letting his right hand drop with the bow, he said: So, what do you think of that? (32–33)[36]

The very degree of complexity that this musical performance without an instrument reaches in the Philosopher's (and Diderot's) description is difficult to imagine in the real world, for it implies not only complex body movements but, at the same time, the reproduction of a piece of classical music through Rameau's voice. The more the text advances, the more frequently Rameau seems to turn to such virtuoso moments, until they progress from solo performance to the even more impossible imitation of an entire orchestra. In the words of the Philosopher:

> But you would have roared with laughter at the way he impersonated the different instruments. The horns and bassoons, he did puffing his cheeks up like balloons, and making hoarse, low sounds; he made a piercing, nasal noise for the oboes; his voice catapulting up and down at incredible speed, he did as close an imitation of the strings as he could; he whistled the piccolos and cooed the flutes; shouting, singing, charging about like a madman, single-handedly doing the dancers, both male and female, the singers, both male and female, a whole orchestra, a whole opera company, dividing himself between twenty different roles. (77)[37]

These moments are not limited to the reproduction and production of music. While telling the Philosopher a story about an abbot at the entrance of the Académie Française who wanted to break down its—metaphorically—with his head, Rameau gives his own—bodily—interpretation of the image in question:

> After telling this little story, my man started pacing to and fro, looking down, with a pensive and a weary air; he sighed, wept, grieved, raised

his hands, and looked up, punched himself in the head so violently that he nearly broke his forehead or his fingers, adding: It seems to me that there must be something in there, but however hard I hit it or shake it, nothing comes out. Then he began shaking his head again, and hitting his forehead even harder, saying: Either there's nobody at home, or they're refusing to answer. (87)[38]

I propose to call this truly singular behavior, which was probably born in Denis Diderot's imagination, "metabolic" because it consists of a contiguity and an exchange between the human mind and the material world, a contiguity within which the mind feeds on corporeality, with the effect of gaining a physical life and of giving back its spiritual energy condensed in physical life to the material world. A more intense visualization and materialization of the inseparability of human self-perception from human perception of the physical world is hard to imagine. It goes along, in Diderot's text, with numerous moments where "Lui" refers to himself or to other persons using animal metaphors, for example wolves and tigers (57/445), apes (58/446), dogs (64/452), and cats (64/453). Even more interesting in this context is the specific status of music as the medium in which Rameau's nephew is leading his life. For music is another—by no means fictional—case of a metabolic relationship between the mind and its material environment. In music, the mind feeds on sound as a primary dimension of the physical world, as its raw material so to speak, in order to become material life and to thus give in return its own energy to the material world, in canonical forms like songs or symphonies.

———

Hegel was not the only major thinker who found Diderot's text and its protagonist fascinating and philosophically challenging. More recently, Michel Foucault dedicated a chapter of his book *Madness and Civilization* to *Le neveu de Rameau*.[39] Not surprisingly, given his own topic, Foucault started out with a focus on "madness," as one of so many labels that the Nephew uses in describing himself. According to Foucault, a specific modality of madness, fictionally embodied by Rameau, "flows back towards rationality"; more precisely, it becomes part of an enlightened "rationality that can only be certain of itself against the background of madness" (218). But while this reading is solidly based on Diderot's text, it fails to pinpoint what is episte-mologically specific about the dialogue between "Moi" and "Lui." Foucault probably comes closer to the energy center of this intellectual dynamic when he uses a "delirium of reality" to describe Rameau's metabolic moments, interpreting them as symptoms of a radically "anti-Cartesian" position. If a problem remains, it has to do with the urge to suggest a single description that is supposed to bring together the multiple aspects that constitute Rameau as a fictional character. Even Starobinski, in spite of his general hesitation to outline a comprehensive approach to Diderot's work, falls under the spell of this urge when he speaks at some point of an *esthétisation à outrance*" as a way to comprehensively describe Rameau.

Of course it is true that Rameau's "pantomines," as the practice of a fic-tional character, mark a possible counterpoint to a philosophy that defines the ontology of human existence as synonymous with consciousness. Intrin-sically, however, Rameau's tendency to embody whatever is not materially present to him seems to be but one zone of intensity within a paradoxical identity that lacks a center among so many dimensions. Even Rameau's met-abolic practice is broken down and fragmented in his unlimited openness to the world and in his refusal to ever settle upon just one premise of behavior. The ongoing play between Rameau's metabolic contiguity to the world and his both complex and never stable profile, permeated by impulses of energy that go into opposite directions, bears a certain resemblance to the figure of the devil—which eighteenth-century philosophy was so proud to have overcome and which, at the same time, had a strong and fascinating comeback in the figure of Mephisto in Goethe's "Faust."[40] I do not believe that Diderot had this potential resemblance between Rameau and the devil on his mind, but, on the other hand, it is interesting to see that the word *diable* has a permanent (albeit always casual) presence in Rameau's language—and, for all we know, also in Diderot's everyday conversations.[41]

The impression, however, of ever-mobile contours of identity in the in-teraction between two protagonists does apply to the relationship between Diderot and his characters. Its proportions are different in different dimen-sions, and what makes Rameau above all similar to his inventor are his openness, his generosity, and the desire to share with others his individual moments of sensual enjoyment. That said, I imagine that Diderot would not have had a clear answer to the question of whether he identified more with the Philosopher or more with Rameau. But we can say that, like Diderot, the fictional Rameau never appears to be rushed. To create a personal order of time is not an issue for either of them. The fictional "Moi," by contrast, proudly insists that walking at Palais Royal in the late afternoon is a part of his daily schedule.

I have tried to argue that the epistemological configuration that assigns an eccentric place to Denis Diderot and his works in our retrospective look at the late eighteenth and early nineteenth centuries does not appear to have been exclusive to his frame of mind. Perhaps we should not even speak of a "configuration," because that frame of mind may well have been the result of an intellectual style without a will to contour, the product of permanent practice without "consequence," rather than a consistent intellectual gesture. We can certainly find aspects and effects similar to this practice—and even more complex structures through which they converge into new combinations—in the works of a small group of contemporary authors and artists, a group by the way that was by no means aware of that potential affinity. One eminent figure in this context is Francisco de Goya, who was thirty-eight years old when Diderot died and survived him by forty-four years. By February 1799, an advertisement in a Madrid daily newspaper announced that a collection of eighty etchings by Goya on "eccentric topics" (*asuntos caprichosos*) was available for sale at a downtown "liquor and perfume store." The short text describing this collection could hardly have been more conventional (and perhaps even more opportunistic) in the capital of a monarchy that desperately tried to appear "enlightened":

> As the author is convinced that, while the critique of human errors and vices seems to be a task of eloquence and poetry, it can also be performed by painting, he has chosen, as an appropriate concern for his art, the intention to ridicule some of the most common extravagances and mistakes that one generally finds in all contemporary societies.[42]

The claim that artistic techniques can be used to ridicule the vices predominant in contemporary society, the implication that this critical function may go together with the display of artistic imagination, and the politely modest hesitation about the efficiency of artworks in comparison to satirical texts: all three of these premises belong to long-standing poetological traditions. If, on the one hand, we have no major biographical reason to suspect that Goya was skeptical about these assumptions, there are, on the other hand, two traces of a certain degree of nervousness that may have accompanied the publication of the "Caprichos."

Only a few days before the collection went up for sale, Goya moved the etching with the caption "El sueño de la razón produce monstruos" ("The sleep (dream) of reason produces monsters") (which is today the most famous one) from the potentially programmatic first position in the collection to number 43. Then, shortly after the announcement and with only twenty-seven copies sold, he withdrew the collection from the market. This does not necessarily mean that Goya had been lying about his intentions because there was some different and politically provocative function that he needed to hide. I rather believe that (and in this he was similar to Diderot) he was vaguely aware of a provocative potential inherent to his work—although this potential did not result from any deliberate strategy.

Especially in the first half of Goya's collection, images and topics that refer to concerns of the general Enlightenment agenda prevail. Educational scenes figure most prominently among them, together with scenes that represent the habit of marrying beautiful young women off to wealthy (and often ugly) old men. This was a motif that, under the motto "El sí de las ninas" ("The Yes of the Young Girls," from a play by Fernando de Moratín, a friend of Goya's) had found specifically strong resonance in Spanish society. But the actual etchings hardly ever correspond to the enlightened expectations that they must first have evoked. Education for example never appears as a generous practice facilitating the development of autonomous and morally responsible personalities. Neither do the "Caprichos" lead us to the unequivocal impression that those young women on the verge of being married off to wealthy old husbands are victims. Capricho 2 already departs from the conventional perspective: its caption "El sí pronuncian y la mano alargan" ("They pronounce the yes and stretch out their hand") seems to attribute at least part of the responsibility for this kind of asymmetrical relationship to the young woman it refers to, for the mask that she is wearing must stand for a strategy of hiding her own identity and intentions. Might the two old men to her right and left be the true victims after all?

We can ask a similar question regarding Capricho 14 and its caption "Que sacrificio!" ("What a sacrifice!"). Here the old man is a hunchback—which by the standards of present-day sensibility would quite naturally mean that the role of the victim would be attributed to him. And even in an eighteenth-century context, the contrast between the expression of enthusiasm on his face and the young woman's gesture of hesitation, together with the dark figures standing next to her, must provoke ambiguous interpretations of their relationship. For the entire collection of the "Caprichos," a series of three different contemporary reactions to each individual etching has been preserved, and these remarks document the confusion that such departures from the expected perspectives in many of Goya's images must have produced. In the case of Capricho 14, two of the commentaries perceive a more or less even distribution of advantages and disadvantages between the two protagonists. While the groom's physical deformation is seen as repulsive, a more comprehensive conclusion states that while he is sacrificing money for the privilege of sharing his bed with a beautiful young woman, the young woman will gain a much improved economic situation for herself and her family: "This is how it has to be! The groom is not among the most desirable (ones) but he is wealthy, and thus the salvation (rescue) of a needy family is achieved at the expense of an unfortunate girl. This is how the world goes."[43] The third commentary, by contrast, corresponds to a more conventional perspective on this topic which identifies a coalition among grooms, families, and the Church against the young woman's interest, and thus reduces the ambiguity of the captions that leave it open which of the two protagonists is making the true "sacrifice": "Their vile interest obliges the parents to sacrifice a young and beautiful daughter by marrying her to a hunchbacked old man, and there is no lack of priests who play the role of the godfather for such weddings."

The affinity between Goya's "Caprichos" and the epistemological horizon that we have begun to identify in some of Diderot's texts depends on the observer perspective inherent to most of the etchings. This perspective often transforms situations that are emblematic of well-established moral positions into scenes of provocative contingency. Goya's etchings must thus have given contemporary observers the opportunity and challenge of confronting themselves with a steeply increased complexity of the world—and pushed them into situations where they had to judge without any predefined orientation (which explains their often hilarious commentaries).

The contrast between the standard expectations and Goya's images was probably even more dramatic in his etchings about education. They show parents lying to their children in order to keep them quiet (2), children so spoiled by education that they are incapable of leaving childhood behind them (4), or donkeys as instructors and students (37–41). Such drastic effects are often the product of subtle distances and shifts between the views of conventional morality and Goya's individual images. Like in Diderot's texts, producing effects of contingency has to do with nuance rather than with clear-cut distinctions.

This very technique becomes most visible in Capricho 43, which must have been both the reason why Goya originally placed it at the opening of the collection and why he changed its location immediately before publication. Capricho 43 is also the only image of the series that includes its own caption in the etching itself: "El sueño de la razón produce monstruos." Here, the three commentaries converge in a reading that understands the sleep (or the absence) of reason as a condition under which disturbing "fantasies" or "visions" arise—and one of the reactions adds that such fantasies can also become the "mother of art" and "the origin of wonders." From a purely grammatical standpoint, however, and due to the double meaning of the Spanish noun "sueño" (as both "sleep" and "dream"), the caption can also be understood in an opposite—and then directly anti-enlightened—sense: "the dream of reason produces monsters." Whether Goya was aware of this ambiguity or had even intended it, we will never know—although the repositioning of Capricho 43 seems to suggest that he anticipated the possibility, and the danger, of an unorthodox reading.[44] The truly interesting aspect here is the tendency, characteristic of the "Caprichos" and their implicit observer perspective, towards interpretative destabilization and effects of contingency based on minimal departures from iconic conventions. In addition to the image's ambiguous caption, the "monsters" depicted in Capricho 43 are less frightening than one might anticipate. They look like owls with friendly, human-like faces—and their plumage seems soft enough to awaken the desire of being touched by them.

Following Capricho 43, we are confronted with a number of images that do not produce effects of contingency, because they present certain motifs without aspects of ambiguity or oscillation. Several of these etchings present aspects of a metabolic relationship to the world, most acutely the particularly unsettling Capricho 69, which shows five naked or half-naked old men in physical contact with four naked children. One old man is holding a child by his or her legs close to a fire, which may explain why a wind is emerging from the child's anus. "Sopla" is the title—which we can read as "blow!" or "it blows."

The most dominant motif in the second part of the "Caprichos," however, features human or hybrid figures that are being carried through the air, hovering, or flying. We can interpret hovering bodies and flying bodies as yet another modality of the metabolic relationship between humans and the world. For hovering and flying—as conditions that are of course not really open to humans—may be understood (as Heinrich von Kleist showed in his essay on the "Marionettentheater") as symbols of a balance between the effect of gravity through which figures are attached to the earth and an opposite effect of elevation (which Kleist relates to an only vaguely evoked religious dimension, whereas Goya associates it with witchcraft and other folkloric traditions).

The contemporary commentaries look helpless in their attempt to rescue the possibility of coherent and even edifying meanings. Capricho 65, with the caption "¿Dónde va mama?" ("Where is Mama going?"), features an obese woman being carried through the air and embraced by several folkloric figures with rather masculine faces. And the commentaries (in this case only two) state:

- Madam is suffering from the waters (dropsy) and they send her on a walk. May God help her to feel alleviated.

- The easy life and the drunkenness of women produce endless confusion and a truly witchlike world.

Both reactions seem at a loss about the meaning to be attributed to the etching. In the impossibility of finding any conventional or at least plausible interpretation, the first of them refers to the institutional framework of a medical treatment (according to the professional standards of Goya's time), whereas the second reverts to a moralistic gesture as it belongs to the satirical genre.

For us the truly important insight seems to be that Goya's art begins to imagine different relationships between humans and their material environment for whose quite literally metabolic forms we have still not come up with sufficiently differentiated concepts. The other affinity between Goya's "Caprichos" and Diderot's *Neveu de Rameau* lies in an effect of semantic openness and of openness to the world. It emerges from the text's and the collection's serial structure, lacking any construction or vanishing point that would bring together the phenomena evoked in a condensation or a synthesis. Both at the end of Diderot's text and at the end of the "Caprichos," we may feel that we have been present at a dismantling of the world as we knew it, a dismantling that becomes the precondition for an explosion into centrifugal perspectives and the emergence of a new and yet unfamiliar metabolism between human bodies and the material world as their environment.

If Goya, at least in the first half of the "Caprichos," tends to confront us with figures that appear generic at first glance only to transform them into scenes of contingency, the German scientist and philosopher of nature Georg Christoph Lichtenberg shares with Denis Diderot, who died when Lichtenberg was forty-two years old, an insistence on singularity that he orchestrates in a multiplicity of different conceptual and practical perspectives. This primarily happens not in his academic writings, which earned him a professorship at the University of Göttingen, great respect in the Republic of Letters, and a place in the history of science, but in his *Waste Books* (*Sudelbücher*), brief notes that he kept from 1765 until his death in 1799. The *Waste Books* have given Lichtenberg the permanent status of a popular author among intellectuals, even today.

In a reflection from the earlier years of the *Waste Books*, Lichtenberg undercuts a tendency to speak about his own time from a "totalizing angle" (as we would say today, with a similarly critical undertone) and thus brings to the fore the dimension of singularity:

> The history of a century consists of the histories of its individual years. In order to describe the spirit of a century, it is not appropriate to sew together the histories of its years, and yet it is helpful for whoever undertakes this task to know the substance of the individual years.[45]

In very few words, Lichtenberg develops a complex view of our intellectual relationship to the past. He does not, in the first place, categorically exclude the possibility of "describing the spirit of a century." What he finds implausible is only an inductive process that would lead from the knowledge of individual years to an overarching and abstract view of a period. To such a process he refers—critically—with the metaphor of "sewing them together" (*zusammenflicken*). By contrast, Lichtenberg suggests drawing "permanent lines" (*stete Linien*)—and this expression must refer to general concepts that are not inductively gained—through individual years because this practice would "always produce new aspects." Over conceptual reduction, he seems to prefer holding individual years against the backdrop of abstract concepts in order to tease out their complex singularity.

This intellectual desire for complexity must have been the origin and the vanishing point for his never-ending remarks about the nature and the functions of language. Their recurrent motif is the highlighting of an asymmetry between the world of objects and language or, more precisely, the incapacity of language to correspond to the world in its endless variety of forms and in the specific modes through which these forms cohere. Seen from this premise, different words can never be truly synonymous: "There are no synonyms, for the words that we identify as such most likely expressed more specific and therefore different things for the people who invented them."[46] With *Einerlei* Lichtenberg refers to singularity as it remains inaccessible to abstract concepts, and in his use of the word *Species* we encounter the same reservation against anything generic that we have already seen in Rameau's ironic remark about the concept of "espèce." At the same time, words in their fundamental separation can never capture the specific way in which different phenomena, especially phenomena belonging to the human "soul," relate to each other:

> It is an inevitable shortcoming of all languages that they only use general notions and therefore hardly ever really say what they intend to say. For

whenever we compare the words to the things they are referring to we will discover that the latter always move in a direction different from the former.[47]

This reflection brings us back, through the phenomenology of the human soul used as an example by Lichtenberg, to the dimension of "nuance" as it also permeates Rameau's perception of the world and the gestures with which he reacts to it. And as, according to Lichtenberg, no single word can ever do full justice to the phenomenon it alludes to, another similarity between Rameau the character and Lichtenberg the author lies in the tendency to come up, over and again, with long lists of words that seem to be—but are not really—synonymous:

> Es donnert, *heult, brüllt*, zischt, pfeift, braust, saust, summet, brummet, rumpelt, *quäkt, ächzt, singt,* rappelt, knallt, rasselt, knistert, klappert, *knurret, poltert, winselt, wimmert, rauscht, murmelt*, kracht, *gluckset, roecheln [sic],* klingelt, [. . .] Diese Wörter und noch andere, welche Töne ausdrucken, sind nicht blosse Zeichen, sondern eine Art von Bilderschrift für das Ohr.

While it is impossible to ever truly "translate" such a series of onomatopoetic words, they may not have been as onomatopoetic as Lichtenberg seems to imply ("image-writing for the ear," *Bilderschrift für das Ohr*), but in their accumulation they become a symptom of the pleasure that he takes in their material being, as the trace of sound on the paper.

If Goya's "Caprichos" feature the production of contingency as a process and the metabolic contiguity with the physical world as a topic in the juxtaposition of eighty etchings, metabolic moments also occur throughout Lichtenberg's reflections on singularity, nuance, and the materiality of language. We witness an obsession with kissing, biting, and eating, and the status of these acts is not always unambiguously metaphorical: "He had no appetite for anything and yet was eating some of everything." "A tiny face not for kisses but for bites."[48] This obsession comes closest to Rameau's "pantomimes" (without of course being their full equivalent) when Lichtenberg describes the strong reactions of his body to moments of emotion, even when the intensity of those emotions is triggered by the mediation of language:

> I have been one of those who react to pieces of prose describing emotions
> with a delight that produces goosebumps: holy music and the thunder
> of timpani have made me believe that I was hearing the steps of the Al-
> mighty and had me shed pious tears. With unspeakable voluptuousness I
> remember the day when, at Westminster Abbey, I walked over the dust of
> Kings and sang those words of the "God of Eternities."[49]

For all of their distance from academic conventions, Lichtenberg's notes
mostly pursue canonical questions of philosophy, and this must be the
reason why their depiction of metabolic layers in human life appears more
attenuated than in the monologues of Diderot's Rameau or in Goya's
"Caprichos." But what matters, in our attempt to unfold the phenomenology of "prose of the world" as the epistemological grid underlying a
specific form of existence, is the recurrent contiguity between passages
remembering metabolic moments in Lichtenberg's life and his concern
with singularity and nuance.

To conclude this chapter, I want to focus on one of the more colorful
fictional characters from the European cultural legacy, a figure who—
seen from our specific point of view—may look like a brother of Rameau's
nephew although (or because?) his role was probably invented as a drastic
counterpoint to everything that the eighteenth century considered to be
"philosophical." I am referring to Papageno, from the libretto, written by
Emanuel Schikaneder, of Mozart's opera "The Magic Flute." I will bracket
the questions that have been in the foreground of long discussions between
musicologists and cultural historians about the influence of Free Masonic
thought on this text, about the theater house at the periphery of Vienna with
its mostly unsophisticated spectators where the opera was first produced in
1791, and about certain doubts regarding the authorship of Schikaneder—
who was also the entrepreneur behind this performance and the first actor
to play Papageno. What I want to elaborate is an intuition about the possible
affinity between Papageno and the "prose of the world" configuration.

That Papageno is not only aware, like Rameau, of the animal side of
human existence as a general condition but must indeed be seen, within the
narrative economy of the different characters, as a hybrid figure between the
human world and the world of birds, becomes immediately clear with his
first appearance on the stage:

Papageno arrives, dressed in feathers. He carries a large bird cage on his back that is filled with various birds. In his hands he holds a small flute.[50]

PAPAGENO:

Der Vogelfänger bin ich ja,
Stets lustig, heisa, hopsasa!
Ich Vogelfänger bin bekannt
bei Alt und Jung im ganzen Land.
Weiss mit dem Locken umzugehn
und mich aufs Pfeiffen zu verstehn.
Drum kann ich froh und lustig
    sein,
Denn alle Vögel sind ja mein.
[. . .]
ein Netz für Mädchen möchte ich,
ich fing sie dutzendweis für mich.
Dann sperrte ich sie bei mir ein,
Und alle Mädchen wären mein.
Wenn alle Mädchen wären mein,
so tauschte ich brav Zucker ein.
Die, welche mir am liebsten wär',
der gäb ich gleich den Zucker her.
Und küsste sie mich zärtlich dann,
wär' sie mein Weib und ich ihr
    Mann.
Sie schlief an meiner Seite ein,
ich wiegte wie ein Kind sie ein.[51]

PAPAGENO:

I'm the bird-catcher, who's always
happy! Hi ho! I'm known all
over by young and old. I know
how to whistle every sound,
and I know all the birdcalls.
That's why I can be merry and
happy, because all the birds
are mine.
[. . .]
I'd like to have a net to catch girls
by the dozens. I would lock
them safely at home so that
they'd all be mine.
When they'd be mine, I'd give
them sugar, but I'd give sugar
right away to the one I love
most.
Then if she would kiss me tenderly, it would be as if we were
husband and wife. She would
sleep beside me, and I would
rock her like a baby.

Later on, the spectators will become familiar with Papageno's habit of comparing himself to all kinds of animals, to tigers, mice, and snails; and they will also hear how Tamino, the typical prince in quest of his romantic princess, and Papageno's friend, is not quite certain whether he should consider him human: "Weil . . . weil ich zweifle ob du ein Mensch bist" (46).[52] Already in his first aria, Papageno describes himself as what Rameau's nephew had called "un diable de ramage," that is, somebody who is capable of copying the voices of all the birds, by whistling and playing his flute, and of thus attracting and catching them. Both his own physical presence and the relation to the birds in his environment constitute an elementary version of what I have described as a metabolic form of life, and this also holds true for Papageno's relationship with "girls": he wants to catch them with a net (as if they were birds) in order to possess them, and he wants to feed sugar to "the one he loves most" and then kiss her, so that they can become husband and wife and sleep next to each other.

But that innocence of sleeping next to a girl and just "rocking her like a baby" is just one side of Papageno's animality; the other side is procreation, and procreation will dominate the relationship with his "Weibchen"[53] Papagena at the end of the opera:

BEIDE:

Welche Freude wird das sein,
   wenn die
Götter uns bedenken, unsrer liebe
   Kinder
Schenken, so liebe, kleine
   Kinderlein!

PAPAGENO:

Erst einen kleinen Papageno.

PAPAGENA:

Dann eine kleine Papagena.

[. . .]

BEIDE:

Papageno! Papagena!
Es ist das höchste der Gefühle,
wenn viele, viele Papageno/a,
der Eltern Segen werden sein (108).

BOTH:

What a joy it would be if the gods
would bless us with children, very
darling little children!

PAPAGENO:

First a little Papageno.

PAPAGENA:

Then a little Papagena.

[. . .]

BOTH:

Papagena! [sic] Papagena!
It would be the greatest feeling
If we would be blessed with many
Papagenos and Papagenas.

A romantic relationship, with its emotional complexity and depth, with tensions, inner fights, strategies, and moments of fulfillment, by contrast, does not belong to the options of Papageno's existence. He can either hold "girls" in his arms very tenderly or procreate with his "little wife," and in this condition we discover yet another bundle of affinities with Rameau who, despite his intelligence and due to his frankness, has no psychic depth either, and can thus admire his wife's perfect body, prostitute her, and not feel any regret when she leaves him.

What Papageno, the birdcatcher and "diable de ramage," achieves with his whistling and his flute, has its equivalent among the more "serious" protagonists of Schikaneder's libretto. I am referring to the "magic flute," a folklore motif that gave the opera its name and that Parmeno receives from the "Three Ladies" before his journey into the foreign world of Sarastro:

ERSTE DAME:

O Prinz nimm dies Geschenk von
    mir!
Dies sendet uns're Fürstin dir.
Die Zauberflöte wird dich schützen,
im grössten Unglück unterstützen.

DREI DAMEN:

Hiermit kannst du allmächtig
    handeln,
der Menschen Leidenschaft ver-
    wandeln:
der Traurige wird freudig sein,
den Hagestolz nimmt Liebe ein.

    (54)

FIRST LADY:

Oh Prince, take this gift from me!
Our Queen commanded us to give
it to you. This Magic Flute will
protect you in danger and Support
you in your deepest sorrow.

THE THREE LADIES:

With this flute you will possess
divine powers. You can reverse
human suffering, convert Sadness
to happiness, and assure that the
Loveless will always be loved.

This second flute will indeed protect Tamino and Papageno because "its melodious tones [. . .] have the power to even delight wild animals" (66), but it does not attract the wonderfully reasonable Pamina, whom Tamino adores and who only seems to react to the simple flute of Papageno (67). Instead of engaging in the metaphysics (or mechanics) of all the flutes and "sets of bells" (68) in Schikaneder's text—a text that was certainly not written for the many sophisticated interpretations that it has received over the past two centuries—I want to highlight one final feature that this libretto shares with Diderot's *Neveu de Rameau*. If Diderot invented an energetically oscillating dialogue between two so profoundly different characters as the Philosopher and Rameau's nephew, the liveliness of Schikaneder's text, quite similarly, emerges not from the contrast between Sarastro's both enlightened and monastic-looking empire and the world owned by the Queen of the Night, but from the interference between, on the one side, these two very serious worlds and, on the other side, Papageno and Monostatus (Papageno's morally evil equivalent). In more abstract terms: the "Magic Flute"—like *Le neveu de Rameau*—is about the interaction, interference, and oscillation between rational and metabolic forms of life. This complex and historically specific intersection of different motifs, concepts, and values that cannot possibly be reconciled not only gave their basic form and flavor to both Schikaneder's "Magic Flute" and Diderot's *Neveu de Rameau*, it may also have corresponded to Masonry, as a complex and highly eclectic worldview whose omnipresence and influence culminated in the late eighteenth century. If Schikaneder tried, not very successfully, to let the enlightened world prevail in the end, Diderot's greater sympathy for the Nephew becomes clear right from the start.

This palpable sympathy for his eccentric protagonist, I believe, belongs to the features that make Denis Diderot a potentially appealing figure to readers in the twenty-first century. Sociologically speaking, Rameau's nephew's way of life resembles, from several perspectives, that of a present-day "homeless person" (he is, indeed, quite literally homeless). But his unconditional will "to be and to stay" at Port Royal, in the material environment assigned to him randomly or by fate; the paradoxical convergence of exuberance, concreteness, and precision in his speech; and his metabolic relation to things and bodies around him (and possibly also the absence of any coherent morality) give this protagonist the status of a potential object of desire for people like us in whose life nothing can escape the suspicion of being "virtual" or "constructed." This is the specific fascination to which I allude, in the title of this chapter and for the lack of a better concept, with the word "ontology," the fascination that is also behind our tendency to separate Rameau's nephew from the Philosopher with whom, at first glance, we believe we more easily identify.

No such ideas, I am sure, were on Diderot's mind during the different stages of his work on the *Neveu de Rameau* manuscript. Even Goethe's enthusiasm might have surprised him, because he did not live to see the full development of philosophical Idealism, which, as a background of contrast, most likely explains the specific popularity of the *Neveu de Rameau* among

German intellectuals. Like most authors of the past whom we consider to be important, Denis Diderot may have inadvertently been ahead of his time (although he was definitely not ambitious about that). While I have already mentioned that his texts, in that way unlike the texts of Voltaire and Rousseau, have never been dominant during any single moment of their reception history, we can discover not only signs of explicit admiration but, more interestingly, symptoms of affinity with Diderot's intellectual style and its epistemological framework among a number of authors and artists from the European generation who overlapped with and followed him.

To mention just the names that have come up so far: Francisco de Goya was born in 1742, Georg Christoph Lichtenberg in 1748, Johann Wolfgang von Goethe in 1749, Emanuel Schikaneder in 1751, and Wolfgang Amadeus Mozart in 1756. Famous as these men were in their own institutional and regional worlds, none of them would probably have known of all the others by the time Mozart died in December 1791. There could certainly not have been any awareness of a vanishing point, however vaguely we want to circumscribe it, in which the works of these authors and artists might have converged and that they would have shared with Diderot. And yet it is tempting to look for a joint condition in those lives that might account for their intellectual affinity. And while it seems impossible to come up with any answers that are not banal, I find it interesting that four of those six protagonists struggled— physically and emotionally—with bodily deficiencies. Early in the year 1793, a serious illness whose exact nature we do not know left Goya almost completely deaf; owing to a malformation of his spine, Lichtenberg was unusually short, became a hunchback, and suffered from breathing and heart problems that produced anxiety attacks; Schikaneder, one year before his death, was diagnosed as "stricken with insanity"; and Mozart, as a contemporary opera singer remembered, was "a remarkably small man, very thin and pale" and quite unhappy about this appearance (and in addition, there is reason to imagine that he showed signs of a behavior that we call "Tourette syndrome" today, that is, a tendency towards obsessive-compulsive body movements, often accompanied by verbal obscenities). Beyond the all-too-obvious assumption that such conditions might have triggered individually specific ways of physically being in the world, I will not try to engage in any further speculations. Denis Diderot, like Johann Wolfgang von Goethe, meanwhile, lived a healthy life by eighteenth-century standards. Unlike Goethe, however, we know that he did not like to travel. His openness, sensitivity to the material world, and imagination probably did not depend on situations of immediacy and physical closeness.

4 | "CHOSES BIZARRES ÉCRITES SUR LE GRAND ROULEAU"

Powers of Contingency in Jacques le fataliste et son maître

ALTHOUGH THE WORD had an unstable meaning and was thus not frequently used in the eighteenth century,[1] we have seen how Rameau's nephew, the protagonist of Diderot's last fictional text, leads a life under the practical premise of contingency, as he proudly refuses to trace (let alone care about) any consistency in his behavior and actions. The fictional "Philosopher's" insistent claim that there should be a joint value of happiness and an obligatory way towards its realization must therefore appear "romanesque" and "bizarre" to the Nephew:

> You believe happiness is made the same for everyone. What a strange vision! Your happiness presupposes a certain romantic turn of mind that we do not have, a singular soul, a peculiar taste. You confer the title of virtue on this weirdness; you call it philosophy. But are virtue and philosophy made for everyone? Enjoy them if you can, hold onto them if you can. Imagine what a wise and philosophical universe would be like; you must agree it'd be miserable as hell. (43)[2]

To most twenty-first-century readers, however (and this is probably no different from the reaction of their predecessors in Diderot's time), this discourse looks counterintuitive. For is not precisely Rameau (the Nephew) the "romanesque" and "bizarre" character, in contrast to the Philosopher, whose energy seems to fade away as he tries to be faithful to his abstract and rational principles? Of course it all depends on the perspective we choose. If Rameau suggests that the Philosopher's consistently moral worldview shows a deplorable lack of everyday realism, he may indeed call him eccentric ("une âme singulière") and "bizarre," the second adjective meaning both "impossible to explain" and, paradoxically as a description for a rational standpoint, "impossible to subsume under a general principle." If, on the other hand, we share the Philosopher's conviction that a conduct along commonly embraced values is necessary and well possible, then Rameau's erratic style of existence must appear "bizarre" to us.

The title of *Jacques le fataliste et son maître* announces that the main character of yet another fictional dialogue written by Denis Diderot—this dialogue between Jacques, the Servant, and his aristocratic Master—will also include a belief in necessity, but this time it is less a belief in the necessity of moral behavior than a belief in necessity as fate and predetermination, to which Jacques endlessly and not only metaphorically refers as the "great scroll written up yonder" (8, 12, 13, etc.).[3] Based on our experience from the previous chapter, that the author, instead of maintaining an equidistant relationship to the reasonable Philosopher and the erratic Nephew, must have developed, inadvertently perhaps, a growing fondness for the latter, we may further assume that, in spite of his frequent Materialistic speculations about a universe functioning according to laws of necessity, Diderot was not likely to fully embrace Jacques's fatalism as an unavoidable postulate of necessity. Rather, he described it as one of those "bizarre" and obsessive personal attitudes that exist without much reason or major plausibility. At the same time, and due to his never-changing openness to the world and its phenomena, such a reaction would not easily become synonymous with a prejudice or an explicit critique of "fatalism."

But we are ahead of ourselves in the analysis of contingency that this chapter will try to develop in a reading of *Jacques le fataliste et son maître*. Before we begin to discuss the text from this angle, we must, finally, ask what precisely we mean when we speak of "contingency." The standard definition calls phenomena or situations "contingent" when their existence appears neither necessary nor impossible. Their emergence (or non-emergence) depends, in each individual case, on specific circumstances that are themselves contingent—which explains why, in everyday English, the concept almost always highlights how certain phenomena are contingent "upon" others. By contrast, the German noun *Kontingenz* (which informs my rather untypical use of the English word) predominantly refers just to the status of situations or decisions between necessity and impossibility (mostly without explaining under what conditions they might or might not become real).

Now this status of phenomena between necessity and impossibility, as we may already have seen thanks to the reference to Jacques's fatalism and to Rameau's inconsistency, can occur in two different dimensions, i.e. in the past or in the future. Looking back, contingency typically focuses on the impossibility of subsuming phenomena, situations, or developments under general rules, which implies that each of them must be considered as "singular." Projected into the future, however, a view of contingency normally opens up horizons of non-decidedness and thereby of choice.

Surprisingly, however, even the realm of necessity assigns a specific place to contingency. For depending on whether the rules of necessity that are supposed to determine the past are expected to be decipherable or not, the relationship between past and future will assume different forms. Whenever such rules are expected to be decipherable and thus accessible (as, for example, in the nineteenth-century discourse of the "philosophy of history"), they may be projected into the future and then produce prognostics with a claim of certainty. By contrast, if we believe that such regularities are systematically unavailable to our understanding, they can hardly have an impact on our behavior and will leave the future contingent for all practical purposes. This, as we will see, is the view of Jacques the Fatalist, although he repeatedly asks himself whether the belief in the "rouleau écrit là-haut" should not actually have stronger, that is more limiting, consequences for his behavior and actions. Seen from a larger perspective, Jacques's metaphor of the "script above" brings together the two dimensions of contingency in a particular way: looking backwards, contingency for Jacques is determination articulating itself in "bizarre" stories without overarching meaning; in relation to the future, by contrast, contingency gives openness and free choice the status of illusions.

The fictional space that Jacques inhabits unfolds both fundamental dimensions of contingency, independently and in their interconnectedness, from all possible angles. This exhaustiveness in the unfolding of contingency as a potentially philosophical problem corresponds to my impression of having been unavoidably and permanently overwhelmed as a reader—while, strictly speaking and for reasons of logic, the actual number of potential perspectives produced by the text may well be infinite and thus quite literally go beyond exhaustiveness. The arguably singular complexity of the text emerges from the structural condition that contingency is not only the recurrent narrative and philosophical topic of the protagonists' conversations but also the one premise that is valid for all levels of the intra-textual framework within which which they interact and from which they provoke their readers' thought and imagination.

To have a comprehensive view or a full memory of *Jacques le fataliste*, in all of its dimensions and in their full condensation, seems quite literally impossible, and this probably explains why most readings and interpretations of the book have been distinctively partial, focused either on the multiple narratives that the characters are telling each other or on their multidimensional framework. Due to my project of describing the text's progressive unfolding of contingency in its totality, however, I will try my best to pay equal attention to the narratives it contains and to the framework within and due to which they emerge.

My main thesis will be that the (near) infinity of perspectives opened up, above all, by the text-implicit Narrator (in the future-directed dimension: for this Narrator is incessantly talking about what his next step should be), my main thesis will be that the multiplicity of perspectives brought up mainly by the Narrator makes it impossible to interpret the stories told by the protagonists (in their inevitably past-oriented dimension) along the lines of coherence and general rules. Rather, the narratives seem to remain "what they are," mainly because those many different perspectives of their frame tend to cancel out each other. To say it in a more abstract and more compact way: future-oriented contingency as multiplicity and uncertainty of perspectives brings to the fore past-oriented contingency in *Jacques le fataliste*, with its typical effect of the "bizarre," that is, with the effect of inconsistency and singularity. Understanding in greater detail the powerful intellectual dynamic emerging from this interplay between the two fundamental dimensions of contingency will then confirm our overarching impression and premise of a potential convergence that can bring together the epistemological contours inherent in Denis Diderot's prose of the world (peripheral as it may have been in his own time) and our own intellectual present at the beginning of the third millennium. For this post-ideological age of ours seems to be shaped, in a way similar to *Jacques le fataliste*, by the tense simultaneity of an oversupply of conflicting perspectives that enable us to give multiple meanings to the world and, on the other hand, by a return to the insistence on "empirically proven facts" that in principle reject interpretation, perhaps as a result of the mutual cancellation of multiple interpretations.

Once again, I fear, our argument has jumped ahead to intuitions that require a much longer process of reasoning and illustration in order to become conclusions. So exceptionally complex indeed is the preparatory reflection process required for any attempt at a comprehensive analysis of *Jacques le fataliste* that it may indeed justify our temptation to anticipate its outcome on a more elementary level. For anticipating the direction in which and the results to which the following pages will try to lead us may reduce the threat and the risk of losing our orientation along the multiple steps of our demonstration. As I did in the previous chapter, I will again start with remarks about Diderot's working process on the text in question, remarks that may also help us to get a sense again of the particular fluidity in his thinking and writing. I will then evoke the broad horizon of major interpretations dedicated to partial aspects and layers of *Jacques le fataliste*, not the least as a backdrop for my own, perhaps overambitious effort to describe and thus understand the text in its full multidimensionality. As a first grounding for this effort, I will describe in detail the potential structure made up by the characters, their roles, and their interactions in *Jacques le fataliste*.

If this structure, as I said before, provides a frame for the stories that the protagonists are telling each other, our focus will subsequently have to shift to these narratives and to the conditions under which they become readable in their specific contexts. As a third (and I believe innovative) step of textual analysis, I will then return to the framework of fictional protagonists and interactions, because I believe that it undergoes several movements of transformation as the text progresses, movements of transformation that, even if Diderot was not fully aware of them, may allow us to discover a further dimension of contingency. In concluding, and similar to the previous chapter, our reading of *Jacques le fataliste* will become the basis from which to look for traces of confrontations with contingency in Goya's art, Mozart's life, and Lichtenberg's notes.

———————

Although it is impossible to exactly identify either the beginning or the end of Diderot's working process on *Jacques le fataliste* through biographical documents and textual details (exactly as in the case of *Le neveu de Rameau*), some references to extra-textual events and to the publication history encourage us to assume that he started the writing in early 1773 and probably brought it to a conclusion by the middle of 1774. These months lie between two important events in Diderot's life: on the one side, the completion of his task as editor of the *Encyclopédie* in 1772, and on the other side, his journey to Saint Petersburg, from which he returned to Paris in October 1774 (some specialists, indeed, believe that the larger part of the text emerged during his travels and his stay in Russia). From 1778 to 1780, *Jacques le fataliste* was then published in the handwritten copies of Melchior Grimm's *Correspondance littéraire* that circulated among a socially select and intellectually mostly competent readership at European courts. Compared to some of Diderot's other major works, in particular *Le neveu de Rameau*, we can thus imagine a relatively compact and concentrated progress of textual production, facilitated perhaps by the ongoing eighteenth-century debates on predetermination and freedom as a possible horizon of reference.

More interesting and revealing probably than this difference in the production history of two major Diderot texts is the fact that, with the work on the *Neveu* beginning much earlier and certainly finishing much later than that on *Jacques*, there were about two years during which both projects must have been simultaneously present on Diderot's mind, which converges with our suspicion that his reflections on contingency and those on existential ontology as a form of human self-reference were jointly emerging as dimensions of a larger concern with epistemological structures of the human condition. The overlapping of different philosophical issues in the writing process of two books may also remind us of how neither a tendency to focus exclusively on individual problems and tasks nor a will to finish thought processes with neatly circumscribed results was compatible with the fluidity of Diderot's intellectual style. Without any doubt, the exceptional degree of his openness to the world, his not only personal generosity, and also his distance from any feeling of being rushed came together in his work both on *Le neveu de Rameau* and on *Jacques le fataliste et son maître*.

Although the work on *Jacques le fataliste* may give us the impression of a greater condensation in the production process, some of its internal semantic and narrative contours show how Diderot's fluid intellectual energy could lead both to effects of infinity and to the impression of narrative and conceptual shifts that were out of the author's control. We will see for example that an open-ended addition of ever new protagonists, with their contrasting points of view, on different levels of the fictional story caused an impression of erasure between these levels, an erasure that opened up logically impossible and yet intellectually stimulating spaces of infinity to be filled by the reader's thoughts and imagination. In the frequent reiteration of different points of view through the same protagonists, coming of course above all from Jacques and his Master, we will discover traces of internal transformations that Diderot may not have intended nor perceived. And while he did not, in this text, as he had in *Le neveu de Rameau*, reach any plausible (let alone necessary) point of narrative or argumentative ending, the final pages of both texts converge in giving us the impression of a sudden exit, an exit provoked by the author's growing confusion about where his text was going (or rather not going). Fluidity as intellectual style must finally have translated into a capacity for "letting go" and, from there, into the (not only metaphorical) possibility for the author of being in "dialogue" with his own thought, as he constantly and inadvertently moved away from previous positions and views.

———

I have already mentioned how the unusual structural complexity of *Jacques le fataliste* and its multilayered openness may have been responsible for a reception history characterized by a lack of readings that can be identified as comprehensive. Even the most eminent and expert scholars who have worked on this text have come up with clearly partial interpretations and analyses, often accompanied by a palpable sense of discomfort coming from that incompletion. Among the essays and books on *Jacques le fataliste*, we can distinguish three main perspectives, without claiming or implying that they correspond, as dominant forms of reading, to subsequent moments of a reception history since the late eighteenth century. In the first place, there have been multiple attempts at understanding *Jacques le fataliste* as part of a larger historical process that is supposed to lead to the bourgeois revolution, and most of these readings make explicit reference to Hegel's theses about the dialectic of master and servant in *Phenomenology of the Spirit.* A second focus belongs, rather, to the "history of ideas" as an academic genre and mainly explores contemporary horizons in the debate over determinism and liberty; thirdly and finally, a smaller number of essays and monographs deals with the status and the possible meanings of the narratives inserted into the ongoing dialogue between Jacques and his Master.

Regarding the sociohistorical readings, it is striking to see how they were biased not only in their main questions and results but also in their selection of textual materials and in their evaluation. Even a scholar as eminent as Hans Mayer, in a 1955 essay,[4] took it for granted that his own leftist sympathies were synonymous with what he imagined to have been Diderot's political position, and with the fictional Jacques's "tendency to forcefully act" (in spite of his explicit "fatalistic" worldview). As a consequence, the Master in his skepticism had to appear "weak and undecided"—and Mayer indeed never asked himself whether the aristocratic readers of the *Correspondance littéraire* might not have tended toward a very different and more nuanced reaction. Without any textual evidence—or, more precisely, against all textual evidence—both Mayer and ten years after him the Romanist Erich Köhler[5] jumped to the thesis that Diderot's narrative must have had an inspiring impact on Hegel's reflections on masters and servants.

The only passage, however, where Hegel explicitly mentions *Jacques le fataliste* is in a short text from 1807 on "Abstract Thinking,"[6] and instead of arguing that the servant might end up arriving at a superior level of *Bildung* in his interaction with the master, it is about a positive aspect in Hegel's view of aristocratic masters that Diderot's text is supposed to illustrate: truly aristocratic masters, Hegel writes, and particularly in France, think in a less abstract way than commoners (*gemeine Menschen*) would in similar situations and are therefore capable and relaxed enough to treat their servants in a "familiar," that is in a more "personal," way. This includes an interest in everyday news and gossip that the servants might provide and also the aristocrats' polite tendency to direct them with reasons and arguments instead of orders.

By contrast, I do not see how the character descriptions and the narrative trajectory in *Jacques le fataliste* can possibly be read as an illustration of the one famous thesis from Hegel's *Phenomenology* to which both Mayer and Köhler (and before them Georg Lukács) refer. This is the idea that the master who "inserts" the servant "between himself and the thing in its independence" will draw less profit for his own independence from this relationship than the servant in his direct confrontation that leads to the "sublation of the thing."[7] As its title announces, Diderot's book gives more space to Jacques as a protagonist than to his Master, and it is also true that the Master remains reactive while Jacques quite regularly takes the initiative towards next steps in their conversation. But to understand this as proof of Jacques's possible superiority to the Master is underestimating the text's sublety. We will come back to the specific dynamic emerging from their relationship in the context of our own analysis.

As for a reading of *Jacques le fataliste* against the background of historically pertinent ideas and arguments, Jean Starobinski has brought together all important perspectives in two essays, from 1984 and 1985.[8] He traces back to Spinoza and Leibniz the brand of determinism that Diderot puts into Jacques's mouth, and above all he shows with ample textual evidence that while Diderot was working on his narrative he reached, in a different philosophical context, an ultimately unavoidable conclusion about the inconclusiveness of the debate between determinism and freedom as absolute principles: "Either everything is random [*hasard*]—or nothing," Diderot wrote in his 1773 "Réfutation d'Helvétius." With much greater philological precision than Mayer and Köhler, Starobinski then moves on to show how Jacques "professes determinism without binding himself to it" (308), how Diderot understands human existence as a complex "mixture of randomness and necessity" (320), and how such views become part of the author's "vitalist materialism" (282) and of the protagonist's "quiet audacity" (*tranquille audace*) (327). What does not come into sight, however, despite Starobinski's lucid description of the book's narrative frame based on the conversations between Jacques and his Master and between the Narrator and his Reader, is the progressive transformation of this frame into a complex intra-textual space of reflection, a space of reflection that makes it possible to think through in an infinity of perspectives the multiple narratives that the characters tell each other.

Inspired by Herbert Dieckmann, one of the all-time authorities on Diderot scholarship, Rainer Warning, in his still-impressive 1965 study of *Jacques le fataliste* and Sterne's *Tristram Shandy*,[9] focused on those narratives as decisive for the question of the epistemological status (or, in pre-Foucaultian terms: the "truth value") of Diderot's text. Converging with Erich Köhler's previously mentioned essay, Warning demonstrated how it is impossible to subsume the events they pretend to refer to under any abstract concepts or general principles. We must understand them as being "singular," as resisting any definitive interpretation, and thus also as incapable of ever being "truthfully" represented (the latter impossibility following from the linguistic premise that, with the exception of names, elements of language cannot stand for phenomena in their singularity). As both Köhler and Warning emphasize, Diderot used the adjective "bizarre" to refer to this aspect of singularity—and we have no evidence that he ever reflected on the impossibility of representing such singular situations or developments. In a final evaluation of his interpretative insights that appears both plausible and, in its long-range perspective, typical for a classical style of literary scholarship in Germany, Warning connects the bizarre, "disillusioning reality" (123) evoked by *Jacques le fataliste* to Flaubert's position in the nineteenth-century history of the novel.

The centrifugal movement that we have seen in these major readings of *Jacques le fataliste*, that is, their tendency to focus on different dimensions of the text and to keep them separate from each other, appears to be a consequence of the text's unusual complexity and openness. If contingency as the status of phenomena between necessity and impossibility is its central thematic and philosophical concern, and if contingency has a potential of unfolding two different spaces of thought in its future-oriented ("freedom") and past-oriented ("bizarre") dimensions, one should expect readings of *Jacques le fataliste* to illustrate both of them—although, as we have seen, most academic interpretations have dealt with them in mutual separation. While this by no means invalidates them, this chapter's specific focus on contingency as a central layer of Diderot's thought and discourse as "prose of the world" makes it obligatory to describe both dimensions in their possible relationships and intellectual dynamic.

———————

The opening sentences of *Jacques le fataliste* belong to the most frequently quoted as well as the liveliest paragraphs in the history of French literature:

> How had they met? By chance, like everyone else. What were their names? What does it matter to you? Whence had they come? From the nearest possible spot. Where were they going? Do we ever know where we're going? What were they saying? The master said nothing and Jacques said that his captain said that everything that happens to us down here, good or bad, was written up yonder. (3)[10]

These first words leave their readers with the task of identifying them as part of an ongoing dialogue between an implied Reader and an implied Narrator (and not yet between the two protagonists evoked in the title). After three impatient and almost aggressive refusals to answer the Reader's questions, the fifth question ("What were they saying?") finally triggers an actual answer from the Narrator, who describes the title protagonists in minimalistic terms, thus introducing the first dialogue between them. Unlike most dialogues between narrators and readers, the conversation between Jacques and his Master begins in scenic form, as if written for the theater.

With these two intertwined conversations, the deceptively simple basic narrative structure of *Jacques le fataliste* is present after only a few lines. What does not become clear, however—and will remain unclear throughout the text—is a potential vanishing point of the Narrator's three initial refusals to answer. Is there a logical principle or aesthetic value pushing him not to engage with the Reader's questions? That the Narrator only reacts to the question regarding the content of their conversation seems to suggest right away a philosophical concentration on determinism as dominant in their dialogue. And yet, why should a Reader not have the right be interested in the circumstances under which the protagonists first met; why would he not want to know their names (famously, the Master will stay nameless until the end) and both the origin and the potential endpoint of their journey?

It will become clear to the implied Reader (and of course also to most of the empirical readers) that the Narrator refuses to satisfy any curiosity for details because he associates it with the genre of the "novel," from which he wants to maintain distance. But, again, where does such a wish for distance from the novel come from? To say that it is informed by the status of *Jacques le fataliste* as an anti-novel is to confuse an academic typology with the pragmatics of actual reading. But then, somehow surprisingly, the Narrator's fourth answer, the answer to the question about where the protagonists are heading, comes in the form of a rhetorical question capable of opening up a philosophical discussion, rather than further limiting the genre within which the two ongoing conversations are supposed to take place.

Only a few pages further, the Narrator returns to his aggressive tone and somehow arrogantly assumes a role of omnipotence over the ongoing narrative, an omnipotence that he may use either to endlessly frustrate the Reader or to live up to the Reader's most eccentric expectations. Referring to a woman who had just appeared in Jacques's fictionally autobiographical narrative, the suddenly omnipotent Narrator states:

> What couldn't this adventure become in my hands, if I took it into my head to tease you! I should make that woman an important character— the niece of the neighbouring village curate. I should stir up the peasants of that village; I should prepare all sorts of combats and love affairs, for, actually, this peasant woman was beautiful beneath her petticoats. [. . .] For the last time, make yourself clear: would you like him to, or wouldn't you? (6)[11]

What seems to become increasingly clear and even contoured in the Narrator's reactions to the Reader's insistent interruptions and questions (e.g. 495, 497, 513, 539) is what the former wants to avoid—but also what he wants to emphasize in the orchestration of both his own conversation with the Reader and in the other ongoing conversation between the Master and Jacques: "It's quite evident that I'm not writing a novel for I neglect to use what no novelist would fail to use. He who takes what I am writing for the truth will be, perhaps, less in error than he who takes it for a fable" (13).[12] So we are left with the impression that the Narrator wants to avoid novelistic effects because he is mainly concerned with "truth" (whatever that word might actually stand for here).

Then and again all of a sudden, the Narrator volunteers to suppress a tendency to interpret Jacques's narrative as an allegory, if only the Reader will spare him his hunger for details:

> You are going to say that I'm joking and teasing, and that, not knowing what to do next with my travelers, I jump over into allegory, the usual resort of sterile minds. I shall sacrifice my allegory, and all the richness I might draw therefrom; I shall agree to whatever you say, if only you stop bothering me on the point of this last shelter sought by Jacques and his master. (22)[13]

In all these—sometimes contradictory—interventions, reactions, and self-commentaries, the Narrator certainly does not appear to be completely erratic. Rather, the impression of an identity is slowly emerging. On the other hand, we can never fully exclude flagrant inconsistencies. Early on, for example, it becomes explicit how very boring the Narrator finds the philosophical (or theological) main topics of Jacques's and the Master's conversation:

> You can imagine, reader, just how far I could push this conversation on a subject about which so much has been said and written for two thousand years, without, for that, advancing the argument the slightest bit. If you are not too happy with what I do say about it, be much happier about what I leave unsaid. (8)[14]

Towards the end of the text, however, we find an expression of admiration and gratitude for Jacques's philosophical competence—which the Narrator wants to see as an orientation for his own philosophical position: "Everything I'm handing to you now, reader, I have had from Jacques, I confess, for I don't like to take credit for the thinking of another" (166).[15]

Based probably on the one consistent gesture characterizing the Narrator, that is the distance he maintains from the Reader's expectation and desire to be offered a novel, a consensus does exist among the most canonized interpretations of *Jacques le fataliste* that the Narrator ultimately opts and stands for truth (*vérité*, *le vrai*, *le réel*) as the principle opposite to novelistic fiction. I have already quoted one of several passages that seem to give textual evidence for this view. Referring to the life story of his captain that Jacques likes to tell, the Narrator again warns the Reader against the possible confusion of taking it for fictional—but this time his argument in favor of truth turns out to be more ambiguous and therefore less solid:

You will take the story of Jacques's captain for a tale of fiction, and you make a mistake. I protest that exactly as the story was told to the master, just so did I hear it told at the Invalides on St. Louis' day, of I know not what year, while sitting at table in the house of a certain M. de Saint-Etienne, commanding officer of the institution; and the storyteller, speaking in the presence of several officers of the house, who knew of the affair, was a serious fellow and not at all a jokester. So I repeat to you, for now and for later, be very careful in this conversation of Jacques and his master if you don't want to take the true for the false, and the false for the true. There now! You've been well warned and I wash my hands of the affair (59).[16]

If the truth claim is already explicitly and profoundly undercut by referring to a story told by Jacques, who is a fictional character, the Narrator's claim of having heard the same story before, from different people and in a different place, could not be formulated in a more ironic way. That he pretends to remember the place and the day when this happened (but not the year) appears as irrelevant to the truth value of Jacques's story as the Narrator's judgment about the face of the "historian" on whom he relies. Without any doubt, such sentences cast an ironic light on the Narrator's discourse and on his pledge in favor of truth (and, if we care to do so, we can see this effect as part of the Narrator's possible larger attempt to fool the Reader).

In addition, we should not forget that, in his conversations with the Reader, the Narrator quite regularly returns to positions of omnipotence over the stories conveyed, which makes his narratives look irreversibly fictional (for only the absolute lack of a world reference can give the Narrator such absolute freedom in the choice of what he wants to tell). Now what conclusion shall we draw regarding the status of an implied Narrator who explicitly opts for truth and then moves on to remember conversations with obviously fictional protagonists? Clearly and from early on, this Narrator emerges as the decisive figure in establishing a relationship between Diderot's text and his real readers. But this by no means implies that the Narrator's role and epistemological status are homogeneous and consistent. On the contrary, precisely due to the Narrator's oscillations and to his central textual presence, no segment of this text can ever have a perfectly univocal meaning and status itself.

A different question is whether Diderot indeed intended and planned such shifting effects for the constitution of the text's semantics and pragmatics.

Literary critics certainly have a tendency to identify the highest possible level of complexity in the interpretation of a text with its author's deliberate project, in particular when the author is a classic writer like Diderot, as if there were some direct equivalence between complexity of thought, on the one hand, and aesthetic (or intellectual) quality on the other. Of course we will never arrive at a definitive answer to the question of Diderot's intention. But his intellectual style and, more specifically, his loose way of writing texts during the later years of his life make it impossible to fully reject the thought that the sublime potential of complexity brought forth by *Jacques le fataliste*'s narrative frame might have emerged inadvertently.

However predominant the conversation between the Narrator and the Reader may be for the text's basic structure, a full appreciation of this fundamental form makes it necessary to also take into account the relation between the two title protagonists. Jacques never stops adhering to the determinist worldview that makes him a "fatalist" (e.g. 50, 73, 76, 91, 160, 162 / 543, 569, 572, 589, 663, 666), and from this perspective his homogeneity as a character indeed stands in contrast to the Narrator's inconsistency and complexity. But we have already seen that Jacques's permanent reference to the "script above" that is supposed to shape every situation, circumstance, and event (without being accessible as a formula that could allow for its projection into the future) boils down to a belief that has no real consequences for his behavior and actions. This said, Starobinski was right in highlighting Jacques's "quiet audacity" (other adequate concepts of description could be "serenity" or "composure"), together with his exemption from any retrospective self-critique, as a result of the conviction that only the "script"—and not his own agency—might be responsible for the course of his life. At some point, Jacques answers the Master's question about the practical value of such an attitude with the strongest possible affirmation of his own identity, so strong indeed that, together with the Master's laconic reaction, it may cast a (secondary) ironic light on Jacques's potential aura of existential wisdom:

JACQUES

I have [. . .] decided to be just what I am. I have seen, upon reflecting a bit on it, that it all comes down to about the same thing if you add:

"What does it matter how one is?" It's another kind of resignation—easier and more convenient.

LE MAITRE

More convenient, that's sure. (77)[17]

Despite such moments of (mostly mild) cynicism in the Master's discourse, and although he will never fully embrace his servant's endlessly reiterated credo, a mutual attachment and sympathy are the deep basis of their interactions: "Jacques, the best-natured kind of fellow you could want, was tenderly attached to his master" (16).[18] The Master responds to this faithful sympathy with an active care that transcends the asymmetry of their institutional relationship:

LE MAITRE

I'm watching over you. You are my servant when I'm sick or well; but I'm yours when you are sick.

JACQUES

I'm very happy to know you are human; it's not too common a trait of masters with their servants. (65)[19]

Sometimes the Master imagines possible past or future situations in Jacques's life, as is common between good friends, for example when he asks whether Jacques would have been able to control his notorious loquacity in a marriage with their "hôtesse" at an inn on the road, whose inspired but continuous storytelling keeps them entertained: "You can't imagine the singular idea that just passed through my head. I'm going to marry you to our landlady and then I'll see what a husband can do, when he loves to talk, with a wife who never stops talking" (107).[20] Indeed, Jacques's inseparability from his Master (59 / 553) reminds the Narrator of Don Quixote and Sancho Panza—although the role distribution between Jacques's obsessiveness and the Master's sober skepticism rather inverts the contrast in the relationship between Cervantes's protagonists (where of course the servant shows sobriety and the master appears lunatic).

Unlike Jacques, the Master has neither a name nor a clear philosophical position, and for the longest time he just reacts to his servant's talking, showing plausible and perpetual signs of boredom: "The master started to yawn; in yawning he struck the edge of his snuffbox; in hitting his snuffbox he looked off into the distance" (44, with the same words appearing in passages on pages 119, 222, and 258).[21] Such gestures and reactions could not be more distant from Hegel's description, in *Phenomenology of the Spirit*, of the productive dynamics that may potentially emerge from the relationships between masters and servants—but they exactly match Hegel's view that a polite suspension of the hierarchy between masters and servants can be regarded as typical of French society.

Only seldom indeed do the Master's interventions go beyond prompting Jacques to continue the stream of his words, and even less frequently does the Master articulate fragments of a knowledge about literature and philosophy that is as pompous and fragile as Jacques's:

LE MAITRE

As for me, I think of myself as a cocoon. And I like to think that the butterfly, or my soul, managing one day to break the shell, will fly off to divine justice.

JACQUES

Your imagery is charming.

LE MAITRE

It's not mine. I read it, I believe, in some Italian poet named Dante, who wrote a work entitled: *The Comedy of Hell, Purgatory, and Paradise.*

JACQUES

Now there's a strange subject for a comedy! (182)[22]

Everything in the Master's behavior during his journey with Jacques seems to justify the fact that the Narrator several times calls him an "automaton," except for some rare scenes where the Master, with no profound or obvious reason, insists in a loud voice and using physical force on reestablishing the hierarchy between himself and Jacques (always after changing from the second person singular to the courtesy form):

MAITRE

I'm telling you, Jacques, to go downstairs and to go immediately because I order you to.

JACQUES

Sir, order me to do any other thing if you want me to obey.

> At this point Jacques's master got up, took him by the lapel, and said to
> him very gravely: "Go downstairs."
> Jacques replied coldly: "I am not going down."
> The master, shaking him violently, said: "Go down, rascal! Obey me!"
> (158)[23]

There is no truly plausible explanation for such eruptions in the Master's
temper—nor for Jacques's stubborn impulses of resistance, which tend to
aggravate them. As such moments seem to simply occur without any reason,
one may say (using a concept that has assumed central importance in the
reception history of *Jacques le fataliste*) that they are "bizarre" accents in the
Master's otherwise flat profile and in the increasingly shallow up-and-down
of his conversations with Jacques.

To finish our description of the book's narrative architecture, we need
to take into account the roles and functions assigned to those other, mostly
peripheral protagonists whom Jacques and his Master either meet on their
journey or evoke in their stories, and who thus occasionally become a reference
in the Narrator's conversation with his Reader. These manifold transitions
and moments of permeability between all different levels of the narrative add
to the fluid complexity of its discursive status and constantly open up further
dimensions in the fictional space to be imagined by the readers. As the hostess
is telling a long story to Jacques and his Master, she is interrupted all of a sudden
by an unnamed voice announcing that a cooper (*tonnelier*) has arrived, and this
voice becomes present in Diderot's text. Likewise, the conventional narrative
discourse in which Jacques's eternally postponed and continued history of his
erotic adventures takes place sometimes jumps to the form of a dialogue that
transforms him into a "Moi" speaking directly to the characters of his story,
who are represented by their respective individual names (193 / 698).

But this fluid complexity and the subsequent erasure of the gap between
different narrative roles, discursive levels, and ontological dimensions again
reaches its greatest intensity around the figure of the Narrator, an intensity
that may well leave the readers' minds in a state of vertigo. This could happen for example in response to the potentially self-ironic remark that the
Master, after listening to a segment of the hostess's story, "is snoring as if he
had listened to his own (i.e. the Narrator's) reflection about the same story"
("Tandis que je disserte, le maître de Jacques ronfle comme s'il m'avait écoute"

[563]). By thus suspending the inevitable temporal and categorical distance between himself and the protagonists of the story that he tells, the Narrator joins the other peripheral protagonists of the same story—a status that is of course logically incompatible with his main role (because he can either be the typical Narrator inscribed into a fictional text, or a protagonist, but not both at the same time).

Earlier on, while the Narrator presents himself to the Reader in his so often assumed position of omnipotence over the fictional plot and over the hostess as one of its protagonists ("Well now, reader. Why don't I stir up a violent quarrel between these three characters? Why shouldn't the landlady be taken by the shoulders and thrown out of the room by Jacques [. . .]?" [96]),[24] he also "warns" the Reader about his own lack of power to prevent the hostess from joining Jacques and the Master and explains this impossibility, as only Jacques normally does, by referring to fate in its form as "the script above":

> Here she is back upstairs, reader, and I warn you that it's no longer in my power to send her away.—Why not?—Because she came back with two bottles of champagne, one in each hand, and it was written up yonder that any speaker who should appeal to Jacques with such an exordium would be heard of necessity. (111)[25]

After a series of quotes and examples in this complexity-driven mood, it would be state of the art in literary criticism to head towards the conclusion that what we have textually witnessed must be a trace of Diderot's intention to stage a mise en abyme, that is to open and trigger a process of reflexive infinity by the repeated crossing and crossing out of categorical borders. But while there is an abundance of passages that could set such an intellectual dynamic in motion (if a reader is only willing to play along), I cannot discover any form of stable sequence or logical syntax that would look like the product of an author's coherent intention.

What we do find, halfway through *Jacques le fataliste*, is an intrinsically beautiful textual fragment between quotes that has no connection at all to the preceding dialogue (or to any preceding text segment) and that the Narrator presents as written either by Jacques, or by his Master, or by himself:

> "The first mutual vow made by two fleshly beings was sworn at the foot of a rock already crumbling into dust. They called as witness to their fidelity

a sky that is never for an instant the same. Everything was changing, in them and about them; yet they believed their hearts free from vicissitudes. Oh, children! Ever children!" I don't know whose reflections these are: Jacques's, his master's, or my own. It's certainly one of the three and it's certain that they were preceded or followed by many others which would have taken us—Jacques, his master, and myself—until suppertime, after supper, up to the return of the landlady, that is, if Jacques had not said to his master: "See here, sir, all these grand aphorisms that you have just reeled off for no good reason are not worth one single fable of our get-togethers of an evening in my village." (106)[26]

It is no wonder that few critics have ever dealt with this passage, because, in its strangely isolated status, it leaves the reader both helpless and with the absolute freedom to confer a meaning on it, if possible a meaning that will provide possible connections within Diderot's text.[27]

If we want to pursue such an option, Jacques's words seem to offer, for once, the concrete possibility of identifying an act of mise en abyme by connecting his reference to the Master's "grandes sentences à propos de bottes" ("grand aphorisms that you have just reeled off for no good reason") precisely to the words between quotes that indeed lack any clear intra-textual motivation. But such an interpretation would contradict the admitted uncertainty of the Narrator, who does not know whether the enigmatic passage belongs to Jacques, to the Master, or to himself as possible authors. So I come back to the impression that we are touching upon a trace of Diderot being a carefree author, that is, an author whom we should not expect to always fulfill our standards of textual coherence and perfection.

For Diderot, the process of writing may often have been a flow that, on the one hand, did not strictly obey the rules and necessities of narrative or argumentative logic, while, on the other hand, it had sufficient coherence not to let open any possible development at each moment of the story. Now if we suppose that the text of *Jacques le fataliste* indeed emerged between a remainder of necessity (some narrative rules are left) and a remainder of impossibility (a few things continue to be impossible), i.e. if it emerged within a field of contingency, then we could perhaps describe its specific function and philosophical movement as a broadening of the mental space of contingency. Contingency would then not only be the philosophical topic whose two dimensions the narrative structure of *Jacques le fataliste* unfolds—but also come into sight as an energy that permeates the text.

———————

We have seen how the deceptively simple narrative frame of *Jacques le fataliste* reveals itself as a condition that produces, quite literally, an infinity of levels and perspectives, and how these perspectives and levels come together in a multidimensional space of thought that does not only allow for the unfolding of contingency as a philosophical problem but also shows traces of being permeated by it. The one side of contingency that we have mostly been talking about so far is contingency as a force that opens ever new future possibilities of thinking, of imagining, and potentially also of acting. It is mainly due to the ever complexifying effects on this side of contingency that it is so difficult, so impossible indeed for us readers to retain the content and the form of *Jacques le fataliste* as a text in its centrifugal complexity.

What has not come into sight yet, except, indirectly, through Jacques's obsession with the famous "script above," is contingency as facticity, contingency as an openness between the necessary and the impossible that, seen from our retrospective, has always already turned into a past of choices made and of events having happened. As I have mentioned before, this second, past-related aspect of contingency becomes present in Diderot's text through a potentially confusing juxtaposition of multiple stories told by the protagonists about themselves and about others. On the next few pages I will try to illustrate how, mainly due to the complexity of the narrative frame, produced by openness and instability as modes of future-oriented contingency, those stories acquire a status of retrospective contingency, of contingency as "facticity"—and this also means a status of "singularity" as the impossibility of subsuming what happened (or is supposed to have happened) under any general rules.[28]

Unsurprisingly, the two dominant stories, in terms of the status of their narrators and also of their textual extension, are those told by Jacques and by the aristocratic Master about their respective lives—and they stand in stark contrast to each other due to their different narrative shapes and tonalities. Trying to entertain the Master with the history of his erotic adventures ("ses amours"), the loquacious servant over and again falls prey to the temptation to convey mostly medical details, which prevent him from finding anything resembling a plot line ("you talk too much" (157),[29] the Master reacts to Jacques's narrative staccato with his usual laconism). The lengthy descriptions of changing states of pain and their treatment all go back to an injury inflicted on Jacques's knee by a "fateful" bullet that of course becomes the emblem and constant reminder of predetermination. Several women take care of him, all of them becoming, in the Master's imagination, potential agents in Jacques's first sexual experience. On the final pages of the book, long after the two travelers have given up on this story, one of those women, Denise, will become Jacques's wife. She is the young woman who, within a drastically improbable concatenation of random events and circumstances that include a former friend of the Master, became the last one to soothe the pain caused by Jacques's injured knee. And while there is reason in the fictional world to believe that Denise never lost her premarital virginity, Jacques's actual initiation into erotic life had taken place in situations (and narratives) far away from her.

The Master first feels an itch to start telling his own "love story" much later in the book, but although its plotline emerges quite straightforwardly, although it develops at a much faster pace than Jacques's, and although it finally provides a point of arrival for the journey, this narrative will trigger the same reactions of boredom in Jacques that his Master had felt in following his story (238 / 747). Unlike Jacques, however, who so likes to embrace ideas and principles with a mythological flavor, the skeptical Master ends up falling victim to a conspiracy. When Saint Ouin, whom the Master believes to be a good friend, realizes that his concubine Agathe has become pregnant, he arranges an erotic encounter between her and Jacques's Master and is successful, later on, in manipulating the legal authorities to assign both paternity and the ensuing financial obligations to the Master. All along, the Master's journey with Jacques had been heading to a village where his legal and Saint Ouin's biological child is living in the house of foster parents—and right in front of this house, the Master of course runs into Saint Ouin, whom he engages and kills in a duel.

It is from a manuscript (no longer from the Narrator's "mouth") that the Reader is then supposed to learn how Jacques and, a bit later, also his Master got arrested after this accident, were able to liberate themselves, and ended up meeting again at the castle of the Master's friend where Jacques had previously encountered Denise. This is the time when Jacques finds employment at the castle and marries Denise. Rumor has it, as the Narrator, transformed into a manuscript editor, conveys in the first sentence of the book's final paragraph, that the Master and his good friend are Denise's lovers. In which case, we read further, Jacques would be able to find consolation in his determinist belief—and fall asleep over his own words:

> "If it's written up yonder, Jacques, that you'll be a cuckold, you may do what you will, my boy, you will be a cuckold. If, on the other hand, it is written up yonder that you won't be, they may do all they like, you will never be a cuckold. Sleep, then, my friend, sleep . . ." And he would go to sleep (270).[30]

Obviously, the narrative contrast between Jacques's history and that of his Master illustrates the conceptual contrast between the truth ("le vrai") of sometimes tedious details on which the Narrator tends to insist and, on the Master's side, the improbable but therefore all the more engaging action ("le romanesque") expected and desired by the Reader. But counter to the preference for truth maintained by the Narrator and embraced by so many literary critics, the two principles seem to cancel each other out in the juxtaposition and ultimate intersection of Jacques's and the Master's stories.

Neither of the two life stories appears to be particularly "bizarre," and this lack of an effect that so fascinated Diderot was not only (and perhaps not even mainly) a consequence of their intrinsic poetic features. If, by contrast, we have reason to assume that the impression of bizarre facticity (and of singularity) will only emerge from plots that have a chance to provoke conflicting reactions and thus to reject any interpretations along the lines of general principles, then the intra-textual availability of multiple perspectives appears to be the decisive condition for that particular appeal. Within the centrifugal form of *Jacques le fataliste*'s narrative structure, Jacques's and the Master's stories can hardly produce this effect because, as both their narrators and protagonists, they are not in a position to produce doubts, conflicting commentaries, or open discussions.

By contrast, Jacques, his Master, and the Narrator often become engaged in thorough and sometimes even passionate debates about stories told by other protagonists. This explains why such stories, much more than Jacques's and the Master's "autobiographical" narratives, do constitute a textual zone of bizarre effects in the readers' view. By concentrating on five of them (there are many more non-autobiographical tales in the text, some unfinished, others remaining bare allusions to potential narratives), we will see how they indeed tend to contain structural arrays capable of provoking interpretations from conflicting perspectives.

The first of them is still told by Jacques but refers to his brother Jean, who was a Carmelite, and to his death in the earthquake of Lisbon, together with a fellow friar (38–43 / 529–35). In their home monastery both had gained a reputation for convincing young women to get married within less than two months after their first encounter with the monks. Whether it was just the jealousy of other monks or immoral practices behind their success that ended up shedding a negative light on the two friars and obliging them to leave and head for Lisbon, will never become clear. But the initial ambiguity gets emphasized as they perish in the context of an event about whose status—as either divine punishment or randomness—European intellectuals were still debating when Diderot wrote *Jacques le fataliste*.

The second story, again conveyed by Jacques, is about his captain's obsessively circular relationship with an officer of the same rank whom at times he considers as his dearest friend and at times as a mortal enemy to be challenged in regular duels (49–59 / 541–53). Here the lens that activates multiple interpretations and makes the case unique is provided by the Narrator's expert commentaries on human nature and its variations: "nature is so diverse, especially in the question of instincts and character" (59).[31] Immediately following this banal and pompous conclusion, the Narrator conveys a much longer story (59–88 / 554–86), which, as he reports, his wife had first heard from a certain Monsieur Gousse ("here's his conversation with my wife" [59][32]). Monsieur Gousse, we read, had been capable both of rescuing the life of a friend by sacrificing his entire own fortune and, driven by greed, of falsifying documents in order to illegally enrich himself. Right from the start an ongoing—and never quite fitting—comparison of Monsieur Gousse's story with the plot of Molière's *Médecin malgré lui* will provide angles for moral interpretation.

Only a few pages after Jacques, the Master, and the Narrator have abandoned their exhaustingly controversial debate about Monsieur Gousse's psyche and fate, the longest and most intensely discussed internal narrative will begin, and not by coincidence it is—very competently—presented (in spite of endless interruptions) by the hostess, a peripheral protagonist whom we have already referred to several times. This assignment of the narrator role to a peripheral character finally gives full distance and complete freedom to the characters of the central narrative for ongoing analyses and debates. The hostess's story deals with Mme de la Pommeraye and the Marquis des Arcis, two members of the high aristocracy, and it contained enough drama and charm to motivate a separate rewriting and translation by Friedrich Schiller that was published in 1785 by the magazine *Rhenische Thalia*. A virtuous, wealthy, proud, and beautiful widow, Mme de la Pommeraye decides to give in to the insistent advances of the Marquis des Arcis and becomes his lover. When, after a few years, the Marquis's passion is fading, Mme de la Pommeraye invents and carries out the cruelest plot of revenge. She arranges for the Marquis to fall in love with, propose to, and end up marrying a young woman by the name of Mademoiselle d'Aisnon, who is in reality a prostitute. But from the moment when the Marquis first faces this painful and potentially damaging truth, the narrative of revenge turns into a singular—and indeed remarkable—case about the unpredictability of the human psyche. For not only does the Marquis decide not to abandon his new wife, against everybody's expectation he will also end up finding fulfillment in their marriage: "In truth, I think I repent of nothing, and that Pommeraye woman, instead of avenging herself, has done me a great favor" (146).[33]

No other plot provokes so many intertwined reactions, opinions, and interpretations among the characters of *Jacques le fataliste* as this novella-length story told by the hostess. Jacques will never overcome his fearful indignation about the consistency with which Madame de la Pommeraye carries out her strategy to hurt the Marquis: "What a devil of a woman! Lucifer is not worse. I am trembling from it, and I need another drink to get a grip on myself" (132).[34] The implied Reader, in his conversation with the Narrator, seems to follow him. To undercut this reaction and driven by his usual intellectual ambition, the Narrator develops a full-fledged "apologie de Mme de la Pommeraye":

> You can hate and you can fear Mme de La Pommeraye, but you cannot
> scorn her. Her vengeance is terrible, but it is soiled with no motive of

self-interest. [. . .] You rise up against her instead of seeing that her resentment makes you indignant only because you are incapable of feeling such deep resentment yourself, or because you don't make such an issue of a woman's virtue. (148–49)[35]

The Master, as so often, does not have any specific opinion but observes, in one of his laconic interjections, what may indeed be most remarkable about this story from a philosophical perspective: "Elle est incompréhensible" (644)—"impossible to understand," because the plot appears to be unique and can therefore neither confirm nor illustrate any general knowledge about human nature.

The narrative with whose brief analysis I will conclude our commentaries on the internal plot structures in *Jacques le fataliste* shows the most eccentric frame of them all. Diderot lets the Marquis d'Arcis, Mme de la Pommeraye's former lover and intended victim, present it exclusively to the Master, in the most straightforward way and without any interruptions (169–79 / 673–82)—which appears immediately plausible because the Master has emerged, in comparison to Jacques and to the Narrator, as the least loquacious commentator. The story is about Father Hudson, an abbot who, quite unlike Jacques's brother, successfully reforms his monastery along the lines of strict morality while he leads, not only in the imagination of the other monks, a parallel life of unlimited erotic luxury. Surprisingly for the reader, however, there is no turning point and no peripatetic moment in the course of Hudson's adventures. While several Church authorities try to spy him out in order to break his authority, he always manages to identify his persecutors and expose them to the type of suspicion that they expected to cast on him.

Rather than following a complex narrative, we thus witness the emergence of a unique and therefore remarkable character, a character who does not provoke, as all the preceding stories did, conflicting interpretations that lead to debate. And yet the Narrator cannot resist the temptation to try yet another intellectually ambitious commentary when he brings together, in his imagination and for the Reader, Father Hudson and Mme de la Pommeraye:

I should like to propose a little question for you to turn over on your pillow. What would the child born of Father Hudson and Mme de la

Pommeraye be like? Perhaps a decent fellow. Perhaps a wonderful rascal. (181)[36]

This question and its inconclusive hypothetical answer have attracted the attention of multiple critics, among them Warning, who states (108) that, by making Mme de la Pommeraye's and Father Hudon's stories intersect (*Verklammerung*), Diderot intensifies the impression of a bizarre reality that resists any interpretation or conceptual analysis. Now, while it is neither possible nor necessary to activate any systematic objection to this view, the text certainly allows for a different reading. Could the contrast between the complicated and indeed intriguing question and its banal answer (which boils down to the truism that "anything is possible") not also shed an ironic light on the Narrator? Could the passage not be, to go one step further, another trace of Diderot as a surprisingly careless author, an author who was not always eager to transform into well-defined philosophical positions the semantic complexities and the effects of contingency that he produced?

In an impressive reading of "The Mme de la Pommeraye Tale and Its Commentaries," I. H. Smith arrived at a similar impression: "All the tales and dialogues in which Diderot's ethical preoccupations are reflected end arbitrarily or in confusion, and leave the reader with the same jumble of sentiments as besets their author."[37] This observation may help us to develop our working hypothesis about the interplay between future-oriented and past-oriented contingency as the structure responsible for impressions of facticity (i.e. of what Diderot was referring to as "bizarre") in *Jacques le fataliste*. So far, we have been assuming that providing multiple and if possible conflicting interpretations that cancel each other out was a sufficient condition for such readings (and that is, from a different angle, a sufficient condition for an experience of contingency).

But then again, why should multiperspectivism as hermeneutic multiplicity and hermeneutic conflict not rather produce horizons of clearly differentiated meanings and thus illustrate how textual "openness" can trigger open panoramas of interpretation, a motif cherished by so many literary critics? I believe that Diderot's text undercuts such possible effects of plurality and difference (and this is probably not only true for *Jacques le fataliste*), above all through that specific third mood of contingency (and carelessness) that permeates the text and pushes the readers to a point where they no longer expect, where they indeed give up on, crystal-clear meanings and deep truths. Once the readers are there, the instability and the frequent discontinuities in *Jacques le fataliste* unleash the powers of contingency as an energy that keeps them in an agitated pace of thought and association, without leading them to specific goals or endpoints of argumentative demonstration. Such a process corresponds to the intellectual style fictionally embodied by Rameau's nephew—and is the extreme opposite of Jacques's stubbornly reiterated return to the position of determinism and its supposed philosophical groundings.

———

The textual presence of an author who must have been serene enough to allow for carelessness and "negligence" (as readers would have preferred to say in Diderot's time) gives us a reason to look for shifts in the main protagonists' behavior and in their positions throughout *Jacques le fataliste*. Not of course for shifts that will take us to deep levels of ultimate wisdom hidden by the author under layers of "superficial" narrative elements but, I insist, for traces of that third power of contingency which, as we know by now, has engaged our reading from the beginning. Against the unfortunate tradition of a politically "enlightened" reading that is blinded by its bias toward the servant as intellectually and ethically superior, we have seen how Jacques, if he had ever been off to a promising intra-textual start, progressively drifts into self-complacency and even into a lack of passion for his own values and arguments. This development may well reflect the author's growing frustration with the limited potential of a character that he must have found entertaining when he first invented him.

As their story advances, the Master indeed needs to remind Jacques not to forget his determinist creed: "Have you forgotten your refrain, and the Great Scroll, and the writing up yonder?" (227).[38] Prompted by similar interventions, Jacques makes a final effort to engage the Master in yet another discussion about freedom of will and its impossibility, during which, with a self-irony that can hardly be attributed to the fictional character, he describes the Master and himself as "two veritable living, thinking machines" (247).[39] But the new conversation will only lead again to a point of silence and thus provoke a sarcastic remark from the Narrator about Jacques's brain:

> After this nonsense and other remarks of equal importance, they were
> quiet. Jacques put on his enormous hat, umbrella in bad weather, parasol in
> hot weather, head covering in all weather, the shady sanctuary under which
> one of the best brains that ever existed used to consult Destiny in major cri-
> ses. [. . .] Jacques then [. . .] perceived a farmer who was uselessly beating
> one of the two horses he had harnessed to his plow. (248–49)[40]

I have already referred to the concluding sentences of the book, where Jacques
of course again invokes "the script above" and falls asleep over the unpleasant
imagination of his newlywed wife betraying him with the Master and his
friend. For me, this scene resonates with the final paragraph in *Lazarillo de
Tormes*, the earliest picaresque novel (from 1554), and with the title character's
threat that whoever reminds him of his wife's visits to a certain archpriest's
house will no longer be his friend. Throughout the long and meandering
conversations with the Master, Jacques never shows a glimpse of the intelligence that Larazillo needed in order to survive in a hostile environment;
but he certainly joins him in preferring a comfortable life to keeping his
honor immaculate.

It is tempting to imagine that Diderot, instead of growing tired of the
Master, became increasingly fond of this protagonist. Towards the end of the
book and as if out of the blue, he makes him find an unexpected desire and
energy to tell his own "love stories"—when his servant asks him about his
noble friend Desglands, at whose castle he had first met Denise:

> So that's the story of Desglands. Is Jacques satisfied, and might I hope that
> he will now listen to my love story or take up his own? (245)[41]

Jacques doubly declines "because the weather is warm, he feels tired, and
the landscape is charming" (245 / 755). But this does not prevent the Master
from beginning his story and indeed bringing it to an ending which, as we
have seen, will reveal the purpose of their journey and its place of arrival.
Above all, the Master shows himself very capable of playing the traditional
role of an aristocrat by confronting and defeating, without Jacques's support,
Saint-Ouin, his treacherous archenemy (265 / 776); by then talking himself
out of jail—and most likely also by sleeping with his servant's wife.

More even than the roles of Jacques and his Master, the positions of the
Narrator have been constantly shifting since the beginning of the book and

thus turned into an impulse for those movements of contingency that constitute the text as a complex space of active thinking. While his self-presentation
as omniscient and omnipotent over the emerging narrative prevails on the
opening pages, followed by a repeated insistence on his preference for "true"
over "novel-like" stories, the Narrator will later on confess that he is "as
curious as the reader" to know more about the continuation of Jacques's
anecdotes, because he completely depends on what the title protagonist is
ready to tell him:

> Don't you think I'm as curious as you are about it? [. . .] Everything I'm
> handing to you now, reader, I have had from Jacques, I confess, for I don't
> like to take credit for the thinking of another. Jacques did not know the
> name of vice and virtue; he held that we are happily or unhappily born.
> (165–66)[42]

Throughout his countless interventions, the Narrator also ends up arriving
at a more respectful and even friendlier tone with the Reader, whom he
initially addressed in harsh and condescending words. He particularly does
so in an apology for certain "obscene details" which, comparing himself to
the grand historians of Roman antiquity, he had judged to be unavoidable
for reasons of truth and full understanding. But his most dramatic moment
comes when the Narrator announces that "he will stop" before Jacques's
history reaches its end:

> As for myself, here's where I stop, for I have told you all I know about
> these two characters.—And how about Jacques's love story?—Jacques said
> at least a hundred times that it was written up yonder that he wouldn't
> finish the story, and I see that Jacques was right. I also see, reader, that
> this upsets you. Well, then, take up the story where he left off and finish it
> however you've a mind to. (265–66)[43]

At this point in the book, any seasoned reader, from our own or from Diderot's time, has long understood that its author does not plan to ever bring
Jacques's autobiographical ramblings to a conclusion. But, on the other hand,
for lack of an internal narrative motivation, nor could any reader anticipate that the Narrator would quit at the point where he decides to do so.
This moment in the Narrator's monologue resembles the sudden decision of

Rameau's nephew to abandon his conversation with the Philosopher. Could it be that Diderot was not particularly good at bringing his dialogues to an ending? May he simply have regularly grown tired of his own stories and their protagonists?

The Narrator—with the author behind him—quickly moves on to a new and final role when he suddenly makes reference to "some memoirs which I have good reason to distrust" (266),[44] and then promises the Reader to reread these notes and to get back to him "within eight days." Once he keeps his promise and indeed comes back at the beginning of the following paragraph, the Narrator, without any further explanation, has turned into "the Publisher":

> The publisher adds: The week has gone by. I have read the memoirs in question. Of the three paragraphs that I find not an integral part of the manuscript in my possession, the first and the last seem original, but the middle one is, to my way of thinking, obviously interpolated. (266)[45]

From a strictly logical perspective again, it is not clear who exactly is "speaking" in the text when this shift from the Narrator to the Publisher occurs. Nor are we able to find out whether the Publisher is supposed to be different from the Narrator or identical with him. In the latter case we can imagine that the Narrator finally "reveals his true identity as that of being a Publisher," whereas the former option would suggest that the Publisher has been "silent" so far—and in possession, from the beginning, of a text with the Narrator role inscribed.

The following page then identifies the "inserted" second paragraph of the "suspicious manuscript" as "copied from *The Life of Tristram Shandy* by Mister Sterne"—and this detail has of course inspired countless literary historians, although it belongs to those frequent textual effects without consequences that are typical for *Jacques le fataliste*.[46] Intentionally or not, Diderot again opens a loop of potential reflection and does not go much further than that. All speculations about the possibility of complicated mises en abyme triggered by the reference to Sterne belong exclusively to the critics' imagination—and may well be regarded as philologically acceptable unless they imply claims about Diderot's intention. All that we really learn in the end from the connection to *Tristram Shandy* is that Diderot must have been aware of its affinity with his own text—and most likely also of some differences between them.

All these textual traces and symptoms of Diderot's intellectual style, as a movement driven more towards complexity and openness than towards cohesion and closure, come together in that third dimension of contingency as their joint effect and vanishing point. *Jacques le fataliste* not only unfolds the future- and past-oriented dimensions of contingency in their interaction; the text also adds the accumulated instability effects of Diderot's carelessness as an author. Together, the three dimensions of contingency provide for Diderot's readers the energy of an extraordinary freedom of thought and imagination, as an impulse whose flip side is the constant risk of disorientation and confusion. Thus the text encourages and triggers truly individual reactions, but it also becomes an ever-expanding intellectual space where individuality can turn into isolation and the depressing realization of being lost.

Again I see a resemblance between this framework and array of intellectual movement created by Diderot and certain paths of thinking that seem globally present and perhaps even dominant today; and again I insist that this intuition of an affinity does not imply any speculations about genealogical or even "historically necessary" connections between Diderot's intellectual style and that of our time. Regarding the now, I am trying to describe the temporality that we inhabit as a "broad present" whose existential horizon is in a process of transformation from being a field of contingency into becoming a universe of contingency.[47] And in this new present I see a number of epistemological conditions reminding me of the specific configuration of complexity underlying *Jacques le fataliste*.

"Field of contingency" is a concept characterizing the standard situation of individual life as it emerged with the new role of the citizen in the bourgeois reforms and revolutions around 1800. In their individual lives, citizens were now granted a space of independent choice within which to shape their existence, a space that was limited (hence "field") between a dimension of "necessity," that is situations not accessible to choice, and a dimension of "impossibility," that is situations open for human imagination but not associated with the range of what humans can actually achieve. From the early nineteenth century on, "necessity" in this sense had been associated with the concept of "fate," and "impossibility" with a number of predicates, such as "omniscience," omnipotence," or "eternity," that were only used for divine beings. During the past decades, however, and partly due to the effects of electronic technology, these two poles have been, metaphorically speaking, in the process of melting. This is what I refer to as the transition from the everyday as a field of contingency towards the everyday as a universe of contingency.

To illustrate my observation: if until recently the sex to which somebody had been assigned, due to certain physical features, was considered fate, this very necessity is now beginning to vanish, with the rising hope for a new agency over sex that has been inspired by the beginnings of transsexual surgery; if eternity used to be considered and imagined as a temporality exclusive to gods, the option of endless bodily life has now become a new and serious goal for medical research. At the same time—and we have already referred to these internal conditions of the broad present—a new future occupied by threats that are moving towards us and a new past that invades the present, instead of falling back behind it, have transformed our present into a zone of overly complex juxtaposition and simultaneity. Both dynamics, the present as overly complex simultaneity and the present as a universe of contingency, provide us all with an unheard-of new intensity of freedom—but this dizzying intensity of freedom also means instability and makes us long for a fundamental orientation and for pre-reflexive values to hold on to.

In this sense, I associate the reading experience facilitated by *Jacques le fataliste* with an existential experience of our present—and I connect the title protagonist, in his specific and very visible limitations, both to a widespread contemporary desire for basic truths without complexity and to the problematic consequences of that desire. A second parallel is, on the one hand, the impression of bizarre facticity as it emerges, in *Jacques le fataliste*, from the discussion of internal narratives among the central characters' perspectives, and, on the other hand, the present-day tension between a prolific production of knowledge elements that present themselves as "factual" and a multiperspectivism that wants to transform every fact into a "social construction." Thirdly, as we tend to use words like "fact" and "facticity" to refer to "elements of knowledge" which, as opposed to "constructions," are not accessible to abstract general concepts and therefore have the status of being singular, we are in need of judgment, that is in need of the capacity to process individual phenomena without having resource to generally valid quantitative or qualitative criteria. Judgment today thus increasingly occupies the former place of rational argument and syllogism, and we will see in the chapter on Diderot's art criticism how central this operation already was within his intellectual practice.

As I have mentioned, the existentially and socially challenging complexity of our present brings to the fore, over and again, a craving for elementary orientation and values—but this same present also lends itself much less to beliefs in homogeneous systems and discourses of world explanation than did the age of overarching ideologies in the first half of the twentieth century. Instead of ideologies, that is conceptual and epistemological master keys, as they used to shape collective life in the past, a type of behavior capable of helping us individually to survive in the present might include skepticism, distance, serenity, an occasional tone of irony, and an occasional readiness to act, all based on judgment.

Seen from this angle, the aristocratic Master is the one character in *Jacques le fataliste* for whose prosaic ways in the world I feel sympathy. Needless to say, such a reaction does not imply any claim of being a finally discovered truthful interpretation or a serious hypothesis about what Diderot wanted to convey to his readers. Biographically speaking, he probably had no intention whatsoever to provide wisdom or moral orientation. He may just have prompted and followed the irregular movements of his thinking, in contact with other minds—but without the idea of lecturing or guiding them. This may also come close to a productive attitude for a present-day reading of *Jacques le fataliste*.

———————

But beside the possible resonance of such a text in the twenty-first century, what have we learned from the analysis of *Jacques le fataliste* about the position and the connections of Diderot's thought in his own time? Unlike those who embraced, developed, and promoted the historical worldview, authors and artists like Diderot and Lichtenberg, Goya and Mozart were not bothered by the contingency effects that followed from the new obsession, among intellectuals, with observing themselves in the act of world observation; nor did they bracket the central question of their "Materialistic" reflections, that is, how world appropriation through the mind could become compatible with world appropriation though the senses; they were playing out the corporeal layers of their existence as a new type of self-reference in their metabolic relations to the world; and instead of exclusively relying on rational deductions and inductions, they used acts of judgment in order to come to terms with a world experience in which individual phenomena resisted general principles. Contingency, Materialism, metabolic self-reference, and judgment were the four main components of their intellectual style on the periphery of the Enlightenment, and while these dimensions of course functioned in a rhizome-like connection, we have by now understood that different texts and different artworks focused on different aspects each time. If the key motif of the *Neveu de Rameau* was the protagonist's material self, the intellectual axis of *Jacques le fataliste* rather pursued the endlessly unfolding dynamics of contingency.

Francisco de Goya quite literally made these connections visible in yet a different configuration. First published in 1798, the etchings of his "Caprichos" produced multiple contingency effects by undercutting well-established positions and figures of Enlightenment knowledge and by showing human bodies in metabolic connection to their material environment. What dominates, by contrast, in Goya's second famous collection of etchings, *Los desastres de la guerra*, are scenes from the bloody confrontations between Napoleon's army as a force of occupation and those Spanish men and women, mostly from the lower classes, who ended up liberating their country in a war of independence between 1808 and 1814 (largely thanks to the emergence of new strategies of resistance and warfare that we have been calling "guerrilla" ever since). But in the repressive political climate after the return of the Spanish monarch to Madrid, Goya never exposed or sold any of the images from *Desastres*. For all of his patriotism, he even spent the final years of his life in France.

If, then, in "Caprichos" situations of contingency mostly emerged from allegorical figures who stood for certain groups of the population (spoiled children, narrow-minded monks, greedy go-betweens, and many others), almost all the scenes of *Desastres* refer to individual events of violence and scenes of extreme physical suffering. In this context Goya seems to react critically to a mode of pictorial meaning production that had been conventional until his time. While each group in a conflict had of course always been scandalized by any act of excessive physical violence committed by the other side, it would redeem its own violence as heroic conquest or courageous resistance. Against the background of this tradition, Goya comments with the caption "Lo Mismo" ("The Same") the image of a Spaniard killing with an energetic blow of his axe a French soldier who lies defenseless on the floor.[48] The implicit judgment is clear: although Goya was politically on the side of the insurgents (with a certain degree of ideological ambiguity), he must have felt that this position should not become a possible excuse for ruthless acts of physical aggression. Another example of the same relation between a scene made present in an etching and the artist's reaction is the image showing a Spanish woman and a Spanish man (the identification is easy because, unlike the French soldiers, the Spaniards had no uniforms in their guerrilla war) who together are disfiguring with a wooden stick and a lance the corpse of a dead French enemy—under the caption "Populacho" ("Low-Life People").[49]

More ambiguous appears the etching with the caption "Y son fieras" ("And They [i.e. These Women] are Savages"). In the midst of a violent confrontation, a woman joyfully penetrates the lower belly of a French soldier with her lance.[50] The word *fiero* has a double denotation to choose from: it can either describe a person with courageous physical strength or someone who goes too far in her or his animal-like violence—and certainly does not deserve admiration. We frequently discover such effects of contingency and their consequences in *Desastres*, and they are similar to the transformation of internal stories from *Jacques le fataliste* into facticity through different perspectives of interpretation that neutralize each other. Already in "Lo Mismo" and "Populacho" there was a potential contrast between the expected "patriotic" interpretation and Goya's apparent refusal to overlook cruelty on the Spanish side. "Y son fieras" makes this relationship more complex because it adds a second layer of complexity to the primary tension between two political perspectives, by activating through the word *fieras* both specific admiration for women engaged in violent action and a critique of their unredeemable violence. Together, the political tension, the surprise about female violence, and the deliberate semantic ambiguity of the caption make it difficult for any observer to subsume the scene represented under just one moral principle. By resisting such coherent forms of meaning, however, the image acquires a status of bare facticity. It exclusively stands for what happened in a specific moment—with no viable interpretation. Scenes of violence in their facticity no longer appear to be "typical cases" but turn into documents of individual moments. And cruel actions in their naked singularity are what Western culture has been calling "atrocity" since Goya's time.

Three etchings from *Desastres* that most editions present at the end of the collection make it clear that undermining the possibility of meaning attribution was something that intrigued Goya more than just as a device of critique and an expression of indignation.[51] The first and the second of these images are clearly allegorical. They show in their center a perfectly beautiful, bare-breasted young woman lying on the ground with her eyes closed. The caption "Murió la verdad" ("Truth Died") leaves no doubt that the immaculate female figure represents truth, as a value that died or disappeared in the horrors of the war. But in the following etching the allegorical figure seems to slightly open her eyes, prompting the caption's question: "Si resucitará?" ("[What] If She Wakes Up Again [If She Resuscitates]?"). The final image of the collection then shows us a very different-looking young woman, so different indeed that, within the Western iconographic tradition, she would definitely not qualify as an allegory of truth. Her breasts are also naked—but she stands, instead of lying on the floor, and she is less svelte and might even be pregnant. "Esto es lo verdadero" ("This Is the Real [Thing]") says the caption. From an ontological and also from a semiotic point of view, a discontinuity that Goya must have felt and willed separates the first two etchings from the third. For the third young woman is no longer supposed to represent a specific value—rather she is "the real" (and not "reality"). And perhaps we should go so far as to say that even "the real" appears too abstract a notion for what is at stake here, too abstract to fully escape the dimension of allegory and representation. The third woman is life (which might well explain the pictorial connotation of pregnancy) because it is life—and not truth—that dies or survives in the atrocities of war.

A nonviolent—but also lifelike—existential dimension of contingency dominated the adult life and probably ruined the final years of Wolfgang Amadeus Mozart. Counter to the traditional romantic aura of the poor artist that used to hover over Mozart biographies, we today know that he disposed of a both steady and remarkable flow of income. Estimates go up to the equivalent of over four million dollars in present-day value as accumulated honoraria for his concerts alone. If, on the other hand, a good number of documents prove that Mozart repeatedly and urgently tried to borrow large amounts of money from friends and admirers, this need most likely had to do with a gambling addiction whose intensity had run out of control: "In one single day, he allegedly gambled more than 2,000 Guldens ($800,000) while playing billiard."[52]

Gambling habits and gambling pathologies were astonishingly widespread during the age of Enlightenment and among some of its proverbial heroes. Thanks to his active participation in the emerging gambling industry, Voltaire disposed of a fortune that made him almost aggressively independent even of the monarchs who volunteered to support him. Lessing, by contrast, not only became the one symbolic protagonist of reason in German cultural history; the years after his wife's death in labor were also overshadowed by a gambling addiction and by considerable debts. Two opposite movements in the field of contingency account for the appeal and for the addiction of gambling. It obviously belongs to the existential range between necessity and impossibility, as gamblers are initially tempted by the hope of manipulating both of these limits. They try to make the impossible possible and to transform contingency into necessity (this is the first level of movement). On the side of impossibility, they refuse to exclude what can be considered as highly but not totally improbable; and on the side of necessity they become obsessed with tricks and with schemes that are supposed to turn luck (contingency) into the guaranteed certainty of success. Once playing becomes a stably destabilizing part of a gambler's life, however—once he has a gambling history—the field of contingency adopts a different (second) form for him. Then the past turns into a trail of facticity, an accumulation of seemingly unfortunate failures that he does not want to interpret as a warning or as a beginning of personal tragedy. The heavier his debts become, therefore, the stronger a gambler feels the urge to change the limits of impossibility and necessity, with ever-growing investments and risks. Looking at the final years of Mozart's life, we can ask whether gambling as a way of indulging in contingency, and debts as its consequence, were but the dark side of an energy behind his specific productivity as a composer, the dark side of an energy that indulged—and was successful—in pushing the limits of multivocal complexity, beyond what had appeared possible before and with an impression of transcendent necessity.

In Lichtenberg's sense of nuance and in his concentration on the singularity of phenomena, we have already identified traces of the powers of contingency. By contrast, there are only a few moments in his reflections that explicitly refer to problems and to the very concepts of contingency or randomness. One of them, in Notebook J,[53] discusses a review, published by *Literatur-Zeitung* in 1791, of Carl Christian Erhard Schmid's *Essay on Moral Philosophy*. Lichtenberg's reaction lets us understand that the central question of Schmid's book was identical with the dominant problem that emerges from Jacques's and his Master's conversations: is it possible to "conceive of a being who could in itself freely cause an action, entirely independent of the influence of any temporal causal series (occurring within the form of time), but at the same time, to the extent that it appears active, must in all of its cognizable actions be regarded as necessarily determined"? Do freedom and necessity go together, and are they in conflict at all? In order to save and preserve the "possibility of freedom," we read, Schmid recurred to the distinction between "matter" (attributed to "Nature") and "form" (attributed to "Reason") only to reach the conclusion ("decisive in this issue of freedom," according to Lichtenberg) that, counter to his (and Jacques's) starting point, everything is "either necessity or contingency."

Lichtenberg agrees neither with this argument nor with the reviewer's alternative philosophical proposals. His main objection is grounded in the conviction that "only the sensory world" is "operative under the form of necessity" whereas human action occurs under different premises and in different forms. This, he adds, is due to time as the "inner sense" that in human actions is supposed to give "the concept of necessity its sense" and form. Lichtenberg's reaction to Schmid's book and its premise, i.e. the intuition of a temporalization of necessity exclusive to the world of human actions, anticipates the most important intuition and premise of Hegel's philosophy and of the historical worldview in whose environment this philosophy would later develop its form and then move on to shape the nineteenth century. But temporalization of necessity never became part of the other, more peripheral type of thinking that Diderot practiced and towards which Lichtenberg felt otherwise inclined, the type of thinking where contingency, instead of being tamed by temporalized necessity, continued to function as a power of instability. Time does not seem to have mattered on the periphery of the Enlightenment.

5 | "LE PRODIGE, C'EST LA VIE"

Metabolizing Materialism in Le rêve de d'Alembert

THE SUMMER MONTHS of 1769 were particularly hot in Paris. While Diderot's wife and daughter were staying at Sèvres and Sophie Volland, as every year, spent time with her mother and her sisters at the family estate in Isle, Diderot worked so intensely ("comme un diable") on different projects that sometimes he did not find the time to get dressed and go out in a city abandoned by whoever could afford to leave—and by everybody Diderot cared about: "I am living in my dressing-gown a lot of the time, reading and writing; writing quite good things about the very bad things I read," he wrote to Sophie Volland on August 31. "I see no one, because there's no one left in Paris."[1] Besides working on the "Dialogues on the Commerce in Wheat"[2] by his Italian friend, the Abbé Galiani, who had just returned to Naples (the text would come out the following year); preparing the publication of two volumes with illustrations (*Planches*) for the *Encyclopédie*; and reviewing several exhibits of contemporary art, Diderot was in charge of receiving and evaluating submissions to Melchior Grimm's *Correspondance littéraire* while the editor was traveling in Germany for several months.[3] This task in particular explains why he complained about "the very bad things" that he had to read and why he mentioned over and again how impatient he was for Grimm to return. But in the same August 31 letter he also referred to those "pretty good things" he was writing himself:

I have written a dialogue between d'Alembert and me. We talk quite gaily, and quite clearly too, in spite of the dryness and obscurity of the subject. This dialogue is followed by a second one, which is much longer and serves to explain the first one more fully. It is called *D'Alembert's Dream*. The characters are: d'Alembert dreaming, his friend Mademoiselle d'Espinasse [sic], and Bordeu the doctor. (194)[4]

Unlike *Le neveu de Rameau*, whose production time spanned more than a decade (1761–1773), with considerable transformations in the dynamics of its content, and also unlike *Jacques le fataliste et son maître*, which took Diderot a good year and a half to finish (from early 1773 to mid-1774), he probably—and uncharacteristically—wrote *Le rêve de d'Alembert* within a few of those hot summer days of 1769, and he only once returned to the text at a later date. This was in 1774, when he added a brief allusion to the new monarch Louis XVI, who early on inspired such high hopes that Diderot compared him to the proverbial "bon roi" Henri IV.

Eight years later and two years before Diderot's death, the work was made accessible all over Europe to the few, mostly aristocratic subscribers of the *Correspondance littéraire*—a printed version did not appear until 1830. As we have seen, Diderot had become quite casual about the publication of his longer manuscripts ever since Catherine the Great of Russia had provided him with a comfortable financial situation beginning in 1765. In the particular case of *D'Alembert's Dream*, however, it may also have been the topic being dealt with that gave him good reason, based on earlier personal experience, to be cautious about distributing the text. But what exactly was the theme that he described as "dry and obscure" to Sophie Volland and that, inadvertently perhaps, he failed to explicitly name in his letter of August 31—nor did he name it in any other letter from those months?[5] Rather than spelling out what the new text was about, Diderot commented on its form, more precisely on a change in the fictional framework that he had decided to insert, hoping that it would help *Le rêve* to fulfill its intellectual function:

If I had wanted to sacrifice some of the richness of the subject matter in return for a nobler tone, I should have chosen Democritus, Hippocrates, and Leucippe; but that way verisimilitude would have confined me to the narrow limits of ancient philosophy, and that would have been too great a price to pay. It is the height of extravagance, but at the same time it is the most profound philosophy. It is quite cunning to have put my ideas into the mouth of a dreamer. You often have to dress up wisdom as folly to gain admittance for it. I had rather they said: "But that isn't as mad as you might think," than: "Listen, here are some great truths." (194)[6]

In the first place we learn, with Sophie Volland, that an issue of great complexity ("richesse du fond") is at stake and not just an exercise in stylistic elegance ("ton"), an issue also whose origins in ancient Greek philosophy (the three historical names mentioned as possible authors of course exclude a wide range of possible topics) must have undergone a major development during the previous years. This most likely was the reason why Diderot replaced his initial choice of a set of Greek protagonists carrying the conversation with the names of three characters who belonged to his immediate environment in Paris. What he regarded as his boldest ("extravagance") and indeed philosophically decisive move ("de la philosophie la plus profonde"), however, was the idea of putting some of the most important thoughts into the mouth of his former *Encyclopédie* coeditor and still friend Jean le Rond d'Alembert, whom the second part of the text presents as speaking in a fever dream. This fictional element in the center of the work, Diderot argues, will make his readers more inclined to accept its eccentric and highly speculative content ("lui procurer ses entrées").

Only eleven days later, in the next letter to Sophie, he comes back to *Le rêve* with a strangely distant gesture ("I think I told you that I had written a dialogue between d'Alembert and me"[7]), congratulates himself on the both necessary and paradoxical duplicity of "depth and madness" ("You can't imagine anything more profound and more crazy"[8]), and then mentions a third part that he had just added and with whose very brief summary he tried to provoke a stronger interest and reaction from Sophie:

As an afterthought I added five or six pages which would make my sweetheart's hair stand on end, so she shall never set eyes on them. But the thing that will surprise you is that there is not a single word about religion and not a single indecent word in the whole piece. So I defy you to guess what it is about. (198–99)[9]

How could these words have helped Sophie to guess what the subject matter ("deviner ce que ce peut être") of a text capable "of making her hair stand on end" ("capable de dresser ses cheveux") might have been? Key to her understanding must have been the hint that there was "not a word about religion" and that this would "surprise" Sophie—for the one topic obsessively (and almost always critically) related to religion in Diderot's circles had long been the monistic worldview of Materialism as a position that would systematically undercut all kinds of metaphysical claims. In 1749, the anonymous publication of *La lettre sur les aveugles* (*Letter on the Blind*), Diderot's first treatise with Materialistic ideas, culminating in an explicit questioning of the existence of God, had led to his imprisonment, on behalf of the monarchy's censorship system, for almost four months at Vincennes—and must have traumatized him enough to stay away, for a good quarter century, from this thematic horizon and its provocative potential. Although he continued refusing to name the very fascination he was now returning to, we can be certain that Diderot finally managed to awaken Sophie's interest because, on October 1, he had reason to write her,[10] in a both unfriendly and condescending tone, that the new text was too long to be copied for her, besides requiring interpretative guidance: "As for this dialogue between d'Alembert and me, how the devil do you expect me to have it copied it for you? It's almost as long as a book. And besides, I've already told you that a commentator is needed."[11]

It remains unclear what Diderot may have exactly meant on September 11 with his reference to a second omission, besides religion, in *Le rêve de d'Alembert*: that is, to the omission of any "indecent words" ("pas un seul mot déshonnête"). For unlike the strong associative relationship then existing between religion and Materialism, there was no single or even exclusive topic with which a contemporary reader would have associated erotic allusions (or their absence). At least we have discovered that Materialism was indeed the both "dry and obscure" philosophical subject matter of *Le rêve de d'Alembert* that, according to Diderot, needed "clarification" and "explanation." After the intellectual play with perspectives of human existence as embodied existence in *Le neveu de Rameau* and after the centrifugal dynamics of contingency in *Jacques le fataliste*, this chapter will concentrate on Materialism as a horizon of problems, concepts, and hypothetical answers that must have originated in a concern about the relationship between world appropriation through concepts and world appropriation through the senses. As I announced in the second chapter, it will add a further dimension to our reconstruction of that loose epistemological configuration (or "epistemological underbelly") and its "prosaic" relationship with the human environment which, since the late eighteenth century, the emerging historical worldview and its rise to the center of institutional social knowledge left at its own periphery as an alternative option of experience and thinking.

Unlike most previous interpretations, I believe that the conceptual and argumentative innovations conveyed by *Le rêve de d'Alembert* were modest, not to say minimal. And yet the work has been celebrated by major specialists "as a bold view of the cosmos, much in advance of its time," as Diderot's "greatest work,"[12] and, even more hyperbolically, "as a text that is unique in the history of philosophy and of literature since Plato."[13] How can a strangely heterogeneous sequence of philosophical reflections in three different tones and discourses deserve such praise (with those who judge being quite unclear about their criteria), and how can it be regarded as "in advance of its time" when, in its own intellectual world, it did not make a true theoretical, let alone empirical difference? The thesis that I try to pursue in answering this question will claim that, instead of enriching the philosophy and science of its time, *Le rêve de d'Alembert* succeeded in transforming the highly abstract intellectual repertoire of Materialism into an existentially appealing, embodied relationship with life, both as a horizon of living phenomena and as the manifestation of a force that underlies the universe, and that it did so partly through the multiple rhythms of its prose and through their effects on our imagination. In other words, *Le rêve de d'Alembert* should be read less as a philosophical manifesto, a survey, or a variation of Materialism than as a mechanism towards its tentative transformation, for the reader, into a body-intense mode of existence. This is what I mean by the phrase "metabolizing Materialism."

As Diderot did not try to systematize or advance Materialism but was just presupposing its existence as the matrix of an ongoing intellectual conversation of his time, we need to briefly describe its map of positions or, more adequately, its field of forces, within which Diderot quite freely moved and to which, above all, his writing would give a new existential status. Authors and works whom we connect with this map and its dynamic today, like Julien Offray de La Mettrie (1709–1751) and his *L'homme machine* (1747); Claude Adrien Helvétius (1715–1771) and the book *"De l'esprit"* (1758) in which he tried to demonstrate that all psychic and intellectual ("spiritual") functions of human life depended on matter; Diderot's friend Paul-Henri Thiry, Baron d'Holbach, with his *Système de nature* (1770); and Diderot himself, largely overlapped in their philosophical intentions, their central concepts and arguments, their knowledge of chosen predecessors from Ancient Greek philosophy, and even in their lineup of favorite metaphors, instead of trying to elaborate individual versions within their joint stream of thoughts. With a clear degree of caution caused by the interventions of censorship in the emerging public sphere, each of the Materialists was enthusiastic about pushing further the shared intellectual movement and to sharpen its potential of intellectual provocation.

This common energy, since the late seventeenth century, had emerged from a resistance against the ontological dualism between *res cogitans* and *res extensa* that was foundational for René Descartes's (1596–1650) writings and for the broad resonance that made them normative in multiple contexts of thinking during the Age of Reason and Rationality. In this sense, an elementary affinity existed between the Materialists and Baruch Spinoza's (1632–1677) *Ethics* where, in the most consequential monistic turn, God was declared to be identical with Nature (*Deus sive Natura*). But for the Materialists, by contrast and as a first premise, being able to think human existence and the cosmos in absence of any concept of God became a central temptation and even the true reward of monism. As they did not care about including any purely spiritual being in their worldview, the concept of "matter" could, in the second place, remain strictly synonymous with *res extensa* as substance—and at the same time become a basis for all three-dimensional phenomena that humans are able to distinguish in their individual forms.

As Karl Marx, trying to give his own thinking about society and economy a dignifying genealogy, made explicit reference to "matter" and to "Materialism" as frequently used words in the debates of the eighteenth century and in his doctoral dissertation even dealt with their presocratic history, we need to insist that his use of these words and its broad resonance have little to do with Materialism before 1800. For Marx they referred to the "conditions of production" in industry and in economy, that is to a horizon of phenomena that, based on a distinction that did not exist yet in his time, was rather "social" than "substantial" in the sense of the Aristotelian tradition.

In a third segment of Materialism's field of forces, after monism and the concept of "matter," we find a decisive bifurcation between two types of assumptions about matter, a bifurcation triggered by the challenge of explaining the existence of spiritual phenomena within a strictly monistic and purely material worldview. It is of course possible to presuppose that there are two different types of matter, one implying elements that lead directly to the existence of spiritual phenomena and another type that does not relate to the mind. Under this premise, however, an ontological dualism ("matter that leads to spirituality" vs. "matter that does not") must undercut the monistic premise of Materialism, whereas the alternative, more consistently monistic option ("there is only one kind of matter and it can produce spirituality"), leads to a fourth step in Materialism's basic questions and distinctions.

This is the step where the Greek concept of "atom," as a minimal unit of matter, becomes relevant. For if there is only one type of matter (and of atoms), then the different possible configurations of its basic units must explain how some of them can become the basis for life, while some others cannot. Most Materialists assumed with Pierre Louis Maupertuis (1698–1759) that all atoms had an inherent capacity for motion and for sensibility and that this potential could be either "inert" or "active." There were two approaches to explaining the transition from "inert" to "active." Some Materialists wanted the contrast to hinge upon different structures in which the atoms were connected. Their antagonists (among them Diderot) preferred to imagine that the distinction depended on the quantity of atoms assembled. The more atoms assembled in close connection, they suggested, the more complex, livelier, and ultimately more spiritual the phenomena made up by them would become (this is where temperature often came in as a condition facilitating or blocking the concentration of atoms and thus their transition from inert to active). In a growing assembly of atoms, the potential dynamic of each atom would be activated; if, by contrast, the number of atoms assembled were decreasing (up to the extreme of individual isolation), then they would stand still, have no lively functions, and approach death (a death, however, from which they were able to return in a fresh movement of assemblage).

In a fifth segment of Materialism, different types of assemblages with large numbers of atoms were considered and distinguished, often under the unifying concept that they were all "machines" (a piano, for example, or a human body as a "machine"), which approach was bound to level traditional ontological hierarchies (above all those implied by *Genesis* in the account of divine world creation). Rather than trying to explain how a piano (for example) was categorically different from a human being, most Materialists liked to insist on the gradual character of such differences. This anti-hierarchical tendency also explains why they were so fascinated by imagining the different (but not "inferior") world experience of humans who were lacking part of their perceptual connections to the world, like the blind or the deaf.

In a further (and, for our survey, final) segment, Materialism approached a cosmological dimension. If the entire universe was basically and exclusively supposed to be matter, and if matter consisted of atoms as its basic units, then the most important question and challenge was to explain, starting from atoms, transformations within the universe, above all the appearance and the vanishing of the species of life. During the eighteenth century, unlike the present-day dominance of a flexible concept of evolution in this context, a much broader variety of models was in debate: between a strict determinism and an absolute claim of randomness, early versions of evolutionism began to emerge (and Diderot was particularly interested in them). But while Materialism, especially among French thinkers, found broad resonance during the eighteenth century, not all philosophers were willing to embrace it. Voltaire and Jean-Jacques Rousseau, for example, remained epistemologically Cartesian, and so did d'Alembert—although Diderot used his name in the title of his most important treatise under Materialistic premises.

Our main problem in reading such texts today has to do with the number of their "scientific" premises, observations, and assumptions that we know are no longer valid—but which, in many cases, we need to understand in order to follow the arguments made and the hypotheses launched. This explains why much of the scholarship dedicated to *Le rêve de d'Alembert* indulges in impressive erudition without ever trying to find specific reasons for the great appreciation that the text has received within Diderot's work. My thesis about "metabolizing Materialism" as its main effect tries to make a step towards the solution of this problem—and to add a point of contemporary existential relevance. For however naive certain details and beliefs of eighteenth-century Materialism may look to us, we should not forget that, as a mode of thinking about ourselves within the world of nature, its premises have ended up prevailing—while many of its most traditional questions remain wide open. We still do not know how exactly "consciousness" (let alone "conscience") emerges from our brains and our bodies, but nobody doubts today that body and brain are indeed the bases of our mind. What we lack much more, however, than a model to solve such problems are discourses through which the existing positive results of science could contribute to making the world more habitable for us. Contemporary ecological politics and eco-philosophy try to improve this situation. But as their agenda, understandably, has become one of mostly "last-minute warnings," they make us feel more what we may be about to lose than what we still have and should probably enjoy even more under the threat of its vanishing.

———————

Without any doubt, Denis Diderot was very capable of dealing with the "dry and obscure" issues of Materialism in a philosophically abstract way. After all, many contemporary readers assumed that he had written large portions of the 1770 *Système de la nature* (attributed today to his friend d'Holbach but first published under the name of a secretary of the *Académie française* who had died ten years earlier[14]), a work whose style fulfilled and even exceeded every possible expectation about conceptual and argumentative rigor. But we have experienced how his more spontaneous inclinations prompted him to discursive forms that allowed for effects of enthusiasm and embodiment, above all on the readers' side. While this tendency likely explains the dialogic form of *Le rêve de d'Alembert,* it had already shaped his *Lettre sur les aveugles—à l'usage de ceux qui voient* (*Letter on the Blind for the Use of Those Who Can See*) from 1749.

The text of the *Lettre sur les aveugles* focused on two fascinations of Materialism hardly present in the *Rêve*, that is (firstly) on trying to imagine the world experience of persons who did not share the full perceptual equipment of other humans and (secondly) on the nonexistence, rather than the absence, of God (this, above all, must have been the aspect to which Diderot's subtitle referred). All discussions in the first part of the *Lettre* were supposedly based on Diderot's conversations with a person who was born blind, "the man-born-blind of Puiseaux"[15] whom he had personally visited, to whom the *Lettre* referred as "notre aveugle" ("our blind man"), and whose behavior and mind it progressively conjured up. One ongoing concern was to document, in almost obsessive detail, how a blind person was able, through organizational devices and a sharpening of his other senses, to compensate for the lack of vision:

> The man-born-blind of Puiseaux works out how close he is to the fire by how hot it is, how full a receptacle is by the sound liquid makes as he decants it, and how near he is to other bodies by the way the air feels on his face. (177)[16]

Another intellectual effort of the *Lettre* was to imagine the contours and inner forms of different mental worlds that some blind persons from Diderot's time inhabited, including their morality, and to do so under the premise and conviction that these worlds were different but not necessarily deficient in comparison to the worlds of those who can see:

> Since I have never doubted the great influence of our senses and organs on our metaphysics and morals, nor that our most purely intellectual ideas, if I may call them that, are closely related to the organization of our bodies, I began to ask our blind man about vice and virtue. (179)[17]

The first, both plausible and surprising, observation that Diderot made, i.e. that "our blind man" did not know any feelings of physical embarrassment or shame (*pudeur*), must have been particularly shocking for eighteenth-century readers, who were so used to the exuberant play of covering and uncovering certain body parts with their clothing. With the second "moral" difference that he perceived, Diderot moved into dangerous territory, for he talked about the impossibility for blind people of inductively gaining, from images of the physical world, the impression of a creator God's existence (180 / 93).

The other protagonist and true hero of Diderot's *Lettre*, with whom his readers could identify and to whom he encouraged them to look up, was the English mathematician Nicholas Saunderson (1682–1739), who had gone blind around his first birthday and would later rise, with active support from the British monarch, to a professorship at Cambridge, to a status of international admiration and indeed celebrity in his contemporary world and, thanks to a number of important discoveries, to a lasting place in the history of mathematics.[18] Saunderson, too, had intensely trained his remaining senses in order to compensate for the lack of vision:

> Saunderson's sight was in his skin. He had such an exquisitely sensitive epidermis that if a draughtsman were to sketch a friend's portrait on his hand, he would undoubtedly have been able, with a bit of practice, to recognize it. (198)[19]

It is important to insert here that, to the best of our knowledge (and most likely also of Diderot's), Saunderson never really did develop the capacity to recognize friends by the contours of their portraits that somebody drew on his hand. Rather than a true feature of his hero's specific relation to the material world, this detail was the product of the author's generous and altogether edifying tendency to push his own and his readers' admiration for Saunderson to the level of suggesting a systematic connection between handicap and genius.[20]

An implicit claim that intellectual as well as moral superiority were inseparable from Saunderson's blindness ended up becoming the premise of the *Lettre*'s culminating pages, which Diderot presented as his translation of a transcript of the blind man's conversation, on his deathbed, with Mr. Holmes, a pastor. Here the experience returns that a person without vision would find it impossible to acknowledge the existing material world as evidence for the existence of a god and creator (it appears that Diderot and his readers shared the assumption that this was bound to happen). But Saunderson moves decisively beyond the bare impossibility of acknowledging the existence of a god by denouncing as a lack of intellectual modesty the human urge to confuse certain limits of understanding with the trace of a divine presence:

> If we think a phenomenon is beyond man, we immediately say it's God's work; our vanity will accept nothing less, but couldn't we be a bit less vain and a bit more philosophical in what we say? If nature presents us with a problem that is difficult to unravel, let's leave it as it is and not try to

undo it with the help of a being who then offers us a new problem, more insoluble than the first. (199–200)[21]

There is a moment of great solemnity in Diderot's text when, almost at the very end of Saunderson's life, during his conversation with Mr. Holmes and after a brief moment of delirium, he invokes a god who, for him and for the author, may well have been synonymous with the nonexistence of God: "*Oh God of Clarke and Newton, take pity on me!*" (202).[22] Above all, though—and this detail must have been of great personal concern to Diderot and most of his readers—the philosopher-mathematician of the *Lettre* dies surrounded by his family, quietly, at peace with himself—and without evoking a god:

> His final farewell to his family is very touching: "I am going," he told them, "where we all go. Spare me your distress, which I feel moved by. The signs of pain that escape your lips only make me more sensitive to the signs that elude my grasp. I feel no sorrow at leaving a life that has been nothing more to me than one long deprivation and endless yearning. Live as virtuously as I have and more happily, and learn to die as peacefully." With that he took his wife's hand and held it tight in his for a while. Then he turned to face her as though trying to see her, blessed his children, embraced them all and begged them to withdraw as their presence was a crueller pain for his soul than the approach of death. (203)[23]

It is remarkable how Diderot's Saunderson, for all of his supposed intellectual and moral superiority, lives this last moment in full and desperate awareness of the lack of vision, which adds a further emotional dimension to the psychological and cognitive focus of the text. Within the larger discursive and philosophical field of Materialism, the two specific topics that the *Lettre sur les aveugles* pursued—that is, constituting a subjective world through a mainly tactile relationship to the material environment and, based on the first experience, arguing against the existence of God—were quite peripheral. They must have been the result of Diderot's concern, in the quite literal sense, with making palpable in his readers' imagination even the most abstract philosophical topics.

But Saunderson's farewell to life in his conversation with the pastor also brought up a topic that would become more central in *Le rêve de d'Alembert*. This was the question about forms of life that had preceded and would follow our own, the question that we have referred to, since the early nineteenth century, with the concept of "evolution." Leading the readers to an unusual temporal distance by the standards of their historical moment, Diderot's protagonist once again produced an immediate relation to his own existence by starting the reflection with the suspicion that life forms without vision must have been quite normal at earlier stages of the cosmos:

> It is therefore my conjecture that in the beginning when the universe was hatched from fermenting matter, my fellow men were very common. Yet couldn't my belief about animals also hold for worlds? How many lop-sided, failed worlds are there that have been dissolved and are perhaps being remade and redissolved every minute in far away spaces, beyond the reach of my hands and your eyes, where movement is still going on and will keep going on until the bits of matter arrange themselves in a combination that is sustainable? (201–2)[24]

Some aspects of this passage show an astonishing affinity with a more advanced version of evolutionism, as we like to profess it today: above all the idea of "failed" strains of development that will not find any continuation ("lopsided, failed worlds" / "mondes estropiés, manqués"), but also the intuition about changing concentrations and condensations of matter ("bits of matter arrange themselves" / "combiner des amas de matière"). And yet I refrain from postulating a specific talent here that would have inspired Diderot to be truly ahead, in his speculations, of his time's positive knowledge. For his true and most recurrent strength as an author, as we see again in the *Lettre sur les aveugles*, was that of connecting scientific complexity and philosophical abstraction to individual situations and individual protagonists that his readers could identify with. In doing so, Diderot managed to transform Materialism into images of life, life in the sense of a self-experience of human existence that was becoming aware in a more differentiated way of its bodily conditions and increasingly also of the body's larger spatial and temporal environment.

————————

From the summer letters of 1769, where Diderot mentioned *Le rêve de d'Alembert* for the first time to Sophie Volland and then immediately proceeded to name the dialogue's protagonists, we can tell that giving life to abstract concepts and facts had indeed become a concern for him. It thus seems appropriate, as we are finally approaching the text, to introduce the characters of *Le rêve*, not just through biographical data and facts but also, as far as possible, with a number of memories and connotations that they must have carried for the author and his readers.

Of course there were multiple reasons for Diderot to choose, as his counterpart for a fictional philosophical debate about Materialism, Jean le Rond d'Alembert, with whom he had organized and edited the *Encyclopédie* until January 1758. First of all, it was easy to imagine such a conversation as part of their former collaboration and ongoing friendship (the beginning of the written dialogue indeed pretends to join such an ongoing debate and thus explain the formulation of its title: "Sequel to a conversation between M. d'Alembert and M. Diderot"[25]). In his work for the *Encyclopédie* d'Alembert had complemented Diderot as a specialist in Latin literature, in the theory of musical composition, and, above all, as a physicist and mathematician (although Diderot frequently referred to d'Alembert as a "géomètre," his greater merits rather seem to have been in the field of algebra). But it must also have been important that, unlike Diderot whose epistemological monism could not help leading to atheism, d'Alembert was a dualist in the Cartesian style and thus most probably a deist. Altogether, their positions within the larger field of Materialism appeared both sufficiently divergent and sufficiently overlapping to make an intellectually fruitful exchange highly plausible. Besides his intellectual profile, d'Alembert had an exceptional life history. Born three years after Diderot, as the natural son of an artillery officer and a woman writer who was also a nun, the infant d'Alembert had been left by his mother in front of the church of Saint-Jean-le-Rond (hence his first name), from where he was brought to an orphanage. Soon, however, his father managed to identify him and anonymously financed his education. While from an early age d'Alembert developed a reputation as an eminent mathematician and scientist, a connotation of social awkwardness surrounded him, at least in Diderot's memory.[26] There were doubts, for example, about whether his relationship to Mlle de Lespinasse, with whom d'Alembert lived beginning in the early 1760s, ever included an erotic dimension. When in 1758, reacting to interventions by the royal censorship, he resigned from his post as editor of the *Encyclopédie*, d'Alembert appeared utterly inflexible in his decision and unable to appreciate diverging arguments. And yet Diderot was successful—unlike his history with Jean-Jacques Rousseau—in maintaining their friendship through several precarious moments. In 1765, during one of the mathematician's recurrent episodes of bad health, he even decided to regularly see Diderot in his apartment, together with Mme Diderot.[27] And aside from that, the impulse of Diderot's text to imagine such a famous, highly learned, fragile, and socially insecure character under the impact of a fever also promised some comic side effects for contemporary readers.

The second male protagonist (beside the author's own presence, which ends with the first part of *Le rêve de d'Alembert*) is Théophile de Bordeu, a physician who was eight and five years younger, respectively, than Diderot and d'Alembert, and ten years older than Mlle de Lespinasse, the only female character. The real Bordeu would become the first researcher to give a definition and assign a specific anatomical status to the concept of "tissue"; he also gave new diagnostic relevance, based on a number of treatises, to the pulse. In one of these publications he compared the human body to a "swarm of bees," which metaphor greatly impressed Diderot. But Bordeu was equally recognized among his contemporaries as a medical practitioner (in this function he helped Diderot's family on several occasions) and as an early specialist in psychological aspects of health care. Indeed, emergency intervention was the thematic focus that he chose for the entry on *"Crise"* with which Diderot entrusted him for the *Encyclopédie*. This convergence between empirical research, practical care, and a tendency towards psychological speculation made Bordeu a protagonist of the Vitalist School, which was then highly recognized in French medicine. At the same time he was a notoriously charming presence in Enlightenment circles.

Whether Bordeu ever really met Jeanne Julie Eléonore de Lespinasse, with whom he occupies the larger part of the *Dream*'s second and its entire final part, will forever remain uncertain. All that we know about her connections to the text's other protagonists has already been mentioned, namely that she shared an apartment with d'Alembert for several years and that Diderot and his wife made her acquaintance in 1765. Like d'Alembert, Mlle de Lespinasse was the child of parents who never married. While the identity of her natural father was never revealed to her, her mother, who lived separated from her aristocratic husband, invented the name "de Lespinasse," together with a story about a father and a mother who had indeed never existed. When Julie Eléonore was twenty-two years old, an aunt discovered her spiritual liveliness, which seemed to belie the very basic education that she had received at a convent, and brought her to Paris, where Mlle de Lespinasse soon became a widely admired protagonist in the most prestigious salons. While nineteenth-century historians of literature later made her letters part of the national literary canon, there is no evidence that Diderot had ever read any of her texts or had an individual impression of her profile or her talents. We must assume that the only reason for her presence in the text was her association with d'Alembert, which means that she was a character whose role was open for Diderot to shape in any convenient way. There have been speculations about her image in the *Dream* reflecting Diderot's view of Sophie Volland, but all that we know they shared was an interest in philosophical issues. It is certainly more important to underline that, from several perspectives, Mlle de Lespinasse ends up occupying functions that are typically covered by the implied author. She is the first to express an interest in the fragmented sentences that d'Alembert utters during his fever attack; she comes up with increasingly daring questions and hypotheses about the status of of the human body; and she will turn to Bordeu, with growing affection, as she tries to find out whether what she imagines about medical topics and questions has any truth value.

In the first of the *Dream*'s three parts, however, it is the role of "Diderot" to provoke new questions and thus provide a dynamic for the intellectual exchange, often against "d'Alembert's" resistance, who occupies a position with which many readers could likely identify and which frequently obliges "Diderot" to sharpen his distinctions and arguments. As for the discursive flavor, this opening segment largely remains within the philosophical tone of the ongoing debates about Materialism. With his fever dreams in the second part of the text, by contrast, d'Alembert will not only progressively join Diderot in the monist beliefs that he was rejecting before, but does so with images and with an insistence capable, on different levels, of transforming concepts into impressions of life. Meanwhile Mlle de Lespinasse not only reads her notes on d'Alembert's words to Bordeu and thus provokes both enthusiastic and experience-saturated reactions of approval and interest; she also feels progressively encouraged to raise issues that end up capturing the doctor's respect and personal interest, besides creating an opening for the presentatation of many individual case histories. Finally, in the short third part, Mlle de Lespinasse and Bordeu are alone for dinner ("D'Alembert had gone out to dinner" [225][28]). Their conversation only returns to topics of Materialism after dessert, when she tries to focus on a phenomenon that indeed found intense interest in their time, that is, the possibility of a "mixture of species" ("mélange des espèces" [169]) and its possible consequences. Their starting point will lead the two protagonists, as no interpretation of *Le rêve* fails to remark, to the problem of whether moral rules and constraints can be derived from the Materialist worldview. As an exclusive focus, the problem leaves unredeemed a different existential dimension that may be decisive for the conclusion of *Le rêve de d'Alembert* —and for the entire text indeed.

———————

We have needed to bring together an unusual amount of historical knowledge to prepare the actual reading of *Le rêve de d'Alembert* because the text was part of an intellectual obsession in the third quarter of the eighteenth century whose contents are mostly forgotten today, because they are scientifically outdated. But this work is also difficult to access because, much more so than *Le neveu de Rameau* or *Jacques le fataliste*, it belonged to a brief and thus quite specific moment in Diderot's intellectual life. The two central phenomena ("les deux grands phénomenes") and concerns from the agenda of Materialism in which its three segments converge, are, as d'Alembert states with strong emotion in his fever moment, "the transition from a state of inertia to one of sensitivity, and spontaneous generation" (177).[29] With the expression "generations spontanées" he refers to the emergence and vanishing of different life forms over long stretches of time, that is, to the topic that has become relevant for us as "evolution." It is certainly characteristic of Diderot's intellectual temperament that both issues, including the "transition from inert atoms to their sensible state," had no possible solutions in sight within the Materialist discussions.

    In this problem-oriented spirit, d'Alembert's opening remark about the difficulty that even he feels in assuming the existence of a god ("I grant you that a Being [. . .] so contradictory [. . .] by nature, is difficult to accept"

[149][30]) immediately tackles a notorious weakness in Diderot's position. Whoever does not believe in God, d'Alembert seems to imply, must assume that
only matter (and he silently supplements: only one type of matter) exists.
This gives his friend the obligation to show how life, above all intellectual
life, can emerge from matter; and the obligation then leads to d'Alembert's
deliberately absurd postulate that a stone must be able to have feelings: "stone
must feel" (149)[31]—because, if it is based on the same matter, even a stone
should possess a potential equal to that of humans. In such precarious situations of debate, Diderot always enjoyed the challenge of making arguments
that looked impossible at first glance. "Pourquoi non?" he says in reaction
to d'Alembert's question whether he can imagine a stone with feelings, and
the attempt to live up to this "why not?" brings him back to the distinction
between basic units of matter in their inert and active state. This distinction
evokes the both vague and very general thesis that certain "obstacles" prevent
inert atoms from being active, which Diderot will illustrate through the
example of food intake as a behavior supposedly removing such obstacles
and thus making matter sensitive:

> What do you do when you eat? You remove the obstacles which were
> resisting the active sensitivity of the food. You assimilate the food with
> yourself, you turn it into flesh, you animalize it, make it capable of feeling.
> What you do to that food I will do to marble, and whenever I like. (151)[32]

The last sentence already announces Diderot's farfetched claim, in reaction
to d'Alembert's sustained doubt about a "stone that feels," that one can grind
a marble statue into dust, use the dust as an ingredient for the humus soil in
a vegetable garden, and thus ultimately, by eating the vegetables, "turn the
statue into flesh." As the passage about eating and digestion as an illustration
for the transformation of inert matter into active matter fails to specify what
exactly might be an "obstacle" to the activation of matter, the final thought
about a marble statue becoming flesh may have struck Diderot's readers more
as a symptom of intellectual impatience, energy, and the will to arrive at an
associative horizon of life than by its precision and scientific competence.

The same impatience becomes evident again in the dialogue when Diderot
makes his decisive conceptual point about adding "sensibility" to "motion"
as a second function belonging to matter. Short of an empirically based

objection to hold against d'Alembert's view that "sensibility is essentially incompatible with matter," Diderot quite aggressively states instead that his friend should feel sorry for himself for not embracing a purely conceptual solution that is tempting—just because it promises to explain what needs to be explained:

> Listen to your own arguments and you will feel how pitiful they are. You will come to feel that by refusing to entertain a simple hypothesis that explains everything—sensitivity as a property common to all matter or as a result of the organization of matter—you are flying in the face of common sense and plunging into a chasm of mysteries, contradictions and absurdities. (159)[33]

Under the pressure of intellectual impatience, Diderot often works over conceptual problems and gaps by mere deictic gestures. One such case is his second attempt to produce evidence for the transition from inert to active matter—when he invites d'Alembert "to sit down and follow, step by step," the development of an egg:

> What is this egg? An insensitive mass before the germ is put into it, and after the germ is in it what is it then? Still an insensitive mass, for the germ itself is merely inert and thick fluid. How does this mass evolve into a new organization, into sensitivity, into life? Through heat. What will generate heat in it? Motion. What will the successive effects of motion be?
>
> Instead of answering me, sit down and let us follow out these effects with our eyes from one moment to the next. First there is a speck which moves about, a thread growing and taking colour, flesh being formed, a beak, wing-tips, eyes, feet coming into view, a yellowish substance which unwinds and turns into intestines—and you have a living creature. (158)[34]

Common knowledge comes to stand in here for (the lacking) scientific observation, whose interpretation might have filled the existing conceptual gap. For at least the Diderot of the dialogue seems content with any illustration, example, argument, or concept that gets him close to the associative horizons of "life" and of "flesh."

But he does not manage to escape the next question that d'Alembert asks, regarding the step between a being that feels and a "thinking being" (*être pensant*). As a first response, Diderot activates the standard explanation of his time, according to which certain larger accumulations of atoms were able to come together in organs resonating with the world and thus fulfilling the function of a memory (which implies a material transition from such accumulations of atoms to all kinds of strings, cords, and tissues)—and which further suggests that only humans dispose of a memory powerful enough to facilitate the transformation of primary resonance into consciousness. Rather than drawing distinctions and descriptions for different functions of the human mind, Diderot seems more fascinated by the Materialist motif of a similarity between different types of "instruments" based on resonance: above all by the supposed similarity between musical instruments like the harpsichord (*clavecin*), animals, and humans, and also by the subsequent idea that, after all, human communication may not be all that different from animal communication: "notice [. . .] that all human intercourse consists solely of noises and actions" (161).[35]

Probably Diderot, the author, was aware, at least to a certain degree, of his intellectual impatience and of the ensuing philosophical incompleteness in the development of some of his favorite motifs and claims. This may have been the reason why he makes the fictional d'Alembert ask whether the different steps leading from basic elements of matter to thinking had a status of contingency or of necessity for him. And unlike the reflections in *Jacques le fataliste* on necessity and contingency in human interaction, Diderot now makes a strong principled claim for necessity permeating the realm of nature. At the same time, he concedes that an impression of contingency (or of a different, softer kind of necessity) will remain inevitable as long as humans are not capable of observing and identifying the full range of conditions that constitute a necessary cause in nature:

> the cause is subject to too many peculiar vicissitudes which we fail to perceive, and so we cannot count infallibly upon the effect that will result. Our certainty that a violent man will lose his temper when insulted is not of the same kind as the certainty that if two bodies collide the larger will cause the smaller to move. (162)[36]

By now we have seen how Diderot's and d'Alembert's dialogue, as the first part of *Le rêve*, concentrates on a repertoire of concepts and images about the transition from inert matter to active matter and about the consequences of this transition, a repertoire that is more impressive for its discursive liveliness and variety than for its focus on systematic transparence. It stops short of addressing issues related to the larger temporal frames of nature ("générations spontanées") by, quite literally, letting the fictional d'Alembert get tired at a certain point of the conversation (which, seen from the continuation of the text and its narrative structure, will end up looking like an excuse to finish a conversation that had gotten boring).

Earlier on, however, in one of the more remarkable passages of the entire text, the dialogue's energy violently transgresses a rule of social tact, and it does so more, as we will see, between the real Diderot and the real d'Alembert than between the text's protagonists,[37] thus indeed reaching an ontologically different dimension. This happens when the textual Diderot, in his first reaction to d'Alembert's skepticism regarding the Materialist thesis about the emergence of thinking, uses private knowledge about the scandalous relationship between his friend's natural parents and about his upbringing in an orphanage as an illustration for his own philosophical point:

DIDEROT

Let me tell you the story of one of the greatest mathematicians in Europe. What was this wondrous being in the beginning? Nothing.

D'ALEMBERT

Nothing! How do you mean? Nothing can come from nothing.

DIDEROT

You are taking words too literally. What I mean is that before his mother, the beautiful and scandalous Madame de Tencin, had reached the age of puberty, and before the soldier La Touche had reached adolescence, the molecules which were to form the first rudiments of our mathematician were scattered about in the young and undeveloped organs of each, were being filtered with the lymph and circulated in the blood until they finally settled in the vessels ordained for their union, namely the sex glands of his mother and father. Lo and behold, this rare seed takes form; it is carried, as is generally believed, along the Fallopian tubes and into the womb. It is attached thereto by a long pedicle, it grows in stages and advances to the state of foetus. The moment for its emergence from its dark prison has come: the new-born boy is abandoned on the steps of Saint-Jean-le-Rond, which gave him his name, taken away from the Foundling Institution and put to the breast of the good glazier's wife, Madame Rousseau; suckled by her he develops in body and mind and becomes a writer, a physicist and a mathematician. How did all this come about? Through eating and other purely mechanical operations. (152–53)[38]

By speaking of Diderot's "tactlessness," I am not trying to accuse the author of a malicious intention to expose his former friend—or his potential rival for recognition in the world of the salons. What I rather imagine is the socially unpleasant side of an openness and of a longing for life that were driving forces behind his prose, an energy also that implied the permanent chance and the permanent risk of blurring or even breaking both epistemological and social borders. This, too, was a level, perhaps the most extreme level, of metabolizing Materialism.

———

In the second, longest, and most complex segment of *Le rêve de d'Alembert*, the tone of the protagonists' words changes considerably. It happens due to the appearance of Dr. Bordeu and of Mlle de Lespinasse, as two new protagonists in the ongoing discussion—but above all, through and in d'Alembert's fever language. The opening conversation between the doctor and the mathematician's companion suggests that d'Alembert had returned home from his conversation with Diderot, seemed worried (*soucieux*), and began to speak with a confusion so alarming that his servant called for medical help. Dr. Bordeu's diagnosis brings comfort: "it's only a bit of a temperature and there won't be any after-effects" (165),[39] and yet Mlle de Lespinasse is sufficiently worried to read to the doctor the notes that she has taken on d'Alembert' words. Unlike these two characters, a reader will of course not only recognize many points of resonance between Diderot's and d'Alembert's previous conversation and the latter's fever discourse but will also see how, in his dreams, the mathematician more and more tends to give in to his friend's Materialist positions.

It all starts with a renewed focus on the transition from inert to active matter—now dealt with, for the first time, as a consequence of the step from isolated atoms to a larger atomic assemblage, which also means that the progress from a "contiguity" to a "continuity" of basic elements is presented as decisive for the emergence of organs, bodies, and life. In this context a notion of the "molecule" comes up that does not quite correspond to today's chemical understanding of a stable configuration consisting of different atoms. Diderot instead used the word in the sense of "a special kind of atom capable of becoming something akin to what would now be called a cell [. . .], a building block that could be vitalistic, compatible with the properties of life":[40]

> And how is this continuity formed? He'll find no trouble about that . . . Just as a globule of mercury joins up with another globule of mercury, so a sensitive, living molecule joins up with another sensitive and living molecule. First there were two globules, but after contact there is only one. The same sensitivity is common to the whole mass. And why not? (167)[41]

The end of this passage ("and why not?" / "en effet pourquoi non?") shows how, with the fictional d'Alembert's rationality being weakened by the fever, he gets more easily carried away by what he remembers from Diderot's provocative thoughts. At the same time we once again see how liveliness and life function as the decisive conceptual horizon of the text: it is by being "sensitive and alive" ("sensible et vivante") that the molecule makes a difference in the emergence of the mind.

Diderot's prose reaches a further level of intensity by putting into the fictional d'Alembert's mouth the metaphor of a bee swarm, invented by the nonfictional Bordeu with the intention of illustrating what an organ—but also a more complex animal, and even the totality of all atoms—is supposed to be and to become. For while his idea of the swarm's coherence depending on each bee "stinging the next one" must have departed from contemporary everyday knowledge (not to speak of present-day scientific observations), it initiates a new, almost ecstatic level of movement in the text:

> Have you ever seen a swarm of bees leaving their hive? . . . The world, or the general mass of matter, is the great hive . . . Have you seen them fly away and form at the tip of a branch a long cluster of little winged creatures, all clinging to each other by their feet? [. . .] If one of those bees decides to pinch in some way the bee it is hanging on to, what do you think will happen? [. . .]

> Throughout the cluster as many individual sensations will be pro-
> voked as there are little creatures, and [. . .] the whole cluster will stir,
> move, change position and shape, [. . .] a noise will be heard, the sound
> of their little cries, and [. . .] a person who had never seen such a cluster
> form would be tempted to take it for a single creature with five or six
> hundred heads and a thousand or twelve hundred wings . . . (168–69)[42]

This is the ecstatic pace of fever language with which Diderot's d'Alembert
begins to engage in cosmological speculations.

Meanwhile, Mlle de Lespinasse observes how his memory of a drop of
water filled with life had inspired a reflection about the universe: "He compared the receptacle, in which he could see so many instantaneous births,
to the universe, and in a drop of water he could see the history of the world"
(174).[43] A few words later, d'Alembert begins to speak about dimensions of
time that Diderot's readers were probably not used to:

> What is the the duration of our time compared with eternity? Less than
> the drop I have taken up on a needle-point compared with the limitless
> space surrounding me. Just as there is an infinite succession of animalculae
> in one fermenting speck of matter, so there is the same infinite succession
> of animalculae in the speck called Earth. Who knows what will follow our
> present ones? Everything changes and passes away, only the whole remains
> unchanged. The world is ceaselessly beginning and ending. (174)[44]

The temporal scale that his fever speech reaches here encourages d'Alembert
to imagine (from our perspective: in pre-evolutionary fashion) the vanishing
of all existing species during a stage of isolation among the basic elements of
matter: "let the great, inert sediment go on working for millions more ages.
It may well be that in order to renew species ten times longer is needed than
their actual duration" (176).[45]

There is no implication of direction, teleology, or necessity in the fictional
d'Alembert's and in Diderot's conception of cosmological time. What impresses them most in the flow of the appearance and vanishing of different
species and objects is their anatomical but also their existential contiguity.
Each thing has the potential of becoming a plant, an animal, and then a
human being, whereas the atoms of humans may well reassemble, on lower
levels of complexity, as animals or things, and even arrive at a transient state
of absolute isolation:

All nature is in a perpetual state of flux. Every animal is more or less a human being, every mineral more or less a plant, every plant more or less an animal . . . There is nothing clearly defined in nature . . . [. . .]

And life? A series of actions and reactions . . . Alive, I act and react as a mass . . . dead, I act and react as separate molecules . . . Don't I die, then? Well, not in that sense, neither I nor anything else . . . To be born, to live and to die is merely to change forms . . . And what does one form matter any more than another? (181–82)[46]

With this hymn to "the miracle of life" ("le prodige de la vie"), the most ecstatic passage of d'Alembert's discourse comes to an ending. If so far it had been Bordeu's role to confirm to Mlle de Lespinasse that all her notes made perfect sense from the perspective of vitalist medicine, these two protagonists now begin to elaborate answers to new questions that, each time more confident and more philosophical, d'Alembert's woman friend dares to ask.

The first of these questions regards her feeling of "togetherness" as an individual. It first comes up as an example for what Mme de Lespinasse believes does not need any philosophical discussion or explanation. But Bordeu provokes her by showing how difficult it is indeed to develop a conceptual description of such primary self-reference, and she reacts, winning the doctor's approval, with the image of a spider for her—Materialist—intuition of the self:

MADEMOISELLE DE LESPINASSE
But if the smallest speck of matter makes one thread of the web vibrate, the spider is alerted, excited and darts here or there. At the centre she is conscious of what is going on at any point in the huge mansion she has woven. Why don't I know what is going on in my own system or in the world at large, since I am a bundle of sensitive particles and everything is touching me and I am touching everything else?

BORDEU
Because messages weaken in proportion to the distance they come from. (183–84)[47]

Long pages follow filled with attempts, between these two protagonists, at unfolding phenomena and concepts like "reason," "emotion," "memory," "will" or "imagination." While most of them look quite interesting to us from a historical point of view, none can appear convincing by present-day standards. This also applies to the many individual cases of malformations and "aberrations of Nature" that Bordeu quotes from his clinical experience in order to satisfy his counterpart's growing curiosity (191 / 116ff.). What I find most interesting here is the impression of a general insecurity regarding the difference between biologically "normal" and biologically "aberrant" forms. As a discursive effect, this insecurity resembles the lack of teleological perspectives in the speculations about morphological differences that emerge within larger dimensions of time. Thus eighteenth-century Materialism explores and plays through an imaginative zone of endless variation, rather than following an—evolutionary or historical—trajectory of elimination and evolution.

The discursively most eccentric paragraph in Le rêve's second segment, however, does not belong to the exchange of ideas and observations between the three protagonists—and it gets barely mentioned (if at all) by most critical commentaries. Shortly after mentioning, from her notes, d'Alembert's comparative associations between life in a drop of water and life in the universe, Mlle de Lespinasse sees and describes, with apparent surprise, the progressive transition of his language into body movements that clearly stand for masturbation (although Diderot's text does not make any direct or euphemistic reference in this sense):

> Then he added with a sigh: "Oh, vanity of human thought! oh, poverty of all our glory and labours! oh, how pitiful, oh, how limited is our vision! There is nothing real except eating, drinking, living, making love and sleeping . . . Mademoiselle de L'Espinasse, where are you?" "Here." Then his face became flushed. I wanted to feel his pulse, but he had hidden his hand somewhere. He seemed to be going through some kind of convulsion. His mouth was gaping, his breath gasping, he fetched a deep sigh, then a gentler one and still gentler, turned his head over on the pillow and fell asleep. I was watching him very attentively, and felt deeply moved without knowing why; my heart was beating fast, but not with fear. A few moments later I saw a little smile flicker round his lips, and he whispered: "On a planet where men reproduced like fish, where a man's spawn was simply spread over that of a woman . . . I should have fewer regrets . . .". (174–75)[48]

Exposing d'Alembert in a scene of masturbation may come across as less shocking than the earlier words about his parents and the origins of his real life, because it is part of a fictional situation and contrasts less with the protagonist's fever language than the intimate biographical details did with the sober philosophical tone of the initial "Dialogue." And yet we see just another effect of Diderot's energy and casual tactlessness transforming a discourse of ideas into prose of the world, with its potentially disturbing effects on its readers. D'Alembert smiles as he imagines a happier life in a possible world where sexual intercourse would be less physically intimate and less socially complicated. And even his woman friend, with whom the real d'Alembert may have never had sex, is "moved without knowing the reason." Concepts and arguments become prose of the world—and thus make intuitions about life existentially present.

As so often, Diderot failed to finish the second part of *Le rêve* with a passage of similar intensity. On the contrary, as the fever-dreaming d'Alembert falls silent and later returns as a mildly jealous observer, the conversation between Bordeu and Mlle de Lespinasse loses direction and peters out in the unstructured flatness of numerous medical case studies and their discussion. If it seems typical that Diderot closes the text with a protagonist's random time constraint (Bordeu needs to see another patient), he probably noticed this flaw and therefore added ("après coup") "a few pages" that he imagined, as we have seen, to be "surprising" and even shocking enough to make Sophie Volland's "hair stand on end." These pages begin at the end of a dinner in d'Alembert's apartment that again brings together Mlle de Lespinasse and Bordeu:

> *The doctor returned at two. D'Alembert had gone out to dinner and so the doctor was alone with Mademoiselle de Lespinasse. Dinner was served, and they talked about nothing in particular until dessert, but when the servants had gone Mademoiselle de Lespinasse said to the doctor:*
>
> MADEMOISELLE DE LESPINASSE
> Come along, doctor, have a glass of malaga, and then you can answer a question which has been going round and round in my mind and which I wouldn't dare ask anyone else but you.
>
> BORDEU
> This malaga is excellent . . . Well, your question?

MADEMOISELLE DE LESPINASSE
What do you think about cross-breeding between species? (225)[49]

The intercourse between different biological species ("mélange des espèces") was a late-eighteenth-century[50] obsession and added to the risk—or the possibility—of turning an already intimate after-dinner conversation into a more directly (or even more drastically) erotic scene. Diderot conjures up this dimension through the protagonists' ongoing attempts to fence off its threat, either by insisting on their morally proper intentions or by trying to eliminate any "improper" connotations.

The clearly intended paradoxical effect of these efforts lies in a palpable and fast-growing tension and attraction between the doctor and d'Alembert's woman friend. Early on, Bordeu asks Mlle de Lespinasse on which of the "physical, moral, or poetic" aspects of the issue in question she wants to focus, and Mlle de Lespinasse immediately—and safely—opts for the last of these (226 / 171). The conversation, however, quickly gets derailed. Bordeu quotes, as an example of "mélange poétique," Horace's principle of combining "useful and pleasurable" perspectives in texts (*Omne tulit punctum qui miscuit utile dulci*), Mlle de Lespinasse assures him that, so far "she can agree without blushing"—and only one page further into their dialogue they have abandoned all questions of textual aesthetics only to agree that no moral argument can be made against sexual "self-gratification" ("les actions solitaires").

A critical consensus has identified Bordeu's attempt to apply the famous Horatian distinction to questions regarding the morals of sexual behavior (together with his predictably libertarian conclusions) as the central subject matter of "La Suite de l'Entretien." But in the actual text, Mlle de Lespinasse quickly becomes bored by Bordeu's highly conceptual arguments about such issues ("These questions are too abstruse for me" [230][51]), and when the doctor repeats his question about the aspect from which she prefers to deal with "le mélange des espèces" her second reply eliminates yet another layer of discursive prudence: "Oh, scientific, scientific" (231),[52] she affirms insistently.

After some further, rather cautious remarks by Bordeau about the lack of experimentally based knowledge regarding the issues in question, the fictional exchange arrives at its final part with a strange fantasy about mythological Satyrs seen as "chèvre-pieds," that is as products of an imagined intercourse between goats and humans:

BORDEU

We might get in that way a vigorous, intelligent, tireless and fleet-footed race which we could train to be excellent servants.

MADEMOISELLE DE LESPINASSE

That's a fine idea. I already seem to see our duchesses' coaches followed by five or six great louts with goat-legs, and that delights me. (232)[53]

The remark concerning a practical usefulness of the "chèvre-pieds" marks a last measure of discursive caution. It vanishes quickly and gives way to very direct language when Mlle de Lespinasse, under the pretext of evoking a reason against breeding "chèvre-pieds," speaks of their probably aggressive, dissolute sexuality: "These goat-men of yours would be terrible lechers" (233).[54] As Bordeau again has to leave, he concedes one final question about the origin of all "these topics of horrible taste" and evokes the "abnormality of the nervous system in young people, softening of the brain in the old, from the attraction of beauty in Athens, shortage of women in Roe, fear of the pox in Paris" (233). Diderot indeed lived up, both literally and ironically, to his promise in the letter to Sophie Volland that there would be "not one dishonorable word" in the text. But it is precisely—and paradoxically—this absence that produces the impression of an erotic atmosphere.

And yet the tension that dominates the "Suite" does not emerge exclusively from the exchange of ideas between its protagonists or from the apparent efforts to prevent their mutual attraction from becoming explicit and even physical. Rather, this central discursive dimension, beginning halfway through the text, intersects with a crescendo of peripheral remarks between Bordeu and Mlle de Lespinasse about their relationship. After d'Alembert's more sober return from the fever dream and his grumpy observation about the doctor's presence no longer being required (to which the two other protagonists pay no attention), Bordeu inserts his compliments for Mlle de Lespinasse into a description of individual human evolution—for which, not unlike Diderot did with d'Alembert in the initial dialogue, he uses his counterpart's physical existence as an example:

First of all, you were nothing. In the beginning you were an imperceptible speck, made of even smaller particles dispersed in the blood and lymph of your father and mother. This speck became a fine thread, then a bundle of threads. So far not the slightest suggestion of the attractive form you now have: your eyes, those lovely eyes, were no more like eyes than the tip of a sea-anemone's claw is like an anemone. (186)[55]

On the following page Bordeu moves on to praise, for the first time, Mlle de Lespinasse's intelligence: "It is a pleasure to talk to you: not only do you follow what is said, but you draw conclusions therefrom which amaze me by their rightness" (187).[56]

At the next occasion, an embrace will replace the compliment: "That's right. Come and let me give you a kiss" (188),[57] and soon Mlle de Lespinasse begins to speak in a tone of aggressive ambiguity: "So treat me just as you like, so long as I can learn" (189).[58] Towards the end of the "Sequel / Suite," as we have seen, all ambiguity disappears. For a moment, Bordeu is disappointed because d'Alembert's companion has abandoned a male-sounding language in which she had been speaking "during four minutes" and returned to a more female tone: "Having been a man for four minutes you take your cap and petticoats and go all feminine again" (230).[59] Finally, Mlle de Lespinasse's farewell to Bordeu is nothing short of a passionate love declaration suggesting a chance of erotic fulfillment in the fictional future: "Well, good-bye, doctor. Don't stay away for ages, as you usually do, and remember sometimes that I'm madly in love with you" (233).[60]

Throughout *Le rêve de d'Alembert* we have discovered three different discursive moments and modalities for the conceptual field of Materialism to become prose of the world and thus awaken and make present feelings of life for the readers. One was Diderot's short (and tactless) narrative about the biological and sexual prehistory of d'Alembert's existence—where concepts became mimetic in reference to a specific person; another was the transition between d'Alembert's dream discourse and his masturbatory movements— where loose associations turned into action and direct experience; and the third was the crescendo leading from Bordeu's flirtatious words to Mlle de Lespinasse's declaration of love—conjuring up the dense impression of an erotic desire that was never explicitly mentioned in the text.

After our reading of *Le neveu de Rameau, Jacques le fataliste et son maître*, and *Le rêve de d'Alembert* we have reason to believe that the tendency towards

such trajectories from philosophical abstraction to existential presence became stronger in the second half of Diderot's work. When, for example,
thirty-three years after the publication of the *Lettre sur les aveugles* and two
years before his death, he came back to the text that had earned him several
months of imprisonment, he did not supplement it with new scientific insights
but with tender memories of Mélanie de Salignac, a young blind woman and
family friend of Sophie Volland. Diderot was much more impressed by her
particular grace and by its impact on her environment than by the specific
worldview that her words and her behavior allowed him to extrapolate:

> She was profoundly rational, charmingly sweet, uncommonly subtle in
> her thinking, and innocent. [...]
>
> Of all the qualities of character, what she valued most were sound
> judgement, gentleness and cheerfulness. She talked little and listened a lot:
> *I am like a bird*, she would say, *I'm learning how to sing in the darkness.*[61]

There is one important, if not decisive, textual element for the metabolizing
transitions from conceptual abstraction to impressions of life's presence in
Diderot's language that I have not mentioned yet, and it is by no means
specific to *Le rêve de d'Alembert*—although its function in this text may be
particularly eminent. In a scholarly essay from 1948, Leo Spitzer first drew
attention to the rhythms of Diderot's prose,[62] but none of his multiple quotes
came from the work on which we have concentrated in this chapter. I agree
with Spitzer's intuitions that Diderot was probably but "half aware" of the
rhythms in his writing ("Der Stil Diderots," 66) and that his half-awareness
may explain why we have such difficulty in grasping and describing them
beyond our first perception. Spitzer convincingly characterized the dominant
form that emerges from Diderot's recurrent patterns of stress and syllables as
"staccato," as "forward-oriented," and as the "driving force" in his prose. And
while I think that the comparison between this specific modality of rhythm
and the male orgasm (71) was above all a product of Spitzer's lifelong ambition to break academic taboos, I find quite illuminating his suggestion that
rhythms may have had a "self-igniting" function for Diderot, incompatible
with and working against sustained systematic thought (72).

But how does Diderot's "staccato" rhythm appear in the layout of a page?
We see its most basic pattern in the passages presented as Mlle de Lespinasse's

quotes from d'Alembert's fever language. They consist in a number of short word clusters, juxtaposed without hypotactic structures, and sometimes separated from each other only by "points suspensifs":

> Never mind, never mind, . . . some holes could no doubt be picked in all this, but I don't care; I never pick holes for the sake of it, . . . so let's go on . . . A wire of pure gold is one comparison I remember him making, a homogeneous network into the interstices of which others fit to form, perhaps, a second network, a tissue of sensitive matter which is in contact with the first and which assimilates active sensitivity here and inactive there. (168)[63]

Jean Starobinski's analysis of *Le rêve de d'Alembert* quite enthusiastically confirms Spitzer's insight about rhythm in Diderot's dialogues and its self-igniting power that conflicts with conceptual systematization: "it is the dynamic process thanks to which systematization can be deferred."[64] He then focuses on the passage where Diderot "tactlessly" describes the origins of d'Alembert's physical existence, and identifies it as an illustration of the "forward-oriented" drive in his prose. As we saw, the passage begins with a monosyllabic answer that Diderot gives to his own question about the original state in the emergence of the "marvelous being" that his friend, the great mathematician, has become: "What was this wondrous being in the beginning? Nothing" (152).[65]

A long, indeed staccato-like sequence of short word clusters follows (most of them introduced, in the original text, by the deictic formula "le voilà"), representing in chronological order individual steps of biological and social evolution: "It is attached [to the womb] by a long pedicle, it grows in stages and advances to the state of foetus. [. . .] The new-born boy is abandoned on the steps of Saint-Jean-le-Rond" (153).[66] In the end this reiteration of similar syllabic patterns will produce an expectation and a tension leading towards a longer, more complex passage where the emerging individual (i.e. d'Alembert) turns into an example of the biological development and the existential fate of humankind. This happens in a language that finally returns to the preceding staccato rhythm:

> Suckled by her he develops in body and mind and becomes a writer, a physicist and a mathematician. How did all this come about? [. . .]
> Anyone lecturing to the Academy on the stages in the formation of a man or animal need refer only to material factors, the successive stages

of which would be an inert body, a sentient being, a thinking being and then a being who can resolve the problem of the precession of the equinoxes, a sublime being, a miraculous being, one who ages, grows infirm, dies, decomposes and returns to humus. (153)[67]

Rather than giving in to the (ultimately banal) temptation to attribute any mimetic functions to the rhythms of Diderot's prose, Starobinski unfolds Spitzer's intuition about its "self-igniting" energy. He speculates that in adapting the flow of prose to those rhythms, by letting them simply happen, Diderot recuperated a state of carelessness ("impudence") that enabled him to transcend not only some historically specific limits of thought but perhaps even the functional limits of language as the medium that we use to express and to convey propositions and contents: "[Diderot's] language posited the notion of an 'ocean of matter' with a great degree of careless certainty, and emphatically liberated itself from spiritualist tutelage. For this to happen, language, declaring its material origins, needed to affirm and exercise all the power it felt within itself: the power to imitate, to parody, to disrupt, then to connect, to change its purview, to create through lateral displacement other voices both similar and different, to generate around itself the presence of listeners both real and imaginary."[68]

Two of the rhetorical powers capable of transcending the dimension of content that Starobinski invokes, i.e. the activation of imagination and the production of presence, are indeed closely related to rhythm.[69] If we can consider human interactions mediated by rhythm as belonging to a type of coupling (between different systems) that is nonproductive (in the sense of leading to a potentially endless repetition of specific forms instead of facilitating their constant innovation), then it follows that rhythms must lead to lower levels in the tension of attention (hence perhaps the liberating "carelessness" typical for Diderot's language). Under the premise of a lower tension of attention, however, humans become open to immediate bodily reactions to the images provoked in our mind by perceptions of the environment, instead of filtering these images through concepts that will defer any physical reaction. In other words, and applied to the functions of rhythm: we react to images provoked by rhythmic language as if the objects of reference for those images were physically present and close to us, that is as if rhythmic language could conjure up the objects that it describes, as if it could indeed make these objects of reference present. Rhythm thus takes over a decisive support function in the process of metabolizing concepts into life—because it operates the replacement of whatever is abstract in our mind through images and by impressions closely connected to objects of reference.

We can further associate the larger context within which Diderot's prose rhythms fulfill such support functions (and this may be the ultimate horizon of Spitzer's and Starobinski's shared intuition) with effects and impressions of intensity. If we trust Deleuze's and Guattari's intuition (from their book *Mille plateaux*) that the word "intensity" invariably refers to processes leading from an initial state of contingency (or entropy) to a final state of extreme condensation, without choice or variation (or, using a metaphor from Physics: to black holes), we can indeed describe the accumulated metabolizing effect of the three fictional conversations brought together in *Le rêve de d'Alembert* as such a progression of intensity. As Diderot states towards the end of the first dialogue, he did believe in necessity (that is in the opposite of contingency) as the governing principle of nature, but he was also fully aware that such a claim could not yet be covered by the density or precision of the scientific observations of his time.

In discursively practical terms, therefore (and as the contemporary debates around Materialism indeed show), the starting point for any reflection on Nature had to be one of contingency, that is, an expectation of multiple possible solutions and answers to most of the shared central questions. *Le rêve de d'Alembert* seems to have transformed such initial situations of openness, contingency, and speculation (as they characterize the first of the three conversations) into a specific drive of necessity, not into a "logical" or "causal" necessity of course, but into a state of existential concreteness and certainty that grew as the text advanced. We can illustrate the line of this trajectory by d'Alembert's fever intuitions arriving at an ejaculation—or by the growing feelings of passion conjured up (rather than being described) in the conversation between Mlle de Lespinasse and Bordeu. To invent such textual processes of intensity requires an author who enjoys being intoxicated by the variations and rhythms of his own language; and it also presupposes a reader who values moments of existential condensation more than the rigors of conceptual and scientific precision.

Outside the textual comfort zone of self-ignition, however, Denis Diderot ended up paying a price for his carelessness and for the ensuing lack of social tact. Although the remarks about *Le rêve* in his letters to Sophie Volland give us the impression that he tried to restrain its circulation even more than in most previous cases, the real Mlle de Lespinasse and the real d'Alembert did learn about the text's existence soon after its production, probably through an indiscretion by Jean-Baptiste-Antoine Suard, a journalist who, like Diderot, frequented the salon of Baron d'Holbach. From the words of protest attributed to Mlle de Lespinasse it does not become quite clear whether she took issue primarily with certain connotations related to the role she played in the text (i.e. with her supposed passion for doctor Bordeu) or with the risk of persecution through censorship to which Diderot had exposed her and d'Alembert, in spite of his own negative experience: "Given his experience of such things, it seems to me that Monsieur Diderot should forbid himself from talking about or from putting words into the mouths of women with whom he is not acquainted."[70]

As for d'Alembert, we know that he "unconditionally" requested the destruction of the manuscript by fire or by shredding. In an indeed "quite mysterious"[71] letter presented as "Envoi" for a presumably revised version of *Le rêve de d'Alembert,* Diderot appears so eager to fulfill this demand on several levels (and thus perhaps to save his already precarious "friendship" with d'Alembert) that he ended up getting entangled in contradictions. Between claiming that he had returned to the original protagonists from Greek antiquity in a revised version of the text or that he had indeed shredded the manuscript and then finally put it together again upon d'Alembert's suggestion, it is impossible to come to a plausible conclusion about his actual reaction to d'Alembert's protest:

> I have satisfied your wishes to the extent allowed by the difficulty of the task and the short time frame you gave me. I hope that the history of these dialogues will excuse their shortcomings. They are the products of the pleasure of becoming aware of one's own opinions; the indiscretion of a few people pulled them out of obscurity; alarmed love desired their sacrifice, tyrannical friendship demanded it, overly eager friendship consented to it; they were torn up. You wanted me to gather up the fragments; I did so [. . .].
>
> I will remind you of the sacred promise that forbids you from conveying them to anyone. I will only make an exception for your friend.[72]

The final two sentences may have pursued the double strategy of both suggesting to d'Alembert that the text had been exclusively written for the author's self-reflection—and addressing to Mlle de Lespinasse a gesture of reconciliation. Any threat of losing friends (and even acquaintances) was so unbearable for Diderot that he often went to the limit of self-humiliation in order to prevent this from happening. The desperate-looking words in his "Envoi" may therefore have come from a sincere impulse. But at the same time Diderot had a singular talent of getting out of stressful situations without much damage or trouble. In the end, *Le rêve de d'Alembert* became available, with the mathematician and Mlle de Lespinasse as protagonists, to the subscribers of *La Correspondance littéraire* in 1782, one year before d'Alembert's and two years before Diderot's death. Mlle de Lespinasse had already died in May 1776.

After taking on, in the two previous chapters, *Le neveu de Rameau* and Diderot's fascination with human existence as embodied existence, as well as *Jacques le fataliste* and the narrative struggles with centrifugal vectors of contingency, our reading of *Le rêve de d'Alembert* has shown how Materialism, as a third dimension in the peripheral worldview that gave form to Diderot's thinking, interested him more for its proximity to intuitions of life than as a repertoire of philosophical questions, answers, and problems. He used this proximity as a launchpad for different transitions towards effects of existential presence that only fictional texts can operate. This exclusive function sets *Le rêve de d'Alembert* further from the works of Goya, Lichtenberg, and Mozart than *Le neveu de Rameau* or *Jacques le fataliste*.

While we can easily show that Lichtenberg at least felt close to Materialist positions, music inevitably presupposes what Materialism tries to lead back to, that is, a sensibility-based relation to our perceptions of the world. By contrast, it appears philosophically complicated to decide whether this transition from an abstract to a life-based world relation can even happen at all in paintings and etchings like Goya's, because they offer neither a purely conceptual starting point nor an internal time along which intensity can unfold. As one of the late-eighteenth-century's most distinguished philosophers of nature, Georg Christoph Lichtenberg indeed predicted, in this way no different from thinkers like Helvétius, d'Holbach, or Diderot,[73] that future descriptions of the mind would progressively "settle on a subtle Materialism," with the word "subtle" probably alluding to the then frequently mentioned problem of observations not yet being available that would have been indispensable for proving how mechanisms of nature functioned according to the laws of necessity:

> Our psychology will eventually settle on a subtle materialism as we learn ever more about one side (matter) and on the other side have reached beyond everything. (F/425)[74]

Certain materialist motifs, like the one about bodies and their organs as "machines," occur quite frequently in Lichtenberg's notes, and they regularly contain promises of future discoveries:

> If the soul is simple, why is the constitution of the brain so complex? The body is a machine and thus must be composed of mechanical parts. That the mechanical in us extends quite far is proven by the fact that even the internal parts of the brain are formed with a design about which we probably do not understand a hundredth part. (F/349)[75]

From a different, much more critical perspective, Lichtenberg identifies signs of an anthropocentricism ("conceptualization innate to men") for which Materialism would be the healthy antidote in the (for him: undercomplex) rendition of the mind as "soul" (J/568).[76] Finally, no contemporary intellectual fashion provoked a sharper reaction of protest in Lichtenberg than Lavater's obsession with interpreting faces as the impression of character traits and moral positions: "If physiognomy becomes what Lavater expects it to become, children will be hanged before they have committed the deeds deserving of the gallows" (F/521).[77]

While such a will to extrapolate meaning from any traces and products of human behavior was about to conquer the realm of music during the early nineteenth century, Mozart did not yet conceive of his compositions under this premise. In a detailed comparison between the last scores of Mozart's life and some of Beethoven's piano concerts, Karol Berger has shown how the impact of romantic subject positions and of their forms of solitude did not indeed begin to unfold before 1800.[78] For all we know, Mozart never cared about being existentially present, present as an individual, in his music.[79] As if they were life or nature itself, he wanted his compositions to find resonance in the sensibility of those who listened—without standing for anything but themselves. And despite their famously scatological content, something similar was probably supposed to work, on a different level, in Mozart's letters to his cousin Marianne from Augsburg. A formal analysis of these texts could show how their author let "rhythms" emerge in their prose and how a "flow of words whose effect grew beyond their conceptual content put the author into a state of rapture."[80] This observation converges with the moments of "self-ignition" that Spitzer and Starobinski discovered in Diderot's texts, including *Le rêve de d'Alembert* as a treatise starting out from Materialism.

Can we pinpoint the equivalent of such transitions between Materialism and the effects of life in Goya's art? Towards the end of the previous chapter I suggested that the bare-breasted young woman whom we encounter at the end of *Los desastres de la guerra* (and who may well have been Goya's pictorial answer to a question about the survival of truth in his time), together with the caption "Esto es lo verdadero" ("This Is the Real Thing"), might have been intended to stand for life. Making life visually present would then turn into the Materialist counterpoint effect of several etchings which, instead of showing scenes of torture, killing, or the removal of corpses, are about the accumulation of dead bodies in their incipient stages of decay: "Enterrar y callar" ("To bury and be silent") (18), for example, "Tanto y más" ("So much and more") (22), or "Muertos recogidos" ("Collected corpses") (63). From the angle of eighteenth-century Materialism, as we have learned, decay was understood as a process of growing isolation between basic elements of matter, a counterpoint indeed to the activation of life through the growing closeness of formerly inert atoms and molecules.

The visual equivalent of this contrast appears particularly condensed, between images of decay and emergence, of death and life, in the final sequence of *Desastres de la guerra*. According to the running numbers at the top left of each etching, the two allegories of the possible "Death of Truth" and the concluding allusion to life are separated by a scene with the caption "Fiero Monstruo!" ("Wild Monster!") that shows a giant, dog-shaped "monster" devouring minuscule human corpses. Now while I do not believe that Goya himself would have associated this grotesque motif with a thought like

Diderot's thesis about digestion initiating the return of dead matter to life, it may not be random that Materialist concepts have a specific potential of suggesting connections between different groups of Goya's etchings. To this observation we may add "Esto es peor" ("This is worse") (37) and "Grande hazana! Con muertos!" ("Great feat! Against dead bodies!") (38), perhaps the two most disturbing scenes of the entire collection, where cut-off parts of dead bodies enter into states of fusion, hybridity, and ultimately metabolism with the trees to which they are bound and attached. All the forms indeed to which I am pointing here in Goya's work seem to share a both conceptual and existential impulse with contemporary Materialism, the impulse to blur and remove categorical borders between things, plants, animals, and humans.

Now while eighteenth-century Materialism cannot fail to look thoroughly historical to us, due both to the rudimentary levels of scientific insight on which it had to rely and to its all-overshadowing later deviation into a dimension of proto-sociology within Marxism, its basic claims have long become intellectual and existential premises too obvious to be even mentioned. Who in our present world (except the occasional creationist) would ever doubt that the human cognitive apparatus and intellectual potential must have emerged from basic configurations of matter? The movement that we have identified as central to Diderot's *Rêve de d'Alembert*, that is, the transition from scientific observations and abstract concepts towards intuitions that conjure up "the miracle of life" as existential presence, found its historical continuation in the "philosophy of life" (*Lebensphilosophie*) as a discourse shaped in the later nineteenth century. While they followed and mostly admired the fast-accelerating growth of scientific knowledge, some of its most eminent thinkers, like Henri Bergson, Wilhelm Dilthey, and, above all, Friedrich Nietzsche, also felt compelled to point out the increasing need to react to this movement with new conceptions of individual and collective existence.

This is not the place to focus on the specific circumstances under which *Lebensphilosophie*, mainly through the resonance that some of its positions found in Italian Fascism and German Nazism, has fallen into wide and lasting intellectual disgrace. That critical reaction is surely still plausible enough to shed a cloud of legitimate skepticism over any attempt at reconnecting directly even with the major works and authors of *Lebensphilosophie*. At the same time, I find it striking to see (although the point hardly ever gets mentioned) how, with some remarkable individual exceptions,[81] philosophy at large has not succeeded in reconquering the space of reflection that *Lebensphilosophie* tried to occupy as a response to the progress of science and the need to rethink the bodily dimension of our existence. We have no new version of a "philosophy of nature" in dialogue with contemporary science (and possibly with new branches of engineering), while the contemporary "philosophy of science" restrains itself to a—normally quite cautious—epistemological critique of advanced research practices and of strategies in the representation of their results. Even Martin Heidegger's deft critique of the existential shortcomings inherent to Newtonian science, in his 1938 essay "The Age of the World Picture," with its insistence on the need to develop a new relation to nature from an angle of *Zuhandenheit* ("readiness to hand") instead of *Vorhandenheit* ("presence at hand"), did not find a continuation in his later, strangely pious musings on the "fourfold" (*Geviert*) as an array for an existentially viable relation to our material environment.

Certain motifs of present-day ecological thought (or "eco-philosophy") do receive broad resonance but remain astonishingly anthropocentric in their always passionate manifestos geared either towards the endless survival of humankind or towards its punishment, "for bad ecological behavior," with threats of imminent extermination. In our unsuccessful struggle to initiate reactions of existential relevance between excessive respect for science and intellectually paralyzing moral premises, *Le rêve de d'Alembert* may function as an inspiring alternative from the past. Its potential has of course nothing to do with any of the historically specific concepts, images, and positions that I have tried to identify in their own context. Rather, the potential inspiration comes from the energy, the freedom, and above all the carelessness with which Diderot noted some provocative thoughts and shifting attitudes during a few warm summer days of 1769.

6 | "QUELS TABLEAUX!"

Acts of Judgment and the Singularity of Phenomena in Les salons

DURING THE LATER MONTHS of 1767, the small group of aristocrats in Eastern and Central Europe subscribed to Friedrich Melchior, Baron von Grimm's *Correspondance littéraire, philosophique et critique* had an opportunity to read what Denis Diderot thought about his own appearance and about its rendition in a number of portraits, among them a large format by his older friend, the court painter Michel van Loo, that was exhibited in the current Salon of contemporary painting and sculpture at the Louvre.[1] Nine times between 1759 and 1781 (with three interruptions), Diderot covered these biannual events for the *Correspondance littéraire,* in different tones and at different levels of precision, and all commentators agree that his writing about art reached its peak in 1765 and in 1767. By then, instead of analyzing pictures and sculptures in the order they appeared on the walls and in some open spaces of the Louvre, he had developed an approach of comparing, discussing, and evaluating the works of different artists in separate, individual clusters.[2]

Within one such cluster, Diderot's reaction to van Loo's painting, announced in the Salon catalogue as "8. Le Portrait M. Diderot," stands out because, beginning with a triple opening reference to himself as the object of representation, as a friend of the artist, and as a thinker, it allows us to sense a will to independence from the genre-specific objectivity claims, aesthetic values, and discursive traditions that had long determined art criticism: "MOI. I like Michel myself, but I like the truth even more" (288).[3] In the words following the pronoun "MOI," Diderot refers to Aristotle's famous statement that he was "a friend of Plato but even more so a friend of truth"; "MOI" refers to his likeness in van Loo's work; but the pronoun also connects with the grammatical subject of the following sentence and can thus give more weight to its content as a personal principle (truth is a greater value than friendship); finally, these words do come together in a syntactical form that often articulates acts of judgment. But as we may assume that prioritizing truth over friendship must have been a moral principle for Diderot's readers, rather than the result of a moral judgment, we will read these words as announcing, in the friendliest possible way, a not entirely positive aesthetic judgment of van Loo's painting.

A series of quick, direct judgments referring to the relationship between the painting and Diderot's self-image follows in the next sentences, where friendly gestures of approval are repeatedly undercut by critical remarks:

> It's quite like me, and he can say to anyone who doesn't recognize it, like the gardener in the comic opera: "That's because he's never seen me without my wig." It's very much alive; that's his gentleness, and his liveliness; but too young, the head too small, pretty like a woman, ogling, smiling, simpering, mincing, pouting; nothing of the sober colouring of the *Cardinal de Choiseul*.[4]

While Diderot sees a certain degree of resemblance between the portrait and himself, he immediately adds that some beholders may not have the same reaction because he is not wearing a wig in the painting.[5] Likewise, his approval of the portrait's liveliness (*vivacité*) turns into much more insistent observations and complaints about a visual effect of effeminacy that stands in contrast to another painting by van Loo exposed the same year, where the Cardinal Choiseul appears "in the color of wisdom."

Our brief initial description of this text already captures a basic structure of Diderot's writing about art. Multiple references to minute details in the works he deals with and his reactions to them follow each other as elementary units without any apparent convergence or necessity. And yet the reader will soon identify a movement towards positive or negative appreciation, due to an emerging syntax and rhythm in these judgments that begin to accentuate one or the other (in this case: the negative) option. As soon as such a tendency has established itself, Diderot feels free to indulge in often ironic digressions that presuppose and ultimately provide some gossip from the cultural circles of Paris. In this spirit he mentions the fancy dressing gown he is wearing in the portrait (in fact, a present from a wealthy female admirer) as a jeopardy for his tax assessment: "and the clothes are enough to ruin the poor man of letters if the poll tax collector were to put a tax on dressing-gowns."[6]

The text continues with a similar alternation between judgments and a subsequent digression. First Diderot praises the attention given by van Loo to the objects that surround him in his working space ("The writing-desk, the books, the accessories are as good as they could be"[7]) and also to the form of his hands (except for "the left hand which is not properly drawn"[8]). Then he moves on to explain the previously complained-of lack of a serious expression on his face by remembering the flirtatious conversation that the painter's wife had had with him (referred to in the third person singular) while the portrait was being produced: "It was that crazy Madame Van Loo coming in and chatting with him that made him look like that and spoilt everything" (288).[9] And against this background he imagines, also quite typically, what a more adequate rendition, achieved in Madame van Loo's absence, could have looked like:

> He should have been left alone to his musings. Then his mouth would have been half-open, his absent gaze would have looked into the distance, the workings of his busy mind would have been visible on his face; and Michel would have done a fine painting. (289–90)[10]

From this no longer ambiguous reaction and from his certainty of what a *philosophe* was supposed to look like, Diderot suddenly advanced to a perspective of posterity and to a profoundly different self-image. How should his grandchildren remember him? Definitely not with the effeminate air that he saw as a contradiction to the seriousness of his writing. The true problem was, as he stated in a passage that I already quoted in a previous chapter, that he had "a hundred different faces every day"—although he then undercut this claim by offering a coherent description of what he believed to be his true appearance:

In one day I would have a hundred different faces, depending on what
affected me. I was serene, dreamy, tender, passionate, enthusiastic; but I
was never like the man you see here. I had a broad forehead, very lively
eyes, quite large features, a head exactly in the mould of an ancient orator,
a good nature which was very close to the stupidity and rustic simplicity
of olden times. (290)[11]

This divergence between Diderot's desire to look "like an ancient orator" and
his impression of "having a hundred different faces," with which he counters
not only van Loo's portrait but any possible representation, is quite difficult
to explain—and may later on help us to trace a preconscious dynamic in his
thinking and writing about art. For the moment it propels him to compare
the painting in question to a number of other portraits and busts, among
which he prefers the work of the otherwise unknown Jean-Baptiste Garand:
"The only person who ever did a good portrait of me was a poor devil called
Garand who caught my likeness in the way a fool sometimes makes a witty
remark. Anyone who sees my portrait by Garand sees me" (290).[12] From this
judgment on, the text loses its concentration on details and conditions of
resemblance and begins to peter out, both with comments about copies made
from different portraits and about general problems that other artists had
encountered in their portrait painting. Such changes in discursive tonality
are not only a further feature of Diderot's writing about art, they also confirm
our more general impression that providing textual contours and closure did
not belong to his strengths as an author.

In its oscillation between acts of judgment with precise references, anec-
dotal and narrative digressions, speculations about possible alternative works,
and comparisons between different paintings that represent identical objects,
Diderot's discussion of the van Loo portrait makes for lively reading—but
it definitely does not offer the possibility of extracting anything close to a
method or a coherent set of criteria that he may have been following. And
yet he wrote at some point that the *Salons* were his best intellectual work
because—and not in spite—of their centrifugal dynamics:

It is certainly the best thing I have done since I began writing, from whatever angle you look at it, the diversity of tone, the variety of subjects, or
the abundance of ideas, which I imagine have never passed through any

head but mine. It is a storehouse of humour, sometimes light-hearted, sometimes more forceful. In places it is pure fireside conversation. In others it is the heights of eloquence and philosophy.[13]

This both ecstatic and again centrifugal self-appreciation has an equivalent in the quite confusing range of critical reactions to Diderot's writing about art. On the one hand, we find the unanimous assessment that, from a historical point of view, the "creation of art criticism in French culture" or even the "invention of art criticism as a new genre"[14] happened in his *Salons*—although hardly any precise description appears as to the form and content of this innovation. On the other hand, there is Starobinski's more differentiated observation according to which "it is *as if* Diderot had invented modern art criticism" ("comme s'il l'avait créée") because, instead of developing a new form of writing, he was the first author to "assimilate the voices surrounding artworks, to freely orchestrate them, and to connect them with literature."[15]

So far, we understand that Diderot's departure into a new genre did not rely on new epistemological criteria or discursive forms. It rather marked a beginning without a possible line of difference or separation to be drawn, which explains why all the laborious attempts at circumscribing the practice of Diderot's *Salons* through a coherent formula have been doomed to lead to eternally repeated enumerations of the same topoi, motifs, and criteria. There is hardly any academic reference (including my own) that does not quote Diderot's self-praise of the art criticism as "the best part of his work," his openness to the revision of judgments, his both frequent and flagrant contradictions, his digressions, his desire to be intensely moved by artworks, and, above all, his own concession that there was a non-coordinated multiplicity of perspectives and values in play.[16]

Diderot's both ironic and pertinent self-characterization as "un chien de chasse indiscipliné,"[17] that is as an "undisciplined hunting dog," reacting to any outside impulse and jumping on every prey (that is on every emotional effect to be had), will become plausible if we go through the perspectives and values that permeated his intellectual involvement with artworks.[18] He wanted to look at pictures "like a deaf man would observe the expressions and gestures of a group in conversation," which most likely meant that he wanted to concentrate on details rather than on the works' all-comprehensive subject matters. But he also followed the tradition, coming from Horace, of dealing with art and texts in similar ways (*ut pictura poesis*). In addition, Diderot wanted his "soul to be struck" by scenes with powerful emotions, and expected from such moments a stimulating effect on his imagination. In a more formal attitude, he tried to identify the "one clear line connecting all the elements of great artworks." And yet he preferred "enormous, barbarous, and wild" objects of reference to impressions of harmony and smoothness. Diderot also appreciated truth without ever caring to specify how it could be identified and secured. And on the negative side, he never abandoned an almost aggressive prejudice against all kinds of allegories and against the discursive routines of mannerism.

However tenaciously many specialists have tried to transform such incoherence into the virtue of a non-dogmatic openness,[19] the characterization of Diderot's art critical practice with which they leave us is quite inconclusive—as they never manage to pinpoint the form or the substance of its supposed historical innovation. The only positive exception beside Starobinski may be Michael Fried's book on *Painting and Beholder in the Age of Diderot*.[20] For instead of trying to extract a comprehensive conception or even a "program" from Diderot's art critical practice, Fried sees it as driven by a new, probably preconscious tendency to let the beholder get "absorbed" into the imagined three-dimensional spaces, a tendency that was "dispersed rather than concentrated, spontaneous rather than systematic," the "residue of acts of judgment and interpretation rather than the object of fixed canons and laws."

Acts of judgment will be the focal object of analysis in this fourth (and final) chapter trying to reconstruct the areas and levels of the epistemological frame that shaped Diderot's work. I have chosen the *Salons* as our textual body of reference here because, as we have seen by now, they emerged from a broad variety of judgment practices on which we will concentrate; knowledge and descriptions pertaining to art history, however, will only be provided and discussed to the degree needed in order to describe acts of judgment in their multiple dimensions ("morphology") and the forms of reiteration and accumulation along which they functioned ("syntax").

To finish our tentative reconstruction of Diderot's informal epistemology with a chapter on judgment was not a random decision. So far we have observed how several dimensions standing in contrast to the epistemology of the historical worldview, as it had established itself in the mainstream of Western cultures between 1780 and 1830, shaped a specific (and peripheral) self-reference and the conception of a relationship to its environment in Diderot's work. From the reading of *Le neveu de Rameau* we reconstructed an experience of human existence as embodied existence and of a specific concreteness in self- and world-perception that followed from it (it can be illustrated by the contrast between the uniqueness of "Rameau's nephew," who has an individual name, and the generic character of the "philosophe" with whom he interacts).

In the analysis of *Jacques le fataliste et son maître* we subsequently saw how Diderot unleashed the existentially and intellectually overwhelming powers of contingency (and of world complexity) in different dimensions and in different temporal dynamics, without trying to subject them to the de-complexifying control of a "necessity" principle. As a side effect we observed how, behind the premise of contingency, transformations unfolded in time without any order or predictability and thus produced narrative impressions of singularity (for which Diderot used the adjective "bizarre"). The three parts of *Le rêve de d'Alembert* then showed how eighteenth-century Materialism brought together in a monistic approach the embodied version of human self-reference and a world reference mediated through the senses rather than through concepts. Being unable to fulfill the promise of Materialism to demonstrate that all relationships and developments within its monism had the philosophical status of "necessity," Diderot reacted to this intellectual shortcoming with an ecstatic affirmation of life and its intensity.

Unlike the historical worldview (and, above all, unlike its further development and systematization in the philosophy of Hegel) Diderot's epistemology made the degree of complexity in the relationships between humans and their environment increase on each level of interaction. In other words: the world emerging from his epistemology had no claims for an inherent order producing the impression of things "falling into place." Therefore, on its ultimate level, Diderot's intellectual work required a practice of individual judgment as a tool to cope with potentially endless existential complexity and to keep such complexity at bay. Judgment often happened as a struggle against overwhelming complexity in his texts, sometimes with desperate and sometimes with joyful overtones. What specific structures and images of the "world" this reiterated practice of judgment ended up producing is one of the questions that we will pursue in the following pages. It will oblige us to develop a specific concept of "singularity."

The actual description and analysis of acts of judgment in Diderot's *Salons* will go through seven steps. We begin with two approaches (steps one and two) to the concept of "judgment," one historical and illustrating different meanings from the third quarter of the eighteenth century, the other systematic and using Florian Klinger's book on *Judging* as a guideline for the distinction of several dimensions coming together in the practice of judgment ("morphology"). After a description of the Salons as a cultural institution of their time (step three), I will illustrate the simultaneous dimensions in the act of judgment with textual examples from Diderot's first *Salons* (step four). For a discussion of the "syntax" of judgment, by contrast, I will use his more complex art critical writing from 1765 and 1767, which will bring us again to the question about possible affinities in the works of Goya, Lichtenberg, and Mozart (steps five and six). The chapter ends with an assessment of Diderot's practice of judgment (step seven) as contributing to the constitution of a specific world concept.

Whoever tries to understand the practice and philosophy of judgment during the age of Enlightenment is normally obliged to take into account Immanuel Kant's *Critique of the Power of Judgment*. From a strictly historical perspective, however, this rule does not apply in our case because the *Third Critique* only appeared in 1790, six years after Diderot's death. In addition, there is substantial reason to doubt that Diderot would have had the patience necessary to pursue Kant's pertinent discussions in their subtlety and argumentative consequence. And yet the two thinkers shared one fundamental premise in their reflection on aesthetic judgments. I have tried to show how judging became a central activity within Diderot's work, due to his fascination for complex situations of contingency but also to the accumulated effects of his frequent incapacity to fulfill the promise of uncovering patterns of necessity in observations of nature and society. Within an incomparably more self-reflexive and rigorous framework, Kant's path to the *Critique of the Power of Judgment* obeyed a similar logic, as it started out from the insight that, in their convergence, *The Critique of Pure Reason* (with its analysis of "under-standing," *Verstand*) and the *Critique of Practical Reason* (with its analysis of "reason," *Vernunft*) did not cover all philosophically relevant reactions of the human spirit to its environment. Between "understanding" and "reason" there remained a horizon of situations for whose description and analysis no pertinent deductive or inductive criteria were available. These exactly were the situations that Kant was dealing with in his *Third Critique* and among which, far from being the only modality in question, the aesthetic judgment became central, with its three dimensions of "disinterestedness," lack of quantitative or qualitative criteria, and the paradox of a quest for consensus in full awareness of its impossibility.

David Hume's 1757 essay "Of the Standard of Taste," by contrast, not only begins from premises similar to Diderot's, it indeed brings into focus certain conditions on which Diderot's practice of judging may have relied. Decisive is Hume's observation that judgments of beauty and taste inevitably belong to the level of "sentiment," which means that they only refer to themselves, are always right, and cannot claim any objectivity. But Hume does concede that certain aesthetic judgments appear more plausible than others, and he does explain this experience with the observation that such judgments are normally based on cultural convention. A good judge for him would be a person with a "strong sense, united to delicate sentiment, improved by practice, perfected by comparison and cleared of all prejudice." I imagine that Diderot would have liked to accept these words as a description of his own practice, although neither comparing artworks nor the bracketing of prejudice belonged to his main concerns.

We can safely assume, however, that the entry "Jugement" in the *Ency-clopédie*, signed "D. J." and probably written by the Chevalier de Jaucourt,[21] and published in 1765, is the historical document closest to the thoughts that Diderot may have associated with "judging." There are three aspects of this text that deserve to be highlighted. In the first place, it associates the practice of judging with situations characterized by a lack of evidence and the ensuing dominance of probability:

> There are certain things that appear before our eyes in total clarity and evidence, but there are many more that we can only perceive obscurely,

and if I may say so, in the dusk of probability. This is why the use and the excellence of one's *judgment* are ordinarily limited to one's ability to examine the force and the weight of probabilities, then to assess them in an appropriate manner, and finally, having done the math, as it were, to determine which way the scales are tipped.[22]

If, secondly, judging takes place "in the dusk of probability" and not in the bright light of evidence, it requires intellectual strength and tenacity, that is, a disposition that Kant would later refer to as the "power" of judgment. Here is the pertinent passage from the *Encyclopédie*:

> *Judgment* [. . .] works to delve into things, to carefully distinguish one idea from another, to avoid being led astray by an infinity of ideas. [. . .] Here, it suffices to note that the accuracy of *judgment* consists to a large degree in its ability to conceive of ideas clearly, and, when there exists some difference between them, to distinguish them in an exact manner. If the mind brings ideas together or separates them in conformity to how they are in reality, its *judgment* is sound.[23]

Finally, the *Encyclopédie* dissociates the competence and power of judgment from erudition and from any extended learning process. Being a good judge is a present of nature: "Happy are those who succeed in forming (a sound *judgment*). Even happier are those to whom nature has gifted this rare privilege."[24] Lichtenberg went even further in the direction of separating the competence of judging from erudition and mental agility when he described sound judgments as the privilege of "great men," that is, of men with firm principles:

> Overly subtle men are rarely great men, and their investigations are often as useless as they are precise. They distance themselves further and further from practical life when they should come closer to it. Just as the dancing or fencing instructor does not begin with the anatomy of the legs and hands, so a sound and useful philosophy can begin much higher than with such subtle meanings. The foot must be positioned in this way, or you will fall down, you must believe this, for it would be absurd not to—these are very good foundations.[25]

Denis Diderot, as we have seen, took pleasure and pride in his practice of aesthetic judgment but was quite vague when reflecting on its conditions.

In the seventh and final chapter of his "Essai sur la peinture," written in 1766, just between his two best and most prolific *Salons*, he comes close to anticipating Kant's observation that the "taste" needed for the appreciation of artworks cannot refer to any stable criteria:

> But what do all these principles mean, if taste is a matter of inspiration, and if there are no eternal, immutable rules of beauty? If taste is a matter of inspiration, and if there are no rules of beauty, how then do we explain those exquisite emotions that well up so suddenly, so involuntarily, so turbulently, in the depths of the soul?[26]

In the first answer to his question, Diderot declares that he will never cease to believe in the legitimacy of such strong feelings. He then tries to argue that "the true, the good, and the beautiful" are qualities close enough to support each other. At the same time he admits to the purely speculative character of this very statement: "it is nothing, it is a purely speculative truth."[27] A bit further in his text, similar to Hume, Diderot tries to give taste a basis in "reiterated experience," and adds that in the absence of such grounding it is possible to rely on "instinct and tact":

> What then is taste? A faculty, acquired through reiterated experience, of grasping the true or the good, together with the particular circumstances that make it beautiful, and of being promptly and strongly moved by such beauty. If the experiences that determine one's judgment are present to one's memory, one will have enlightened taste; if the memory has faded, and only the impression remains, one will have instinct and tact.[28]

Later on, Diderot plays with "sensitivity" as a basis for taste, but then plausibly undercuts this idea by stating that a particularly high degree of sensitivity can become a problem for the capacity to make distinctions. He finishes the treatise by stating that in order to recognize a "work of genius" ("ouvrage de génie"), which by definition must be unique, genius is also required on the side of the beholder:

> Hence the uncertainty of success for any work of genius. It stands alone. One cannot appreciate it unless by comparing it directly with nature. And who is capable of making such a comparison? Another man of genius.[29]

Diderot's reflections on the judgment of taste are typical for a circular movement of thought in which eighteenth-century authors, including, on the highest level of conceptual and argumentative sophistication, Immanuel Kant,
got entangled whenever they tried to analyze the practice of judgment in
general and aesthetic judgment in specific. A lack of evidence (and of stable
criteria) was assumed as the general condition that made judgments necessary. Once judging took place, however, it triggered a retrospective urge to
identify possible criteria on which it could have been based. But as there was
no way to satisfy this urge, it ended up leading back to the conclusion that
every practice of judging started out from a lack of evidence.

In order to escape such circularity we need to stop asking for criteria of
judgment and to replace this question by an analysis of the internal complexity constituting acts of judgment, a complexity that brings together several
intellectual dimensions and operations. In his book on *Judging*,[30] Florian
Klinger has, with remarkable conceptual precision, lived up to the challenge
of this task. I will use the results of his work for the development of an abstract description of the act of judging, which will then inform our historical
analysis of Diderot's practice of judgment in his *Salons*.[31]

In the actual practice of judgment we are normally not aware of the multiple converging dimensions that Klinger distinguishes within it. Judging,
despite its intrinsic complexity that is only revealed by philosophical analysis,
can be (and indeed mostly is) experienced as part of our ongoing, habitual
processing of the everyday. As some reflections from Diderot's time have
already shown us, acts of judgment become necessary and occur whenever
evidence is lacking, and it is precisely this lack of evidence that accounts for
the impression of complexity that they project. Now while all dimensions
of judging go back to a lack of evidence as their basic condition, they by no
means all belong to the same ontological level. Strictly speaking, therefore, I
should not refer to those dimensions, as I have done and will continue to do,
as a "morphology"—because we normally presuppose that all the forms making up different morphologies (for example in the grammars of languages)
belong to the same level of reality. If I use the noun in spite of this problem, it
is from the perspective of a description in which their joint pertinence to the
act of judging may bracket the ontological difference between the multiple
dimensions in play.

From a historical point of view, we can observe considerable fluctuations regarding the importance to human life that is attributed to judging. Klinger underlines (and I agree with him) that this appreciation appears particularly high in our early-twenty-first-century present, and he follows an intuition by Jean-François Lyotard, who stated, more than forty years ago already, that the key condition identified by Kant as specific to the aesthetic judgment (the unavailability of stable quantitative or qualitative criteria) has become a general premise for judging today. But this central historical aspect of Klinger's book will not play a role in the way I use his analysis for the description of Diderot's practice of judging. Nor will I pay specific attention to the fact that the judgments occurring in Diderot's *Salons* are exclusively aesthetic judgments. For, as I mentioned before, this chapter focuses on Diderot's performance of judging as part of his general—and clearly peripheral—epistemology, using texts from the *Salons* as one among several possible illustrations of this practice. (Not much would change if I described the same act using materials from a different textual basis.)

The first dimension dealt with in Klinger's book is "rightness" (*Richtigkeit*).[32] Here he develops a number of aspects belonging to the "lack of evidence" as a basic precondition of judging. Rightness can be seen as the central premise of a non-metaphysical worldview in which, firstly, we are often confronted with a lack of evidence that is impossible to overcome and with contingency as its consequence; in which, secondly, we do not believe that logically cogent solutions are or should always be available; and in which, thirdly, we have not lost the confidence that some judgments can be more useful and more appropriate (*richtiger*) than others. However similar different situations of contingency may sometimes look—and practically be—under certain conditions, they are always unique, specific, and singular cases, whereas the reasons that we invoke in order to make and to explain judgments always belong to a higher level of abstraction. We can say, then, that, within "rightness," the sphere of the "singular" and the sphere of the "general" converge.

Judgments will necessarily produce "forms" (Klinger's second dimension) because we typically choose, in situations of contingency, one among several possibilities that are available—and not the other(s). This moment of choosing comes to mind above all when we speak about judging. "Form" is the dividing line between the option(s) selected and the option(s) not selected. Each artwork that Diderot wrote about could be judged either as good or as bad (in his view), it could excel in color or in its attention to detail, it could appear pathos-laden or all-too-abstract, and he always seemed eager to mention what potential options he had not chosen. Subsequent acts of judging will produce accumulations of such forms in which they may converge ("fit") or diverge, and I use the concept of "syntax" for such cumulative effects. We may find sequences of judgments and of the forms they produce predictable, boring, repetitive. Impressions of this kind, however, will not prevent each sequence from being individual and fresh when it first appears (they are all based on acts, and are therefore performative).

The third dimension of judging is its "positivity" (*Setzung*).[33] Positivity, Klinger explains, constitutes a status and a level of reality from which speculations (for example) are excluded—because speculations present their contents as mere possibilities (of seeing the world). Through judgments, by contrast, we produce forms that immediately become factual and thus part of a (non-metaphysical) reality. Even judgments that we subsequently revise or contradict (as so often occured in Diderot's *Salons*) remain factual because when they first happened they were events whose facticity cannot be undone.

"Measurement" (*Anmessung*)[34] opens another dimension of judging that refers to reality. Acts of judging not only add new forms to reality; in doing so they also and of course presuppose that reality exists. Trying to make good (and not only random) judgments, we want to take into account the existing reality, with as much of its complexity as we can possibly perceive and process. We may also be concerned about how the forms we produce will "fit" or will change reality in ways that we are hoping for. Whether this ends up being the case, however, can neither be certain in the moment of judgment nor become clear in an immediate retrospective. We may therefore go so far to say that whether a judgment was good, not so good, or bad is, again, a question of judgment. A judge or an art critic cannot be described as being "right" or "wrong" in the same way as somebody working on a mathematical equation can, and yet we are certain that in the long run it is possible to tell good judges from bad judges, good art critics from bad art critics.

The fifth dimension of Klinger's analysis is "relevance." Judgments will transform contingency into necessity, not into "necessity" in the sense of a logical coherence but into the necessity of a form that needs to be taken into account. "Relevant" objects or conditions are precisely those that need to be taken into account under specific circumstances, and "relevance" therefore includes the awareness that certain forms need to be taken into account and will become important (or not) within larger contexts. Each judgment and each form as its product thus have their specific status, their specific functions, and their specific importance within larger horizons, ultimately within the horizon of the world as a whole.

"Power" constitutes the sixth dimension of judging according to Klinger, and I would like to elaborate this aspect from two different angles (Klinger only mentions the first of them). Judgments are events, and as such they make something happen. In this sense Klinger's (and even Kant's) concept of "power" converges with its use in speech act theory, where it refers to its "performative" dimension and its functions (for example the "power" by which a speech act performed by a state employee transforms two persons into a married couple). But I also want to point to the "power" of judgment as an energy required in order to produce forms in situations of contingency—an energy required because we normally hesitate to make decisions in the absence of evidence or necessity. This second meaning of "power" sometimes comes close to aspects of aggression, for example when Diderot feels obliged to make harsh judgments about individual paintings although he knows that this will be detrimental to the reputation of the artists judged (and in some cases the artists so negatively judged are among Diderot's friends).

Finally, there is the dimension of "poetics." Its precondition and pertinence lie in the unavoidable "opacity" of judging, which stems from the challenge of producing forms in situations that are short on evidence (and without recourse to metaphysical principles). The poetics of judgment transform this opacity into an experience of the contours and of the forms produced, and according to Klinger this transformation may produce intensity (different degrees of intensity, he specifies, depending on the degree of innovation produced by the form in question). For "language games" of aesthetic judgment, Klinger further suggests, this production of intensity is the only reason for existence (I would prefer to say, more cautiously, that intensity often appears to be the main reason but hardly ever the only reason for the existence of language games of aesthetic judgment). At any event, the very effect of intensity may help us understand why Diderot was so convinced that in his art criticism he had reached the best and most enjoyable part of his intellectual activities.

———————

In order to understand the discursive forms that Diderot used and developed in his art criticism, it is indispensable to have some historical knowledge about the Salons and the *Correspondance littéraire*, as the two institutions to which his practice constantly referred and within which it emerged. The decision to publicly display contemporary paintings and sculptures was made by the Académie Royale de Peinture et de Sculpture in 1663,[35] not by coincidence at a time when some observers first dared to think that the national art and literature of the present could compare to and even compete with the works of Greek or Latin antiquity. The first Salon opened during Easter week of 1667, for fourteen days, and from its beginning the exhibit was designed and organized as an event to be repeated every other year.

Astonishingly few structural changes occurred between this beginning and the final Salon, held during the French Revolution in 1791. From their inception, the shows were financed by the king and took place in the Louvre, although it took some time for an ultimate itinerary to emerge in which the works could be seen (the one invariable element of all Salons was a portrait of the king, presented as the first painting). Like the space of the exhibit, its schedule also changed several times, oscillating between April and August, until in 1746 a permanent decision was made to hold it in the summer, and to keep it open for around twenty days. While the number of works shown never had an official limit, about one quarter were sculptures and the total number had never gone over two hundred and twenty until, in 1765, it jumped to four hundred and thirty-two, where it remained until 1791.

Throughout the long century of their existence, the Salons remained under the administrative responsibility of the Académie Royale de Peinture et de Sculpture, with its very hierarchical internal structure. Only members of the Académie (whose number, unlike the Académie Française as a language academy, was open) were allowed—though they were not obliged—to show their artworks, which became a reason for many aggressive strategies and confrontations in its election process. Every two years, the Académie Royale appointed a member (normally not one of the most distinguished artists) to take over the role of the *tapissier*—the person in charge of choosing the paintings and sculptures to be displayed and determining their places along the itinerary of the exhibit (which, due to different light conditions and thematic configurations, had a considerable impact on the visitors' reactions).[36]

In addition, the *tapissier* organized the opening act, represented the Académie and each Salon in the emerging public sphere, and edited a catalogue (*Livret*) in which all the artworks shown were listed and briefly described, without any interpretative commentaries. While admission was free, a non-negligible price had to be paid for the *Livret*, which makes it all the more remarkable that in some years up to twenty thousand copies were produced and sold, in several reprints. Without any doubt, by 1750 the Salons had become a highly popular event in the cultural life of Paris and belonged to the few occasions where members of different social estates were jointly present: "Great noblemen would complain about encountering lackeys there [. . .]. City folk were plentiful, and seemed very happy when they could find a volunteer guide, some well-spoken boy who had studied the *Livret* closely. The *beaux-esprits*, or the intellectuals of the time, were also regulars, some claiming that they came every day."[37]

As the *Correspondance littéraire* tried to provide a detailed and well-informed inside impression of the intellectual life happening in Paris for a handful of aristocrats all over Europe (among them the Empress of Russia, the sister of Frederick II of Prussia, the Queen of Sweden, and the King of Poland), its editor Melchior Grimm was thus under the unconditional obligation to cover the Salons. For several years he fulfilled the task himself until, in 1759, he asked Denis Diderot to take over. Ironically, and only one year before Diderot wrote his first "Salon," he had formulated a skeptical comment about the genre in question and about the competence it required:

> [Our] simple men of letters [. . .] know nothing of drawing, nor of lighting, nor of colour, nor of the harmony of the whole, nor of the artist's touch, etc. At any moment they risk lavishing praise on a mediocre creation while disdainfully overlooking a masterpiece of the genre.[38]

Although he did not believe that artists were in a principally better position to judge their own works from an aesthetic point of view, Diderot became active, throughout the twenty-two years of his involvement with the Salons, in trying to acquire first-hand expertise in all technical aspects of artistic production and increasing his knowledge of the art-historical canon. He took advantage of his voyage to Saint Petersburg to see several important museums and collections, he eagerly visited the studios of contemporary French artists, and he used every opportunity to walk through the Salons with them. And yet Diderot was aware, as he confessed to Grimm in 1763, that his knowledge and his experience would never become fully adequate to the multiple levels and dimensions of the task assigned:

> To describe a Salon in a way that would please us both, do you know what I would need to have, my friend? All the different kinds of taste, a heart sensitive to all charms, a soul susceptible to infinite modes of enthusiasm, a variety of styles to correspond to the variety of paintbrushes.[39]

As we are now approaching the actual texts of Diderot's *Salons*, it is important to remember that the readers of the *Correspondance* were of course not able to see the works he was writing about, which partly explains why his practice of judgment often appears intertwined with lengthy descriptions of the paintings and sculptures in question, descriptions indeed that we may find unnecessarily detailed in an age of photographic reproduction. And yet I imagine that the rhythm of Diderot's judgments must have been more in the foreground of his first readers' attention than the actual images evoked. Given the highly restricted (almost secret) conditions under which the *Correspondance* circulated, Diderot no doubt felt the temptation to be particularly outspoken and blunt in his criticism, to a degree indeed that he would most likely have avoided if the artists had been able to read his texts.

Ultimately, he remained ambivalent between his desire to have a greater number of readers than the *Correspondance* provided and his relief at the honesty and directness that he could afford there without exposing and hurting the artists in public:

> At times I feel torn between conflicting sentiments. There are moments when I would like for my work to fall from the sky, printed and bound, in the middle of the capital; more often, when I reflect upon the profound pain that this work would cause for a great many artists [. . .] I feel I would be upset if it were published.[40]

In the first two *Salons* that he wrote in 1759 and in 1761, we see Diderot on his way towards an intellectual and discursive practice intended to familiarize readers with artworks they had no chance to see. As I mentioned before, he followed the order of paintings and sculptures as outlined by the *Livret* in his first installment, but from 1761 on, he began to shape a more independent view that brought together the different works of individual artists exhibited. What Klinger calls "rightness," that is, the lack of transcendent or authoritative criteria, was the central and almost obsessively invoked premise in the morphology of Diderot's incipient art criticism and in his acts of judgment. As if casually using a point from Kant's analysis of aesthetic judgment, Diderot, in a remark to his friend Grimm that prefaced his second *Salon*, wrote about the expectation that his and his friend's opinions about different paintings and sculptures would most likely diverge:

> Here, my friend, are some of the thoughts that went through my head when I saw the paintings exhibited at this year's Salon. I jotted them down without thinking about how they're arranged or written. Some will be true, others false. At times you will think me too harsh, at others too indulgent. I will condemn what you might have approved; I will praise what you might have condemned; you will be left unsatisfied when I am left content. Little does this matter to me. My only concern is to spare you a few moments that you can put to better use.[41]

Such words indirectly spoke to the subscribers of the *Correspondance* as much as they were explicitly addressed to Grimm, and they thus set the tone of an informal conversation (in whose early stages Grimm occasionally intervened[42]) rather than that of a more formal philosophical treatise. Sometimes this tone, as a premise of judgment, prompted Diderot to imagine, with friendly self-irony, how much he would like to be in possession of one or the other among the works described and how Grimm, visiting his home, could disagree with the choice—while being unable to completely ignore the paintings:

> I wouldn't mind having this painting at home. Every time you came over, you would say bad things about it, yet you would look at it.[43]

In other cases, especially when he was referring to younger artists, the insecurity of his judgment made him postpone a final verdict: "This man will either become a great artist, or he will come to nothing. We must wait."[44]

Much more frequently, however, the lack of transcendent criteria did not prevent Diderot from making clear judgments and thus producing multiple forms of sharp distinction between what he liked and disliked. Paradoxically, his basic insecurity seems to have given him an exceptional degree of freedom in the expression of his reactions and opinions. This becomes particularly obvious in the contrast between his concluding evaluations of the Salons of 1759 and of 1761. It was devastating, in general and in the convergence of different, more specific perspectives, for 1759:

> We have many artists; few are good, not one is excellent. They choose fine subjects, but they are impotent. They have no spirit, no warmth, no imagination. Their choices of colour are almost always sinful. A lot of planning, no ideas.[45]

Two years later, Diderot's judgment became even more decided, but now in the opposite direction; it was so positive indeed that the impression encouraged him to claim a general status of superiority for French contemporary art:

> Never have we had a finer Salon. Almost no painting was absolutely bad; there were more good paintings than mediocre ones, and a large number of excellent ones. [. . .] They no longer paint in Flanders. If there are painters in Italy and in Germany, they are more scattered. They are emulated less and receive less encouragement. France is therefore the only country where this art sustains itself, and even shines.[46]

It appears unlikely of course that French art had truly changed for the decidedly better within barely two years. Rather, I understand this black-and-white effect as a symptom of the joy that Diderot took in making hyperbolically strong statements and in thus engaging the emotions of his readers.

Applied to individual works and individual artists, this tone often produced the positivity of absolute condemnations and of absolute praise—with the ensuing effect of personal rankings, always protected by the distance of the *Correspondance* from the public sphere and the eyes of the actual artists. Often enough, Diderot did not even care to give reasons for his judgments or to describe the perceptions on which they were based:

There is a poor *Adoration of the Kings* by Colin de Vermont. Jeurat's *Carthusians in Meditation* is even worse: no silence, nothing wild, nothing that reminds the viewer of divine justice, no ideas, no profound adoration, no inner reflection, no ecstasy, no terror.[47]

Even his own failure to remember certain works mentioned in the *Livrets* could lead to negative value judgments: "I have no memory of seeing [...] Challe's other paintings. You know how it is to overlook mediocre compositions with disdainful absent-mindedness."[48] In this growing spirit of confidence, Diderot began to elevate his own enthusiasm for individual works and also, quite surprisingly, his resistance to details in other paintings that did not completely convince him, into praise or condemnation of the artists who had created them. In a passage from the *Salon* of 1761, one such positive reaction to the effects of "audacity and force" in a work by Jacques Dumont le Romain even ended up prevailing over Diderot's otherwise unconditional prejudice against any type of allegory:

> You know that I have never approved of the combination of real and allegorical beings, and the painting with the subject *Proclamation of Peace in* 1749 did not make me change my mind. Real beings lose their reality next to allegorical figures, and the latter always add a certain obscurity to the composition. The piece in question is not without impact. It is painted with audacity and force. It is certainly the work of a master.[49]

Measurement as another dimension of the act of judging clearly became more important to Diderot between the Salon of 1759 and that of 1761. Any detail that he identified as improbable compared to his own perception of reality got excluded from favorable evaluation. Here is an example referring to yet another "Adoration des Rois," also remarkable as an early case of the ironic digressions that Diderot would indulge in during later years:

> Tell me how a dyed cushion might have found its way into a wretched stable where mother and child took shelter, and where the breaths of a couple of animals were what kept the newborn warm in the harsh weather? Apparently one of the kings had sent ahead a squire to deliver a cushion, so that he might prostrate himself more comfortably.[50]

Holding paintings up against his own view of reality also turned into a basis for proposals by Diderot on how the artists should have imagined and represented historical or mythological scenes:

> It is not enough to show me Psyche's curiosity to see Cupid; I must also be able to perceive her fear of waking up. Her mouth should be half-open and she should be too scared to breathe. It is her lover that she is seeing, seeing for the first time at the risk of losing him. What joy to behold him looking so beautiful![51]

From measuring individual works by ideas of his own about the representation of certain subjects, there was but a brief step to comparing works exhibited in the Salons with the paintings of canonized masters or with the effects of other genres and national traditions. Diderot thus liked to invoke Rubens's exuberant imagination and to point to Italian taste as a standard for drastic effects that he then made converge with visions of his own, often to the detriment of lesser-known artists:

> Finally, there is a *Souls Passing from Purgatory to Heaven* by one Monsieur Briand. The painter relegated his purgatory to one corner of his painting, from which only a handful of lost figures emerge onto an immense canvas [. . .]. In order to do justice to such a subject, he would have needed the powerful mind, colors, and imagination of a Rubens, and to attempt to create what the Italians call an *opera da stupire.* A fertile, audacious mind would have opened up the pit of fire along the bottom of the painting, taking up its entire length and depth.[52]

On the opening page of his inaugural *Salon*, the emotional impact that paintings and sculptures had on Diderot—or the lack thereof—already appeared as the central (if not the only) criterion of relevance in his practice of judgment. He described such "effects" both as inescapable and as impossible to be conjured up by any beholder's will to engage. Or, from a different angle, Diderot presupposed that the beholder's (his own) psyche was the decisive subjective context in which the objective forms, colors, and contents of artworks could unfold certain functions—or not: "I recall that the Annunciation is depicted in a dry, stiff, and cold manner; it is without impact."[53] Some paragraphs further, by contrast, he admitted that a sick person painted by Joseph-Marie Vien had "made an effect" on him (65). But despite such passages and although the dimension of relevance did indeed already occupy an important place in his early *Salons*, Diderot was often disappointed by the experience that certain of the exhibited works, and among them, specifically, many of the sculptures, did not "speak" to him:

> Perhaps there are some beautiful works among the paintings I have not discussed, and among the sculptures, which I do not talk about. I refrain from doing so because they were mute, they did not speak to me.[54]

One reason for this disappointment may have been a lack of reflexive familiarity, on Diderot's part, with the inclinations of his own taste. Probably he was not sure yet what type of art he most resonated with. Only in later years did Diderot become fully aware (and explicitly state) that paintings with morally charged subjects engaged him more than any other genre, which caused a considerable shift in the focus of his art critical writing and in the forms of his judgments.

Unlike the perspective of relevance, the dimension of power left hardly any traces in the judging practice of Diderot's *Salons*. We can certainly speculate that while well-circumscribed institutions define the effects (the "power," in Klinger's language) of different acts of judgment with great precision (the most obvious example being a court of law), less formal situations (among them a visit to an art exhibit) have their horizon of "power" in the spontaneous emotional impact that moments of subjective experience can produce—which would mean that in these institutionally informal cases, "power" converges with what I have been referring to as "relevance." At the same time, we have seen how, once Diderot had overcome initial doubts and insecurities, judging turned into an activity that came easily to him and thus required no effort or power of self-convincing. There is, finally, an interesting passage in the first *Salon* where he decided to exclude the power of erotic details in a certain painting from its aesthetic evaluation. For he associated this specific power more with the erotic excitability ("the vice") of the beholder than with the artist's "talent" and "judgment":

> There is sensuality in this painting: bare feet, thighs, nipples, buttocks. It is perhaps not so much the artist's talent as our own vice that makes

it eye-catching. The colors are quite vivid. The women busy serving the main figures are judiciously muted: real, natural, and beautiful, without causing any distraction.[55]

As for the poetics of Diderot's early *Salons*, they started out from a very elementary level. Judgments without much nuance and sheer exclamations often went together and set the tone. Each exclamation was of course drawing a line between works considered irrelevant and works to which he wanted to direct his readers' attention and about which he obliged himself to write, as the subscribers of the *Correspondance littéraire* could not see them. In most cases, exclamations thus marked moments of positive value judgment for Diderot, happy moments also because, as he said in a note to Grimm at the beginning of the first *Salon*, he was most enjoying his impulses of admiration and praise:

> Many paintings, my friend; many bad paintings. I like giving praise. I am happy when I admire something. I should like nothing better than to be happy and admiring.[56]

By contrast, he hardly ever made the effort of going through complex comparisons, and he did not yet allow himself to open up the staccato of acts of judgment to those long digressions whose generic and intellectual fluctuations would later on dominate his critical discourse.

Rather than relying on conceptual self-reflection or on discursive experiments, Diderot let the opacity of his reactions turn into unintended transparency in moments of carelessness that probably emerged from his rhythms of judging and from the intensity that they produced. If we take such passages seriously, they lead us to the impression that a casually malicious and condescending attitude towards the artists largely informed the writing of Diderot's *Salons*. Well-painted erotic details, for example, invariably turned into occasions for him to imagine impulses of primary carnal desire in the production process of a work:

> The [nymph's] head is youthful, graceful, truthful, noble. Wondrously soft flesh abounds, and scattered throughout are details so realistic that we are led to believe the artist spared no expense on his models. But how does he manage to find such beautiful models?[57]

Grotesque physical or sexual fantasies and word plays triggered by the paintings often appear between passages of detailed critique and devastatingly negative jugdments:

> And this *Judgment of Paris*? What can I tell you? It seems that the scene ought to be set in a landscape that is remote, silent, deserted, but rich; that the goddesses' beauty ought to keep both spectator and judge in a state of uncertainty; that only a stroke of genius could discover Paris's true personality. Monsieur de la Grenée did not see such difficulties. Little did he suspect that the setting should be sublime in its effect. His young Satyr amusing himself with Pan's flute is bustier than a young girl. The rest is color, canvas, and time wasted.[58]

Altogether, there was more energy than subtlety, more spontaneity than recognizable personal style in the different dimensions (in the "morphology") of Diderot's early judging practice. He certainly did not care yet about coherence in his criteria and preferences. Already between 1759 and 1761, however, the task that he had taken over without enthusiasm began to matter to him: probably less because of any particular appreciation of the artworks he was writing about than because of the opportunity to process his thought and his capacity for emotional resonance on a high level of intensity.

───────────

As I have already mentioned, there is well-grounded consensus among specialists that the quality of Diderot's art critical texts, in terms both of discursive mastery and of palpable enjoyment, reached its peak in the *Salons* of 1763, 1765, and especially 1767.[59] From a structural point of view, it also becomes obvious how the much larger texts that he now began to dedicate to individual works first opened up for serial accumulations of the forms emerging from his acts of judging and thus produced an effect to which I have already referred as the "syntax" of his practice. It was through this syntax, I believe, and through the ever more frequent digressions as its consequence, that Diderot's art criticism had a profound influence on his relation to the world around him, an influence that made him more attentive to the singularity of individual phenomena and more willing to engage with them.

At the same time, and while he continued living up to the task of giving his readers a full survey of the works exhibited every other year, it was during the 1760s that Diderot developed a preference and a more differentiated sensitivity for a then-innovative genre of painting concentrated on particularly pathos-laden subjects. Within this context, he dedicated by far the most pages to works by Jean-Baptiste Greuze, who profited in the Académie Royale from Diderot's appreciation in his polemic about the new style. Despite a number of sophisticated recent attempts to make Greuze's work valuable for our present-day taste on the basis of a multi-leveled historicization, I think it is difficult—not to say improbable—to find aesthetic pleasure in those paintings today. For along with a comparative degree of resistance to the convergence between moral intentions and pictorial exuberance that is the core of Greuze's works, we have also lost some of the desire for direct emotional resonance that was so natural for Diderot and his contemporaries.

Now if, in our analysis of the *Salons* of 1759 and 1761, we tried to illustrate above all the dimensions and forms of Diderot's judging practice, I will now concentrate, in relation to five individual paintings, on how the cumulative effect of subsequent acts of judgment transformed his awareness regarding the specificity of the works in question and even regarding the specificity of the phenomena represented. In other words: instead of subsuming paintings under generic concepts, his discourse increasingly made those artworks and their objects of reference emerge in a new status of singularity.

A particularly enthusiastic text, written in 1763, referred to one of several portraits of Greuze's wife painted by her husband. After an opening sentence that anticipated Diderot's excessively positive judgment by alluding to the "unlimited" price this work might fetch one day, he continued with a series of exclamations that praised "truthful" aspects of Mme Greuze's appearance and of her clothing, without making a clear distinction between her beauty and her husband's achievements as a painter:[60]

> I swear this portrait is a masterpiece that will one day be priceless. What elegant, truthful chestnut hair! How charming the effect of the ribbon tied round her head! How beautiful the long braid raised by her hand as she sits it on her shoulder, and that twirls around her arm! This is how one paints hair![61]

Diderot then concentrated for a moment on the equally "truthful" rendition of her hands as a technical achievement of the artist, only to return to the previous perspective that had not distinguished between the portrait and the person portrayed: "You should see the care and the truthfulness with which the inside of this hand and the folds of the fingers are painted. What finesse and what variety in the coloration of the forehead."[62]

At this point we notice a discursive shift. Diderot refers to other critics who had found the image of Mme Greuze too "serious and earnest," which allows him to mention that she was pregnant when her husband produced the portrait. From being just a general portrait of Mme Greuze, the painting thus turns into a representation of Mme Greuze at a specific moment in her life:

> Her face has been criticized as too serious and earnest; but is that not characteristic of a woman with child, a woman who is aware of the dignity, danger, and importance of her condition? [. . .] Should she not also be criticized for the yellowish tinge of her temples and forehead, for her bosoms that grow heavier, for her sagging limbs, for her belly that is beginning to show?[63]

From yet a different angle, Diderot adds the impression that this work overwhelms all the paintings hanging close to it ("this portrait kills all those around it"[64]) and thus arrives, after more praise for Greuze's technique, at a different type of relationship between himself and the female body represented, a relationship that would become central to his art critical writing:

> Her lower face, the shadow cast by her chin onto her neck, are painted with unimaginable thoughtfulness. It would be tempting to reach out and touch her chin, if only her expression were not so severe as to stop both the viewer's praise and his hand.[65]

The separation between the different body parts in a series of individual judgments was no doubt a condition for this desire to touch Mme Greuze's chin—with which Diderot enters the space of the painting in his imagination. This is the effect of "absorption" described and analyzed in Michael Fried's study of late-eighteenth-century art in France. We see, for the first time, a transition from the rhythm of judging into a digression that will fill an imagined three-dimensional space, as was about to become typical for

Diderot's *Salons* in the mid-1760s. On this basis we are no longer surprised to read that, in the end, Mme Greuze appeared to be alive and looking back at Diderot (and his readers):

> Stand on the other side of the staircase from the portrait, look at it through a telescope, and you will see nature itself. I challenge you to tell me that the figure portrayed does not look back at you, that she is not alive.[66]

He concluded the passage with an explanation, disguised in the form of a piece of advice for Greuze, about the emotional condition that would forever enable him to produce such superb effects: "Ah! Monsieur Greuze, how different you are when your brush is moved by affection and not financial interest!"[67]

When, two years later, Diderot wrote about a different portrait of Mme Greuze, again painted by her husband, he first seemed to directly connect with his motif of emotional and erotic attachment as a premise for great art: "This painter certainly loves his wife, and quite rightly."[68] But soon his judgments went into a different direction, as they oscillated between reservation, appreciation, and rejection:

> There was a portrait of *Madame Greuze with Child* in the last Salon; her interesting state drew your attention, and then the beautiful colouring and the truth of the details bowled you over. This one is not as beautiful, but the whole effect is graceful, the pose is good, the posture is a sensuous one, there's an enchanting delicacy of tone in the two hands, but the left hand is poorly conceived, and it even has a broken finger, which offends the eye. (242)[69]

If Diderot initially seemed undecided, his acts of judgment increasingly turn to the negative side, starting from the sentence about the "broken finger." Even a detail that he had earlier on highlighted as evidence of Greuze's commitment to nature and truth, that is the "yellowish" color of Mme Greuze's skin, now irritates him as excessively realistic:

> The colour tones in the forehead are too yellow; we know that women who have had children are often left with these marks, but if one wants to imitate nature to the extent of portraying them, they must be softened; this is a case where you have to beautify nature a little, since it's possible to do it without losing the resemblance. (243)[70]

And while some more positive views follow each decidedly critical judgment, right to the end of the description ("But the shape of the mouth, the eyes and all the other details are delightful" [243][71]), Diderot does not return to his enthusiasm of two years earlier about Greuze's art and the beauty of his wife.

The contrast between these texts written two years apart helps us unfold some further perspectives on what I mean by "singularity" as a consequence of the syntax in Diderot's judgment practice. In the first place, positive or negative reactions noted earlier had no impact on each new, present act and process of judging; secondly, Diderot took each work or object of reference in the context of the specific situation where he encountered it, her, or him (Mme de Greuze during her pregnancy was not the same as Mme de Greuze two years later); and a third level connected to singularity was the ongoing changes in Diderot's own disposition, humor, or memory. Finally, such singularization effects in the objects and persons represented seem to have encouraged Diderot to imagine himself interacting with them in the imaginary space.

Even in cases without critical counterpoint or ambiguity, as we saw in the text about the earlier portrait of Mme Greuze, the staccato of Diderot's judging brought to the fore impressions and effects of individual differentiation. While he admired all of Jean-Claude Vernet's land- and seascape paintings, without exception ("it's always the latest work of this master that is called the finest" [309][72]), he submitted each of them to an analysis that highlighted and praised its different elements in detail:[73]

> I don't know what I most want to praise in this piece. Is it the reflection of the moon on the rippling waters, or the dark heavy clouds and the way they move, or the vessel sailing along in front of the moon, reflecting it and drawing it to itself from its immense remoteness, or the reflection in the water of the little torch that sailor is holding at the prow of his boat, or the fire whose reddish glow spreads over all the objects around it, without destroying the general harmony, or the whole effect of the darkness? (309)[74]

Paradoxically, even the comprehensive vision ("The whole effect of the darkness" / "l'effet total de cette nuit") turns into an aspect of singularity here, set apart from all the observations on painterly details that Diderot is accumulating.

An analogous process unfolds along a text that marks Diderot's discovery of Greuze's moralist art in a painting entitled "La Piété Filiale" ("Filial Piety")[75] that was part of the Salon of 1763:

> First of all, the genre pleases me; it is a moralistic painting. What now! Hasn't the paintbrush spent long enough—too long, even—devoted to debauchery and vice? Should we not be happy to see it compete at long last with dramatic poetry in its power to move us, to enlighten us, to improve us and to invite us to live virtuously?[76]

Again Diderot presents elements of the work (in this case a group of family members and the furniture of the room where they come together) in great detail, without clearly distinguishing between the subject matter and its representation, between his aesthetic judgment and his identification of elements that make up the painting; again he lets himself be absorbed by the scene evoked, to the degree of believing that he has heard the sick father's voice:

> The principal figure, occupying the center of the scene and commanding the viewer's attention, is a paralytic old man stretched out in his armchair; his head rests on a bolster and his feet are up on a stool. He is dressed; his sick legs are covered by a blanket. He is surrounded by his children and grandchildren, most of them eager to be of service to him. There is something very moving about his handsome face. He appears so grateful for the services rendered; he has such difficulty speaking, his voice is so weak, his gaze so loving, his complexion so pale, that only the heartless would fail to find this painting heartrending.[77]

Diderot continues with a patient description of each of the eight persons who make up the scene, insisting that the differences between them are carefully developed: "Everyone here displays exactly the degree of concern appropriate to their age and character."[78] Towards the end of his analysis he comes back to this appreciation in a more decided and most radical tone. The beauty of the work and its impact on the beholder, he writes, emerges from the "uniqueness," from the singularity of each of the persons invoked:

> This painting is beautiful; very beautiful. Shame on whoever looks upon it with equanimity, however briefly. The old man's character is unique. His

son-in-law's character is unique. The drink-bearing child is unique, the old woman is unique. No matter how one looks at it, one is enthralled.[79]

When Diderot finally asks himself how Jean-Baptiste Greuze has been able to produce a painting that he finds so moving, he comes up with a characterization of the artist that resonates with his own self-characterization in his critique of van Loo's portrait: he describes Greuze as a man with many traits of identity: "he is blunt, gentle, disarming, scathing, gallant, wretched, cheerful, cold, warm, serious or mad, depending on his subject matter."[80] This is where the practice of judgment quite literally begins to atomize previously stable identities.

Several times, in following Diderot's comments on different paintings, we have now arrived at a threshold between his real observer world and imaginary worlds that the pictures conjured up for him. But we have not yet focused on an individual case where he crossed this limit decidedly enough to engage—and get lost—in a digression leading him through the imaginary realm. This is exactly what happened when he wrote about yet another work by Greuze displayed in the Salon of 1765 under the title "The Girl Weeping for Her Dead Bird / La jeune fille qui pleure son oiseau mort."[81] The text again begins with an exclamation, in this case with an exclamation that assigns the work to the poetic and painterly genre of the idyll and thus to a specific emotional tonality:

What a pretty elegy and a pretty poem! What a fine idyll Gessner[82] would make of it! It would serve as the illustration to a piece by that poet. It's a delightful painting . . . ! (236)[83]

Diderot does not hesitate to rank the piece as "perhaps having the strongest affective impact[84] of all the artworks shown in the current Salon." Then he continues with a particularly long sequence of details and acts of praise for their rendition, most of them in the form of exclamations:

How naturally posed she is! What a lovely face! and elegant hair! What expression there is in her face! Her grief is profound, she is completely absorbed in her misfortune. What a pretty catafalque that cage makes! How graceful is the green garland twined round it! And oh! that lovely hand! that lovely arm! Look how true the detail is in those fingers, and

those dimples, and that softness, and the touch of red with which the
pressure of the head has coloured the tips of those delicate fingers, and
the charm of it all. (236)[85]

As we have already seen with other persons portrayed, his focus on the girl's
hands and fingers prompts Diderot to imagine that he is touching her—while
he also feels that such a contact would be inappropriate: "You could go up
to that hand and kiss it, if you didn't respect the child and her grief" (236).[86]

With this bodily impulse of his imagination, however, he crosses the
threshold between his observer position and the space occupied by the girl,
to whom he immediately begins to speak:

> But, little one, your grief is very profound, and very very thoughtful! Why
> this dreamy, melancholy air? What, all this for a bird? You're not crying,
> but you're distressed, and there's a thought behind your distress. Come,
> child, open your heart to me, tell me what it is, is it the death of this bird
> that makes you so sad and withdrawn? (236–37)[87]

Half beholder and half fictional character in the space of the painting, Diderot
seems convinced that the "true" reason for the girl's tears and affliction is
not the death of her bird.[88] So in order to comfort her, he confesses what he
believes has happened, and this is a story about how, in the absence of her
mother, the girl has been seduced by a boy and lost her virginity. After many
more tears and a long silence, she finally reacts with a final, half-hearted
attempt at insisting on the bird as the original explanation for her affliction:

> What about my bird? . . . You're smiling . . . (Oh, my friend, how lovely
> she was! if you could have seen her smiling and weeping!) I went on:
> Well, what about your bird? When you forget yourself, do you remember
> your bird? When it was nearly time for your mother to come back, the
> one you love went away. He was happy, contented and walking on air!
> How hard it was for him to drag himself away from you! . . . What a look
> you're giving me! You see, I know it already. (237)[89]

At this point Diderot is lost indeed in the imagined scene of the conversation,
"lost" to the degree of describing the girl's beauty to his friend (Grimm?) as
if she were a real character and not a product of his imagination provoked
by Greuze's painting.

What finally facilitates his exit from the imagined space will be the critique of a painterly detail triggered by his friend's question about the girl's age:

> How old is she, then?—What shall I answer, and what sort of question is this? Her face is fifteen or sixteen, and her arm and hand eighteen or nineteen. It's a defect of this composition which is all the more noticeable because the head, leaning as it is on the hand, means that one of the parts is wrong for the other. Place the hand differently, and no one will notice that it's a little too strong and well formed. What has happened, my friend, is that the head has been taken from one model and the hand from another. (239)[90]

And yet the text ends with the recommendation not to give too much weight, in the evaluation of this work, to Greuze's mistake: "The painter may have done as well, but not better" (239).[91]

We have for once followed the full movement in the description of an individual work, starting from Diderot's rhythm of judging to the threshold that he crosses to become part of Greuze's painting, and from there to the fictional conversation in which he gets lost and from which he only returns when he has an (imagined) impulse to critically focus on a detail of the work. In this narrative, the girl becomes an individual character to whom Diderot reacts with openness and empathy by reassuring her, perhaps against his true moral conviction, that there was no reason to worry and that the boy who has taken her virginity will keep the promise of marrying her: "What would I do? what would become of me? what if he didn't care about me? . . . What nonsense! Don't be afraid, it won't happen, it can't happen" (238).[92]

On a more abstract philosophical level we can speculate that Diderot's intense reaction to this painting may have implied the question, clearly serious and relevant for a father in the eighteenth century, what advice an older man should give to a girl who had lost her virginity. Perhaps he entered a fictional scene in which he could give the girl consolation because he found himself unable to come up with pertinent answers in a more serious discourse of ethics and morality. The text would then illustrate his tendency, identified and analyzed by the great Diderot scholar Herbert Dieckmann, to engage and indeed get lost in digressions whenever abstract thought and established systematic discourses did not yield the solutions that he was hoping for. According to Dieckmann, Diderot "was aware of the irresistible inclination to follow his thoughts in an informal way instead of guiding or structuring them according to a predetermined plan."[93] This was certainly true for his art critique and for the syntax of judgment as its central level, as they produced views of the world filled with profiles of singularity and individuality for things and objects, profiles to which Diderot could react with openness, empathy, and generosity.

At the same time, such acts of judging and the ensuing digressions, like most other intellectual practices in Diderot's work, unleashed an energy under whose impact his tactlessness became a jeopardy—all the more so as he was aware of the restricted circulation of his *Salons*. Even Jean-Baptiste Greuze and his wife were not spared. The rather unfavorable commentary dedicated to Mme Greuze's portrait in the exhibit of 1765, for example, would end with the insinuation that the artist was eager to attract the beholder's attention to his wife's breasts—although they did not offer an erotically appealing sight:

> The neck holds the head up beautifully, it's beautifully drawn and coloured, and joins on to the shoulders just as it should. But that bosom, I can't bear to look at it, and yet at fifty I'm still not averse to bosoms. The painter has made his figure lean forward, as though to say to the spectator: Look at my wife's boson. I'm looking, Monsieur Greuze, and your wife's bosom is flabby and yellow; if it's really like that, so much the worse for you, her and the picture. (243)[94]

At other occasions, among them a devastating remark about Pierre-Antoine Baudouin's paintings shown in the Salon of 1767, the energy of judging burst into wordplay that was as humiliating to the beholders as to the artists:

> Always the same little pictures, little ideas, frivolous compositions fit for a little madam's boudoir or the little house of a little fop; just right for minor abbés, small-time lawyers, major financiers and other people with no morals and trivial tastes. (171)[95]

Sometimes Diderot allowed himself to write in such aggressively condescending words even about painters whose work and personality he highly appreciated,[96] as was the case with Claude Joseph Vernet:

It appears that all our artists decided to get worse this year. Those who used to be excellent are now merely good; the good have become mediocre, while those who were poor are now execrable. You might have trouble guessing who inspires me to make this remark: it is Vernet. Yes, the same Vernet whom I love, to whom I owe much gratitude and whom I so enjoy praising.[97]

From 1769 on, Diderot returned to progressively shorter forms of discourse than he had been indulging in during the previous years. By 1781, in the final *Salon* of his lifetime, he had arrived at brief, often centrifugal, both very clear and clearly subjective judgments that were now exclusively based on the "effects" they had on him. This was the case in two statements about paintings by Hubert Robert that evoked a fire at the Paris Opéra and the ruins of the Coliseum in Rome:

The Opera going up in flames is not without effect, but it is a hard, dry effect. There is not enough air, and the figures are not very well drawn.

The interior of the burning auditorium pleases me more: it is more balanced, but I still don't like the figures. However, the figures are well grouped together.

(THE RUINS OF THE COLISEUM OF ROME) strike me as having the same tone. There are masses of figures in the painting, and they have some effect. I should have only liked to see some variety therein that wouldn't destroy this effect. This would add harmony and would contribute to the magic of the scene.[98]

Most Diderot specialists have associated this change in his art critical writing with a lack of inspiration due to old age and with a growing impatience with the task he still had to cover for the *Correspondance*. But it may also have been the result of a more deliberate reaction, based on the frustration with his experience that, instead of providing him with growing security and more solid criteria, the ongoing practice of judging the Salons had been progressing in the opposite direction, that is, toward ever more internally complex descriptions, more centrifugality, and a greater awareness of how inescapable this drift was within his form of art criticism.

Written between 1776 and 1777 in their earliest version and never published before Diderot's death, the *Pensées détachées sur la peinture* (*Isolated*

Thoughts on Painting) seem to reflect a paradoxical tension between knowing more each time and yet becoming increasingly insecure and succinct in his acts of judging: "although I grow less ignorant from one Salon to the next, I am more reserved and more timid."[99] To speak so openly and self-critically about his subjectivity as the only basis of writing about art, a basis that he had learned he would never overcome, must have felt like a defeat for Diderot—and was therefore a courageous act of sincerity:

> Furthermore, remember that there is no basis on which I guarantee either my descriptions or my opinions: my descriptions, because there is no memory on earth that can faithfully recollect so many different compositions; my opinions because I am not an artist, nor even a collector. I am only telling you what I think and I tell you this in all sincerity. If it so happens that I contradict myself, it is because from one moment to the next I am affected in different ways; I am equally unprejudiced when I praise and when I withdraw such praise, when I condemn and when I track off from my criticism . . .[100]

This is yet a different self-reflexive discovery of singularity, of singularity as central premise for the practice of judging and of the undercutting consequence that it had for all objectivity claims concerning the writing about art. If, biographically speaking, the insight was sobering for Diderot and may have pushed him towards greater succinctness and fewer digressions in the final *Salons*, the interplay between subjectivity and singularity was about to become the foundation of his role as a decisive innovator in the history of art criticism. For instead of considering effects of singularity as an inescapable shortcoming, modern art criticism begins by affirming the experience that serious judgments need to emerge from subjective reactions.

Once Diderot had realized how impossible it was for him to bring all of his judgments and their criteria into a state of coherence, he began to feel an energy—rather than the confirmations of moral principles:

> I've no hatred for great crimes, firstly because they make fine paintings and fine tragedies; and then, because great, sublime actions and great crimes are marked by the same strength of purpose. If a man were not capable of setting fire to a city, another man would not be capable of leaping down a precipice to save it.[101]

To justify a fascination with crimes by highlighting their status as a precondition for morally positive actions does not appear quite persuasive. But as Diderot must have felt disillusionment about his judging practice and its supposed lack of moral foundation, he may have been blind to its status as a source of the energy that he felt—and rather sought the basis of this energy in certain subject matters displayed by the artworks. Now "intensity"—in the very same sense that Diderot associated with the word "énergie"—is the most important aspect of Florian Klinger's reflections on the rhetoric of judgment.[102] If the language of judgment, he writes, occurs as a "creative engagement with the world," then its strength, that is, the improbability of the forms produced through judging, together with the frequency of its acts (in their syntactic sequence), account for a surge of intensity. Regarding Diderot's critical language and converging with our reading of *Le rêve de d'Alembert,* we can then say that the practice of judging, through its intensity, had its existential status as a core dimension of life.

———————

And what was the status of judgment in the works of Goya, Lichtenberg, and Mozart? Regarding Goya, we of course need to acknowledge that while pictures became a favorite object of judging durng his lifetime, they can under no circumstances become the real site of a judging practice. For if judging is an act that inevitably produces changes in the world by imposing forms upon phenomena experienced in their contingency, it requires a temporality open to the contrast between a "before" and an "after," a contrast that pictures in their simultaneity cannot offer. This said, we have seen how Goya's art frequently—and perhaps centrally—confronted its beholders with immediate, almost aggressive provocations to judge, provocations that went far beyond their general status as potential objects of aesthetic judgment.

The pronounced ambiguity of Capricho 43, with its caption "El sueño de la razón produce monstruos," was only the most emblematic case of such provocations towards judgment. Even more existentially captivating must have been an intellectually similar impulse inherent to the dimension of atrocity as it appears in the *Desastres de la guerra*—that is the impulse to undermine the hitherto dominating moral comfort of reacting to scenes of cruelty from partisan perspectives. Beholders of the *Desastres* were obliged to face, for the historically first time perhaps, the moral failures of protagonists with whom they sided politically. Finally, and unlike the effect of the two allegorical scenes about "Truth Dead" and "Truth Resurrecting" in Goya's *Desastres*, I frankly do feel compelled to life by the beautifully disturbing image of that young and perhaps pregnant woman ("Esto es lo verdadero"), compelled to become part of her world and to find out, through judgment, what the life evoked by this work could be all about.

Lichtenberg too, as we saw earlier, had a clearly practice-oriented perspective regarding questions of judgment, but unlike Diderot he lived to be exposed to Kant's *Third Critique* and the ensuing debates. But instead of philosophically distinguishing among different types of judgment and their respective dimensions, Lichtenberg seems above all to have felt the urge and indeed even the necessity of coming to terms with situations of contingency through the practice of judgment. Not only did he recommend relying more on "great" than on "overly subtle men" in such moments of choice, he also experienced self-doubt as a more productive intellectual premise for judging than certainty:

> Anyone who reflects on the history of philosophy and natural science will find that the greatest discoveries were made by people who regarded as merely probable what others advanced as certain. [. . .] Such a philosophy is all the more to be recommended in that we accumulate our ideas and opinions at a time when our understanding is at its weakest.[103]

While we can see in this statement an affinity with the cumulative dimension of Diderot's judging syntax (as a reaction to uncertainty), Lichtenberg went even further in that direction. For he noted that while our relationship to the world was inevitably "idealistic" (in the sense of even "the belief that representations and sensations are caused by objects outside of us" being "just another representation or idea"), only those among us could be right who "believed that we are not being deceived" by those representations and sensations. For otherwise, he added, we would have neither a point of reference ("a point of measurement") for our judgments, decisions, and actions, nor a basis to deal with persons "who do not themselves reflect very much. When philosophy speaks, it is always compelled to express itself in the language of nonphilosophy."[104]

As Lichtenberg's reflections on the practice of judging were clearly more penetrating than Diderot's, he also managed to be at peace, both for practical and for philosophical reasons, with the situation of ontological groundlessness that never ceased to worry Diderot—never enough though to ultimately prevent him from judging. For Mozart, finally, acts of judgment must have been so deeply inserted into his activities as a virtuoso performer and above all as a composer that they never became accessible to him. An appropriate dimension with which to illustrate this condition is his choice of musical keys, a practice that has been the object of both sophisticated and endless discussion among specialists. Mozart himself, by contrast, hardly ever mentioned keys in the ongoing list of his works.[105] In Wolfgang Hildesheimer's outstanding biography, this question leads back to emotional situations and to an internal logic within the emergence of individual works. He reached the conclusion that for Mozart, the act of composing was "purely technical" and thus separate both from extra-musical dimensions and from the levels of consciousness-based self-reflection.[106] In the few cases where Mozart tried to invent music to suit preexisting texts written by himself, no convergence between the two media can be identified from the outside.[107]

It is thus remarkable—and perhaps even potentially suggestive for our understanding of Diderot—that Hildesheimer describes Mozart as a person who never saw himself as distant from his everyday world and therefore never thought that he needed to "communicate" or to "reveal" anything specific to other people.[108] This may explain why the existing portraits show no similarity to each other, no similarity that would allow us to imagine Mozart as a well-contoured personality. Instead of blaming this lack of convergence among the different portraits on the artists' lack of talent or competence, we should ask whether Mozart, without ever trying to set himself apart from his environment, could have cared at all about presenting a coherent and lasting personal image. In other words: the divergence between the portraits may have reflected—and may still reflect for us—a centrifugal reality (and also a lack of concern about it).

Here we discover yet another interesting affinity with Diderot's remark about having "a hundred faces every day"—except that it would probably never have occurred to Mozart to write from a similarly complex position of self-observation. The two characters converged, however, inasmuch as neither of them particularly wanted to project a coherent image. In different ways and with different degrees of intensity, they both lived their lives as an ongoing confrontation with the world's contingency, which obliged them to constantly engage in acts of judgment. The rhythm of this never-ending sequence transformed their worlds, including their self-images, into spheres of singularities.

———————

By now we have understood why it is so particularly difficult to trace stable discursive and intellectual forms in Diderot's practice of judging. For judging, above all, emerged as a core dimension of living one's life in a world whose face had become a face of contingency. More than by design, reflection, or retrospection, the practice of judgment was processing the contingent world in its ongoing present, which explains why even thinkers capable of writing about it from a philosophical angle, like Lichtenberg, emphasized the need to simply practice judgment as an indispensable function of life. But we have also seen how this practice transformed the contingent world into a world of singularity. Ultimately, the movement towards singularity had to affect even the agents of judgment whose authority and claim to objectivity was thus progressively weakened and undercut. As Diderot's self-critical reactions to his own *Salons* after 1767 have suggested, an awareness of this process and its consequences may have established itself earlier in the case of aesthetic judgment—but was by no means exclusive to it. After all, his conviction of being "a man with a hundred faces" came from Diderot's own everyday experience and not from the artworks, which according to him did not do justice to this condition.

By presenting the world as an assembly of phenomena under the premise of singularity, the practice of judgment contributed to an openness and to an engagement in which authors and thinkers ran the risk of getting lost. They became, to use one of Diderot's metaphors, "unruly hunting dogs" ("chiens de chasse indisciplinés"). Many of the texts about individual artworks in Diderot's *Salons* petered out into details, anecdotes, and digressions from which he did not return to a more focused perspective. The main bonus related to the practice of judging thus came as a surge of energy and as an increase of existential intensity, both of which may have been behind Diderot's early enjoyment of and euphoria over art critical writing as the "best cultural activity of his life."

But he was not yet able to see things this way. Rather than with energy and intensity, he associated his euphoria with a centrifugal "variety of objects and ideas" that ended up turning into frustration for him.

7 | "PROSE OF THE WORLD"

Who Is Denis Diderot (and What Is the Encyclopédie*)?*

NOTHING WAS LESS TYPICAL for Denis Diderot's work than the kind of clear and decided distinctions that make up philosophical systems. If we want to know about his "profile" or his "positions," we need to engage with contours in motion and with movements of thought that lack both predictable direction and unequivocal conclusions. That Rameau's nephew (the protagonist marked by the text with the pronoun "Lui") turns out to be a truly thought-provoking presence in the conversation with "Moi" (a role supposed to be close to that of the author, as a *philosophe*) happens as the result of a surprising and potentially "bizarre" (as Diderot might have said) reading process. Numerous details and passages in *Jacques le fataliste*, I am fully aware, continue to stand against my suggestion that we sympathize with the Master's cynical allure and crisp agency rather than with his servant's consistent determinism. No hermeneutically coherent argument will ever be able to prove that the mathematician's fever dream and the erotically driven conversation of Mme de Lespinasse with Dr. Bordeu provide the decisive intellectual energy for the discussion of Materialism in *Le rêve de d'Alembert*. And the discourses making up Diderot's *Salons* leave us uncertain about his personal appreciation of many individual paintings and sculptures.

But who then was Denis Diderot in his lively and intense presence—acknowledging that the presence of an author remote from us by two and a half centuries can only emerge from his texts, and that the texts in question give us no contours or positions? Who is Diderot, with the present tense reminding us of the intuition that an affinity may exist between his intellectual style and some of our worries and inclinations in the early third millennium? Such questions bring back what I consider to be the basic—and paradoxical—crux of Diderot criticism. On the one hand, his very lack of a conceptual "system" or well-rounded intellectual "identity" most likely explain why he has always been a readers' favorite among the great French *philosophes* of the eighteenth century; on the other hand, and unlike in the cases of Voltaire or Rousseau, this lack has also made it impossible for Diderot's work to fulfill particular functions or to address particular questions in historically specific situations. His texts have provoked an infinity of commentaries and studies on microscopic problems; there are several well-documented and even well-written biographies; but we have no comprehensive concepts with which to describe Diderot, no well-rounded image, no coherent *Anschauung*. Herbert Dieckmann, arguably the most eminent specialist within a good hundred years of Diderot scholarship, wisely held back from such comprehensive statements and interpretations; and even the great Jean Starobinski must have felt the impossibility of living up to the task when, in the memorial year of 2013, he ended up republishing his superb Diderot essays as a collection—rather than bringing them together in a new monograph.

———————

And yet again, who was Denis Diderot? In our contemporary language, such a question presupposes a distinction between personal (individual) identity and public (social) identity, a distinction that we can emphasize and make visible by reserving the pronoun "Who" for personal identity (that is for all those—often difficult to distinguish—features that seem to make somebody unique), while we connect the word "What" with public or social identity (that is with somebody's perception in the public space and with the image that she or he is able to project). We can then say that, with very different results, Voltaire and Rousseau lived along the distinction between personal and public identity, while this description does not quite apply to Diderot who, just to mention one example, never wrote apparently "personal" letters with the intention of seeing them circulating "publicly" and being recited among admiring readers (as above all Voltaire so often and so masterfully did).

As for Diderot's "personal" identity, I have mentioned several times his insistence on the strong divergence between different existing portraits of his, a divergence that he wanted to associate with a specific personal fluidity or even agility, depending on different environments and impossible to interpret as the articulation of one true self: "In one day I would have a hundred different faces, depending on what affected me. I was serene, sad, dreamy, tender, violent, passionate, enthusiastic."[1] Even more surprisingly, Diderot saw—and sometimes was worried about—a similar fluidity in his public image and perception. He felt proud of his reputation as an indispensable presence in the world of the Parisian Salons and liked to associate this status, in a twice-removed metonymy, with the specific sound of his voice, for which he used the word *ramage*, normally applied to the voices of birds.[2] In a letter to Mme Necker, however, written on September 6, 1774, upon his return from the stay in Saint Petersburg, he expressed concern that in the "aviary" (*volière*) of Parisian socialites this talent (i.e. "his already not so melodious sound") might appear affected by the impact of the "hard and barbaric bird voices" that he had heard in the meantime:

> I will soon be returning to the aviary from which I escaped fifteen months ago. Won't my already not-so-melodious *ramage* have suffered under the hard and barbaric voices of the Moravian, Helvetic, Belgian, Prussian, Polish, Slavonian, and Russian birds with which I have been living?[3]

Besides the fluidity[4] on both the "personal" and the "public" side, there were several other features of this form of identity or self-reference that were remarkable—and most likely rather eccentric than typical for Diderot's time and social world. In both of its potential dimensions, his identity seemed inseparably related to the body, first through a face that expressed his state of mind at each moment (but was not the articulation of a true inner self) and then through the sound of a voice that assigned him a specific role in the social world. The rhythms of change in both dimensions appear to have been quite different, as Diderot spoke of "a hundred faces per day" on the personal side and of several months of exposure to new social environments having perhaps transformed the sound of his "voice." That both sides of his identity indeed included a bodily dimension made it impossible for either of them to become completely external of the other side and observe it, which meant above all that from the angle of his personal identity he did not quite succeed in observing (in being reflexive of) his social identity. Finally, for a person experiencing himself as materially embodied in both identity dimensions, it did not seem plausible to occupy positions outside the material world.

Variation and fluidity were not only characteristic for the form of Diderot's identity; they also permeated his social life, his work, and his psyche. There was no single figure or friend that he considered more central or more beloved than all others (except for, and probably due to the physical matrix of their bonds, his daughter Angélique and, late in life, his grandchildren). Intense erotic moments certainly belonged to his existence but hardly ever turned into obsession (despite his being the author of some earlier narratives that we can classify as "pornographic" by eighteenth-century standards). After tender beginnings, his mutual affection with Sophie Volland stayed alive in their exchange of letters for two and a half decades, due to their shared intellectual passions, and it never seriously interfered with the mutual ill-humouredness that kept Diderot and his wife Anne-Toinette attached to each other. Although he had a great many friends at a fond half-distance, in different places and on a variety of social levels, Diderot invested whatever was required to prevent such relationships from falling apart. As he believed he was shy, the thought of losing friends must have been unbearable to him. And yet he was also notoriously tactless whenever he got carried away by the spirited rhythms of his writing—and perhaps by trusting his charms too much. One of his greatest admirers, Catherine of Russia, had a small table placed to separate herself from Diderot because he had frequently touched her arms and her thighs during their long conversations.

With the one exception of the voyage to Russia (and there were always "exceptions" in this life), Diderot permanently inhabited the space of Paris and its periphery, interrupted by occasional visits to his provincial hometown Langres. In Paris, however, he talked, corresponded, and worked with a large number of fellow intellectuals (not only due to the business of the *Encyclopédie*), participated in multiple circles of sociability, and had a curiosity for the world of different professions (who else could have referred to the "gardener of the Opéra Comique" as if he were a friend?). But Diderot was not good at pursuing long-term purposes and plans (the monumental exception being his achievement of securing the realization of the *Encyclopédie*). Wishes and suggestions from friends easily derailed him ("on fait de moi ce qu'on veut") as he enjoyed pursuing the flow of his associations. He thus spent more than a decade, with floating changes in purpose and complexity, writing *Le neveu de Rameau*, whereas it took him just a few days to finish *Le rêve de d'Alembert*, a treatise of similar length. Not only was none of his texts free of contradictions and passages that seemed put together all too carelessly; above all, he had a hard time inventing structurally convincing conclusions and thus often left his readers with the impression of incompletion and of an impatience that he likely never felt himself.

There was no center nor clear hierarchy in Diderot's intellectual interests and projects, and this lack may have contributed to some astonishing changes in the reception history of his books. If his role as editor of the *Encyclopédie* filled the center of his active life and must of course count as Diderot's major contribution to the process of Enlightenment, it also was an occupation that bundled contributions on endlessly different topics and in endlessly different styles, often transforming them into centrifugal intellectual impulses. At the same time and as if in compensation for his lack of conceptual clarity, Diderot was fascinated by nuance and detail, as Hegel admiringly stated several times. While he enjoyed, as we have seen for example in his *Salons* from the mid-1760s, inventing narratives about himself, the forms of systematic self-observation, self-reflection, and self-analysis did not belong to his intellectual repertoire; and while his political concepts and projects were far from innovative or even revolutionary, his incessant judging practice made phenomena appear in their singularity, which gave him an aura of openness to the world, tolerance, and generosity. More than conceptual precision or argumentative complexity, the production and activation of rhythm and energy as a source of life seem to have been the vanishing points for all of Diderot's intellectual activities.

"Metabolism" may be the one concept and metaphor that best captures his intellectual style.[5] Not only because, faithful to the fascination with Materialism, Diderot thought of his embodied existence as being part of and in exchange with nature as its environment—so that many objects of the world, above all savory food, heavy wine, and music, stimulated his imagination, his desire and his will to physically appropriate them; at the same time, the etymology of the word "metabolism" and its specific use in biology can open further pertinent intellectual connotations for us. Quite literally, the supposed Ancient Greek meaning of the concept is to "throw across" (in German *hinüberwerfen*) and seems to refer to an act of throwing that does not care about where the thrown object will go—as opposed to the etymologically similar word "project" (going back to Latin *pro-iecere*) that stands for a well-circumscribed image or concept of a future situation to whose realization one wants to actively contribute. In metabolism, by contrast, deliberate choice occurs neither in the absorption of the environment through the body nor in what the body processes and returns to the environment. Likewise, as we have seen, Diderot was both enthusiastic and careless in his exchange and communication with the intellectual environment of his time and of the past. He assimilated whatever ideas or images found his attention, worked on them, and gave them back to the world in his texts, changed but without any specific shape or determination. Similar to the biochemical operations of metabolism also, it was often unclear which of the elements, processed and returned, "belonged" to him or to the authors whom he had read. In other words: Diderot's metabolic relationship with the world was far from being subject-centered and was therefore particularly generous indeed.

The concept and image of "metabolism" can also help us go beyond the standard—and descriptively empty—reference to the *Encyclopédie ou dictionnaire raisonné des arts et des métiers* as a life-culminating achievement facilitated by nothing but an unusual investment of working time. Half a century ago, Jacques Proust already argued against this view of Diderot's twenty-five years spent in charge of this project, from 1747 to 1772:

> How many *Neveux*, how many *Fatalistes*, how many tales like *Is He Good? Is He Bad?* has posterity been denied because of that quarter-century spent on effectively mercenary tasks? This time could very well be called a long, sad, grey interlude. So we try and save Diderot as best we can: we hold him up as an example of abnegation, and especially of courage, because he needed courage to keep the enterprise going as he did, at times

alone against all, risking his freedom in the process. In reality, things were not so simple.[6]

Sheer "abnegation" and exclusive concentration on a single project for such a long time would indeed not have suited Diderot's personality and intellectual style. Proust therefore insisted that it was the Chevalier de Jaucourt who served as "factotum" for the enterprise, with a contribution of about 17,000 among the total of 71,818 articles, which implies that at times Jaucourt finished four texts per day, sacrificing "his time, his fortune, and his talent (if he ever had one)." As a co-editor and, after d'Alembert's withdrawal in 1758, as sole director, Diderot had to take care of the conversations and correspondence with around four hundred authors that he had recruited. In some (probably not too many) cases, he also edited or even rewrote texts that did not fulfill the expectations.

Regarding the "courage" required for this task, and unlike with his own individual publications, his challenge was above all to use, against interventions from the official state censorship system and from the Church, the protection of highly placed supporters, among whom Mme de Pompadour of all people proved to be the most reliable. He also had to decide on strategic moves in order to minimize potentials for conflict, for example by replacing Paris, the place of publication mentioned in the first seven volumes, with Neuchâtel (today in Switzerland, then a municipality under Prussian protection) for the remaining volumes that ended up being printed and sold between 1765 and 1772. As there was reason to believe that under this new condition the authorities in power were ready to ignore the continuation of the work (which was a covert act of tolerance), we can say that diplomatic intelligence, good social connections, and, above all, restraint from overreaction in the face of moments of crisis were more vital for Diderot than the so-often-invoked "courage."

The intellectual level of his involvement first became visible in the authorship of the "Prospectus" that circulated for promotional reasons beginning October 1750 (the article "Encyclopédie" is an extended version of this text) and, later on and even more importantly, in his commitment, both as an editor and as an author, to the entries covering "The mechanical arts / Les arts mécaniques" (the title of the *Encyclopédie* refers to them as "trades (or crafts) / métiers"). Along with ample information about the content and some commonplaces, by Enlightenment standards, about the possible functions of the project, the "Prospectus" presented and discussed the basic structure of the *Encyclopédie* as an epistemological problem. To answer the—first of all—practical question of how the totality of knowledge available could and should be structured, the editors had adopted the "tree of knowledge" from their original model and inspiration, that is, from Ephraim Chambers's English *Cyclopedia*, first published in 1728, which had used a historical principle of knowledge differentiation as a blueprint for its basic outline and structure. Truly astonishing, however, and similar to the spirit of some conversations in *Jacques le fataliste*, was Diderot's fundamental skepticism regarding the possibility of this (or any other) structure of knowledge corresponding to an inherent order of the world. He seemed fully aware of how impossible it was to avoid the arbitrary character of such a project:

> The tree of human knowledge could have been constructed in several different ways: by mapping the different parts of our knowledge either onto the various faculties of the soul, or onto the things that are the objects of this knowledge. But as choices became increasingly arbitrary, the harder it was to make editorial decisions. And oh! how much arbitrariness did we encounter! Nature offers us nothing but individual things, infinite in number, with no fixed or definite divisions. All objects follow one another by imperceptible shadings. In this sea of objects that surrounds us, certain things might be visible, like rocks that seemingly pierce the surface and dominate everything else. But this is an advantage they owe solely to particular systems of thought, to tenuous conventions, to certain events that are extraneous to the physical arrangement of things and to the true principles of philosophy.[7]

Three concepts in this quote are specifically important. In the first place, Diderot uses the word "arbitrary" with the intention of pointing to a fundamental condition shared by all structures of knowledge that one can possibly come up with—and thereby denies the existence of any necessary structure(s) of the world. Secondly, he insists that nature will only offer us things in their singularity ("Nature offers us nothing but individual things" / "La nature ne nous offre que des choses particulières"). Finally, he speaks of a "sea of objects" around us and thus adds a further metaphor to the repertoire of expressions highlighting the world's complexity.

Astonishingly and in conformity with his Materialist atheism, Diderot does not make any concession to the possibility of a structure inherent to the world seen as divine creation. Theology, defined as "science (or knowledge) of God / science de Dieu," only appears next to other disciplines of knowledge, without any attribution of superiority thanks to revelation.[8] And while in his later article "Encyclopédie," published in 1755, he seems more concerned with the rhythms of knowledge growth, none of them leads to the idea or the image of an ultimate, transcendentally based certainty:

> We do not know how far a given man can go. We know even less how far the human race would go, what it would be capable of, if it were not halted in its progress. But revolutions are necessary; there have always been revolutions, and always will be.[9]

Now while this epistemological discussion that Diderot opened up in his presentation of the *Encyclopédie*—the discussion about systematizing the assembled knowledge and about the future conditions of its continued production— does fulfill our historicist expectations of an "advanced" eighteenth-century thinker, I believe that his decisive innovation, underestimated until today, came with the impulse, both editorial and documentary, towards "les arts mécaniques," that is, towards those worlds of practice-oriented production of knowledge that, at least to a certain degree, structurally overlap with our present-day concept of "engineering." As the "Prospectus" shows, Diderot was fully aware of the intellectual status of his initiative and the subsequent logistical problems:

> Such is the substance of what we had to set forth for the public concerning the sciences and the fine arts. The section on the mechanical arts required no fewer details and no less care. Never, perhaps, has there been such an accumulation of difficulties, and, to conquer them, so little help from books. Too much has been written on the sciences; not enough has been written well on the mechanical arts. For what is the scanty information available in the various authors, compared to the extent and richness of the subject?[10]

After explaining, from different perspectives, the shortcomings of previous efforts in this direction, Diderot very clearly highlighted his two specific interests: "the operations of the artisans and the description of their machines."[11] Beside his texts on the "mechanical arts," the initiative also provided the core of the visual program for the eleven volumes, with 3,129 illustrations

(*Planches*), that were printed between 1762 and 1772 and had been, in spite of their later publication date, part of the project from its beginning. The *Planches* constituted a truly revolutionary type of "description" for the then existing crafts and, as their reference to the workers as "artists" shows, they stood at the beginning of multiple changes in their social and epistemological status during the nineteenth century.

Not unlike his reaction to Grimm's commission to cover the Salons for the *Correspondance littéraire*, when Diderot started visiting the studios of numerous painters and sculptors in Paris, he followed his impulse to be in immediate contact with a world that had hitherto been unknown to him:

> Thus everything impelled us to go directly to the workers. We approached the most capable of them in Paris and in the realm. We took the trouble of going into their shops, of questioning them, of writing at their dictation, of developing their thoughts and of drawing therefrom the terms peculiar to their professions, of setting up tables of these terms and of working out definitions for them, of conversing with those from whom we obtained memoranda . . .[12]

In every sentence of the respective passages throughout the "Prospectus" we can feel the pathos of an initiative that truly mattered to Diderot and to which, due to his own intellectual practice and without any condescension, he was convinced he could make an authentic contribution:

> We have seen some workers who have worked for forty years without knowing anything about their machines. With them, it was necessary to exercise the function in which Socrates gloried, the painful and delicate function of being midwife of the mind, *obstetrix animorum*.[13]

This intersection between, on the one hand, the practice of the "workers" who lacked conceptual knowledge and, on the other hand, his own discursive competence that lacked a physical connection with the world of the "mechanical arts" must have shaped the specific style and the aesthetic quality of the *Planches*, where utmost precision and countless details appear immersed in a space of sober luminosity. Diderot once again experienced one of his initiatives and its consequences as a metabolic encounter with the objects of the world in their singularity:[14]

There are some trades so unusual and some operations so subtle that unless one does the work oneself, unless one operates a machine with one's own hands, and sees the work being created under one's own eyes, it is difficult to speak of it with precision. Thus, several times we had to get possession of the machines, to construct them, and to put a hand to the work. It was necessary to become apprentices, so to speak, and to manufacture some poor objects ourselves in order to learn how to teach others the way good specimens are made. It is thus that we have become convinced of men's ignorance concerning most of the objects in this life and of the difficulty of overcoming that ignorance.[15]

He did not, however, go beyond the beautiful paradox of "poor objects" (produced by *philosophes*) that would teach individual "others" (that is, practically competent craftsmen) how to produce really good ones. Engaging in the discourse of knowledge transfer, available since the advent of the mercantilist economy, to try to add to the practical quality and market value of emerging industrial work at large would probably have been too much of a long-term strategy for Diderot.

And yet I agree with Jacques Proust's observation that it was through his insistence on the inclusion of the "mechanical arts" in the program and in the active work of the *Encyclopédie* that Diderot "sketched out the broad lines" of an innovative approach to politics,[16] rather than through his texts on explicitly political concepts.[17] In entries like "Droit naturel" ("Natural Rights"), "Pouvoir" ("Power"), "Puissance" ("Power"/"Force"/"Might"), "Représentants" ("Representatives"), or "Souverains" ("Sovereigns"), he unfolded a conception, conventional among Enlightenment authors and their readers, of politics as a contractual relationship, based on mutual goodwill between monarchs and their subjects. The *Planches* and the articles on the "mechanical arts," by contrast, were not only part of a departure towards nineteenth-century industrialization and bourgeoisie, we can also read them (and the attitude that served as their matrix) as an early stage of a style of knowledge production and epistemology that was "hands-on" enough to leave the subject/object paradigm behind, world-open enough to conceive of itself as an inner-worldly form of practice, and successful enough to become revolutionary in a nontraditionally political way.

But I would like to resist the obvious temptation (and plausible option) to interpret and present Diderot as a precursor of "engineering," of the ensemble of practices that has, during the past decades, overcome all sorts of prejudice and condescension formerly assigned to keeping it on a modest level, at best, in the intellectual and academic world. For one thing, he was far away from all early forms of historical thinking, especially from the mentality of "progress" as it began to take shape towards the end of his lifetime, and he had no ambition therefore to "anticipate" anything at all. At the same time and on similar grounds, we should avoid thinking of possible affinities between Diderot's intellectual style and some challenges of our twenty-first-century present as being mediated by a "genealogical continuity" or, even more inadequately, by the trajectory of a "historical development."

For reasons of principle I cannot imagine a true structural similarity between our lifetime and Diderot's. A potential comparison between the two situations would have to take place on a level of typological abstraction that would make it irrelevant for our purposes. I will also refrain from discussing convergences between possible epistemological configurations belonging to the eighteenth and to the twenty-first centuries which, among other problems, would oblige us to go back to the question of whether something like a coherent epistemology underlying Diderot's works really existed. It will be more appropriate and more productive to ask, as an exercise and experiment in historical imagination, how "somebody like Denis Diderot," with his "metabolic" intellectual style and with his "prose of the world" attitude, might behave under the daily intellectual challenges of our present—and I mean the present of the no longer so early twenty-first century.[18] Out of the potentially endless and, it appears, unavoidably tedious descriptions of this global[19] present, I will only mention two features. Compared to the not so remote memory of our everyday as a "field of contingency"—that is, as a sphere of choice and freedom surrounded by the horizon of "necessity" or "fate" (conditions of life and events that we cannot determine) and by the horizon of "impossibility" (conditions of life that we may imagine and sometimes desire, without them being in human reach)—many of us now experience the everyday as a "universe of contingency," where nothing remains necessary and nothing appears impossible. This implies a beautiful conquest and increase of freedom but also the burden of being exposed to a permanent situation of overwhelming complexity. Secondly, this universe of contingency has become our new present, a present that, counter to the present of the historical worldview described by Baudelaire as an "imperceptibly short moment of transition," tends to contain everything, not only all memory about and knowledge accumulated in the past (and now preserved and kept available by electronic technology) but also a future apparently occupied by dangers that seem to be moving towards us (including the danger of a self-inflicted end of the life of humankind on our planet).

Somebody like Denis Diderot would, above all, necessarily look like an alien in our world, like a Kasper Hauser perhaps but without the transient charm of Hauser's youth. And contemporary intellectuals who strive to be either "political" or "professional" might find his reactions and opinions either scandalous or not worth discussing. While they try their subjective and collective best at keeping the complexity of our universe of contingency under the protective lid of political correctness, with its set of "ethically" argued norms of behavior and its rules of speech control ("trigger warnings"), a reborn Diderot might indulge in the same complexity and perhaps even find a mildly ironic sympathy for those contemporaries who react to it with a longing for old-fashioned, "fundamentalist" values and for apparently "strong" leaders to follow. If such a twenty-first century Diderot could miraculously survive all attempts at marginalizing, excluding, and even silencing his possible enthusiasm for all new phenomena and potentials of thinking, he might surprise the peers of his future (our present) with a staccato of deliberately arbitrary judgments that produced a worldview of singularity, nuance, and generous differentiation, instead of bracketing what cannot be labeled as "globally human."

For sheer lack of specialization and any institutionally confirmed claim to competence, Diderot-Hauser would not find employment on the job market today, especially in academia, where hybrid transitions and oscillations between different discourses and styles of thinking are always praised but create confusion because they make it impossible to assign an applicant to one or the other department and discipline. Tenure committees and search committees would quickly diagnose his metabolic way of processing knowledge as a deplorable "lack of clearly stated purpose." As for his private life, and I imagine that this would happen both in the academic world and the nonacademic middle class, his lifelong attachment to a religiously orthodox wife would trigger as much frowning as his extramarital love relationship that sought neither sexual fulfillment nor the existential excitement of erotic "experiments." For lack of sustained self-observation and self-reflection, Diderot would not help appearing problematically pre-Freudian and without any kind of well-circumscribed "identity," while his tactlessness would get him into more serious, perhaps even legal trouble than in the late eighteenth century. His insatiable search for energy, finally, would have to be diagnosed as a self-destructive addiction.

At this point, I interrupt the play in historical (and also anachronistic) imagination—before it begins to project the impression of using Diderot for an embittered satire of present-day life. My true intention was of course to suggest, by inventing some contemporary situations in which Diderot would look utterly inadequate, that a specific affinity exists between his style, energy, and rhythm and some both intellectual and existential needs of the early twenty-first century. Diderot's work certainly offers us no practically or theoretically relevant answers, not a single one; but as an example from the past his figure may have the potential to remind us (or to help us re-imagine) what an intellectual can at best be within society today. This is not somebody who has, finds, and develops solutions to follow. More than ever, an intellectual today should be a thinker who provides others' minds with excess energy and with possibilities of arguing and imagining in ways that nobody has done or dares to do—especially in an environment whose specific challenges threaten to produce a cast of mental paralysis.

———

Hegel, as we saw in the second chapter of this book, felt a quite literal fasci-nation with Diderot's thinking and writing. Over the two and a half decades during which his work emerged, he frequently turned to texts by Diderot, texts of different content and flavor. Not because he had a stable place or a recurrent function for them in his philosophical system but because he must have sensed—rather than identified and embraced—the presence of a relation to the world that his own thought had a hard time accounting for and which therefore obliged him to make his concepts and arguments more complex.

"Prose of the world" served as the one notion from Hegel's repertoire under which he subsumed Diderot and his own pleasure in reading him:

> This is the prose of the world, as it appears to the consciousness both of the individual himself and of others:—a world of finitude and mutability, of entanglement in the relative, of the pressure of necessity from which the individual is in no position to withdraw. For every isolated living thing remains caught in the contradiction of being itself in its own eyes this shut-in unit and yet of being nevertheless dependent on something else, and the struggle to resolve this contradiction does not get beyond an attempt and the continuation of this eternal war.[20]

I have tried to illustrate how "finitude," "mutability," "entanglement in the relative," "no position to withdraw," or "isolated living things" are concepts that indeed capture Diderot's style—precisely because they are not well-rounded and thus correspond to the energy and obsessions, the unpredictability, the nuance, and the individualizing focus of his writing. In the best possible case, our analysis of some of Diderot's texts should have filled Hegel's description with more *Anschauung*. Likewise, we can now come back to what Hegel calls "ordinary thinking" as a description of the practice through which Diderot transformed the contingent world he was coping with into horizons of objects in their singularity:

> *Ordinary thinking* has nothing to do with an inner connection, with the essence of things, with reasons, causes, aims etc., but is content to take what is and happens as just this bare individual thing or event, i.e. as something accidental and meaningless. In this case there is nothing of the Understanding's dissection of that living unity in which the poetic vision keeps together the indwelling reason of things and their expression and existence; but what is missing is insight into this rationality and significance of things which therefore are without substance for this ordinary thinking and can make no further claim on a rational interest. In that event the Understanding's view of the world and its relations as connected by certain categories is exchanged for a mere view of a world of successive or juxtaposed accidents which may have a great range of external life but which is totally unable to satisfy the deeper need of reason.[21]

Hegel's ambiguity in relation to a form of intellectual practice both so alien and so fascinating to him becomes visible in the "great range of external life" that he concedes to "ordinary thinking" as a style that is otherwise judged as "totally unable to satisfy the deeper need of reason"—and we can imagine that Diderot might not have been completely unhappy with such a characterization. For what Hegel evokes and criticizes as "a mere view of a world of successive or juxtaposed accidents which may have a great range of external life [but are] totally unable to satisfy the deeper need of reasons" strikes me as an adequate characterization of Diderot's metabolic intellectual style and a changed, but not necessarily intellectually changed, relation to the world as its result.

Even more importantly and paradoxically, however, it was Hegel's inability to ultimately pinpoint what attracted him in Diderot's texts and, also, his subsequent reactions to them under a premise of productive negativity that helped us draw a first outline of "prose of the world" as a possible—and certainly vague—epistemological matrix underlying the work of Diderot and of some other eminent protagonists in the culture of his time. It is as if all of them both inadvertently and systematically negated some of Hegel's central negations. If the "subject," as Hegel's concept of human self-reference, was exclusively spiritual in most cases (with some notable exceptions, above all in his *Enzyklopädie*), we have seen how it always and invariably included the body and its sentiments in Diderot's view; if Hegelian history processed the world's complexity into "necessary" forms of progress or decadence, the world remained overwhelmingly—and sometimes joyfully—complex for Diderot; if the spirit and the material world were originally separated by Hegel's master narrative to finally come together in a self-reflexive union, Diderot's Materialism tried to develop a monist view that did not allow for such ontological divergence; and if judgment for Hegel was a tool to discover regularities and "laws" in the interactions between spirit and matter, it served Diderot as a permanent practice that opened up the world as a universe of phenomena in their concreteness and singularity.

Profoundly different from Hegel in this respect too, Diderot did not care about long-term, overarching "programs" or intellectual and political "positions." If Hegel and the style of thinking to which he gave definitive form became decisive for how we still today understand the shaping influence of the "Enlightenment" on the "process of Modernity," the place we can retrospectively assign to Diderot and his work has to be at the periphery of the Enlightenment (and of course I imply that this has been an intellectually productive position ever since Diderot's times). He was connected to the authors and to the more central thinkers of the Enlightenment, but the scholarly attempt to and habit of subsuming him under the concept of an "Enlightenment thinker" has bracketed and neutralized what may be most appealing about his work. Perhaps the time has come to negate this negation—without of course bracketing Hegel and his legacy. It may indeed be a productive privilege of the periphery to do away with institutional brackets and limitations altogether, that is, not to move on to an attack on "mainstream thought."

8 | "JE NE FAIS RIEN"

The Last Three Years of Diderot's Life

ON JULY 28, 1781, three years and three days before he died, Denis Diderot wrote a letter to Angélique de Vandeul, his beloved only child[1]—and this text would become the last document in which he spoke about himself.[2] Angélique's moral and aesthetic education in alignment with the ideals of the Enlightenment had mattered so much to her father that he constantly feared exposing her to conflicts with her mother's strictly religious values.[3] In September 1772, at age nineteen, Angélique had married Abel-François-Nicolas Caroillon de Vandeul, the son of a well-to-do family from Langres, thanks to a large dowry that Diderot had tenaciously negotiated with his future son-in-law and that the stipend from Catherine the Great had made possible. Soon the new father-in-law used his contacts in the political and business world of Paris to promote Angélique's husband, and by 1781 Abel was well on his way towards considerable wealth in the emerging iron industry.[4] The couple had two children, continued to commute between Langres and Paris, and enjoyed a reasonably comfortable life by the standards of their social class and historical time.

The opening words of Diderot's last personal letter show that it was prompted by a loving request from Angélique and that her father was struggling to live up to her expectations:

My child, I don't know if you take great pleasure in reading what I write, but you do know that writing has become an ordeal for me, and yet this doesn't prevent you from demanding one more of my letters. This is what one might call sheer force of character, and clearly preferring oneself over another.[5]

Line by line we get the impression that casual topics and the flow of his prose no longer came easily to Diderot and that he was painfully aware of it. At some point he wrote about how his social connections were "dissolving"— and that he was not unhappy about it: "It is with some satisfaction that I see all my social connections dissolving."[6] But Angélique, he added, would not lose anything from this change: "Vous n'y perdrez pas." The openness to the world that had entertained, nourished, and energized Denis Diderot for so many years was now closing down to a narrow focus on his family, and he felt resigned to the process.

Counter to what Angélique had assumed, no new interests and projects brightened his life: "You ask if I'm working in moderation? I'm not doing anything,"[7] he wrote. In this situation, like many old people, Diderot filled his time by reading novels, discovered that they were good at dispelling bad moods (*vapeurs*), and therefore decided to "provide" regular novel readings to his wife. He now spent most of the day with her—and seemed to find her less annoying than during the forty previous years:

I give her three doses of *Gil Blas* every day: one in the morning, one in the afternoon, and one in the evening. When we've finished *Gil Blas*, we'll take up *The Devil upon Two Sticks*, *The Bachelor of Salamanca*, and other gay books of the sort. Several hundred such readings over several years will end up curing her. If I were absolutely certain of success, this chore wouldn't seem hard at all. What is satisfying is that she regales every visitor she receives with whatever she has retained from these readings; and conversation doubles the effectiveness of the treatment. I'd always thought of novels as frivolous things, but I've finally discovered that they're good at dispelling bad moods.[8]

But talking about novels did not quite spark up the letter, and so Diderot closed with another dry reference to his wife, who had turned to preparing jellies of currant and apricot for Angélique's family and wanted him to pay for the sugar. But above all he was relieved to have filled up several pages:

Your mother is making you currant and apricot jellies. She was given the fruit, and she makes me pay for the sugar. For a man who despairs at writing responses, here's a sufficiently long one.[9]

A good two years earlier, from Sèvres, where he liked to spend the springtime in the country house of his friend, the jeweler Belle,[10] Diderot had still been writing to Angélique in a very different tone, with the warmth of paternal affection and with a melancholia about the distance that separated him from his daughter and grandchildren:

> Your absence made the city sad and the countryside beautiful, especially when the sun would melt in the water, and the meadow would come close to disappearing between the two arms of the Seine, just beneath our terrace. I raged, as you do, against how consistently good the weather was. At night, it often seemed I could hear the leaves on the trees trembling under raindrops. I would get out of bed in my nightshirt, and seeing only a starry sky, or a beautifully purple horizon, I would get back under the covers and feel saddened by what the others would find enchanting when they awoke. And thus I would conclude that a good father is often a very bad man, and at the bottom of my heart, I secretly carried this honest, tender, and human sentiment: let all others perish, so long as my children prosper. And yet I am persuaded that, in the case of one's children, the less we judge them, the more we love them.[11]

These may not be the most stylistically brilliant sentences about a landscape and a sentiment triggered that Diderot ever composed, but they are quite exuberant in their detailed description of the fluid contiguity between rain, colors, and complex emotions—and thus produce an impression of liveliness, which only a few months later he was no longer able to evoke. Rather than just stating facts about her activities, it had also been his habit to chat with friendly condescension about Angélique's mother, as in the same letter from Sèvres:

> I almost forgot to tell you about the two great misfortunes that befell Madame Diderot. That ingrate Bibi flew off, and the treacherous Collet—a tom who's married to Colette the cat—maimed one of her canaries and skinned the back of her female canary with his claws. There is no perfect happiness in this world.[12]

Above all, in the letter from Sèvres, Diderot still talked fondly and with some self-irony about his grandchildren and sent greetings to them and their father—whereas in the letter of July 1781 they would all remain unmentioned:

> Embrace Caroillon for me; I love your little children madly, even though they think of me as ill-bred, ever since I was unable to tell them where Charlemagne died. Be gentle with their little brains and their delicate chests, and don't stuff either their heads or their bellies unnecessarily.[13]

What, then, happened to Denis Diderot between May 1779 and July 1781? These must have been the years when a progressive deterioration of his health due to dropsy and emphysema[14] undercut and even dissolved his exceptional gift of transforming every contact with the material world into energy and intensity of life. He most likely had become a man who started breathing heavily and had to halt after each few hundred yards of walking. He also complained about no longer being able to concentrate at night and work by the light of a candle. And thanks to having acquired an expert knowledge regarding the most recent medical insights and discoveries of his time,[15] Diderot had fewer illusions[16] about death being immanent than his friends and probably even his doctors.

How did his life change once he had lost the unique energy that had formerly turned him towards the world in permanent enjoyment? How did he imagine dying? Aside from a constantly reiterated reliance on posterity and future readers being able to fully appreciate and redeem his work, a rhetorical figure that strikes me as quite conventional,[17] Diderot neither avoided nor indulged in speaking about his death. Perhaps he also remembered some earlier Materialistic discussions that had problematized the concept in question, drawing some serenity from them:

> Alive, I act and react as a mass . . . dead, I act and react as separate molecules . . . Don't I die, then? Well, not in that sense, neither I nor anything else . . . To be born, to live and to die is merely to change forms . . . And what does one form matter more than any other?[18]

We do know from the testimony of numerous friends that Diderot was hoping for death "to come suddenly" (he spoke of "*une mort subite*"), without long anticipation, physical suffering, and, above all, without time for his wife to call a priest for the last rites.[19] To imagine his own death as "sudden" must have added a new layer to the existential dimension of contingency that so fascinated Diderot. But while such thoughts did not seem to bother him much, his family and friends hesitated to let him know about the death of beloved ones. He may never have known about Sophie Volland's death on February 22, 1784,[20] and the Langres branch of the family decided not to notify him when his granddaughter Marie-Anne de Vandeul passed on March 15 of the same year.

What changed Diderot's behavior and, we may say, even his values more profoundly than any reflections on death was the progressive vanishing of his energy—that probably affected his carefreeness. For the first time since Catherine the Great had secured the economic basis of his existence, Diderot again cared about the publication (in 1782)[21] and success of a text, more precisely that of his last original work, an essay entitled "Sur les règnes de Claude and de Néron" ("On the reigns of Claudius and Nero") and dedicated to Seneca, whose Stoicism he admired.[22] Disappointed by the ambivalent (or worse) reactions, Diderot then started thinking about the publication of his complete works. But he never got beyond some preparatory financial initiatives, asking his friends to pay him back money that he had lent them, thus belying his formerly legendary generosity:[23]

> Listen, my friend. I am working on an edition of my complete works. I have four copyists who cost me almost 120 livres a month. I am exhausted, and I am begging you to come to my assistance. You owe me 349 livres. If you can repay this sum without any inconvenience, so much the better; if it is an inconvenience to you, so be it.[24]

At the same time, and unlike his publicly known habit of being in conversation with many different positions, Diderot became increasingly thin-skinned now in situations of controversy and tension. He accused his friend Grimm, for example, of behaving like "a courtier" because Grimm did not chime in with the public enthusiasm over Raynal's *Histoire des deux Indes*.[25] When, in the late summer of 1781, Diderot received notice from the Scottish Society of Antiquarians that he had been elected an honorary member, he answered in English and blended his expression of gratitude with a bitterness over the treatment that he felt he had received in France during his entire life:

> I should have had the honour of answering you sooner, if I had not been prevented by a disorder more troublesome than painfull, but from which I have little hopes of getting perfectly free. Your letter came very seasonably to make me amends for past suffering, and to give me firmness against those to come. I cannot forget the persecutions I have suffered in my own country; but with that painfull remembrance, I shall place that of the marks of esteem I have receiv'd from foreign nations.[26]

Diderot certainly had multiple reasons to feel resentment towards institutions and certain antagonists in France. But while he had never before made much of it—either for considerations of strategy or due to a natural disposition that worked against paranoia—he quite literally began to feel persecuted during his last years, when he could have enjoyed almost universal respect and admiration.

———————

Without his former vitality, however, there was not much left for Diderot to enjoy, and we can imagine how he permanently and somehow impatiently hoped for death—as a sudden event. On top of all the other changes in his character, he may also have wanted to accelerate the flow of time for the first time in his life. The long-awaited final moment seemed to finally arrive in February 1784, with an acute health crisis that Angélique remembered in detail:

> On the 19th of February 1784, he started violently coughing up blood. "Now it's over," he told me, "we must soon go our separate ways. I am strong, it might take two days, two weeks, two months, a year . . ." I was so accustomed to believing him that not for an instant did I doubt the truth of what he was saying; throughout the course of his illness, I always entered his house trembling, and always left thinking that I would never see him again. [. . .] On the eighth day of his illness, as he was chatting away, his head became troubled: he uttered a nonsensical phrase, understood that it was nonsensical, tried to correct himself and repeated the error. At that moment he stood up: "Apoplexy," he said to me as he looked at himself in the mirror, showing me his mouth that was drooping slightly, and a cold, motionless hand. He went into his bedroom, got into bed, embraced my mother, bade her farewell, embraced me and bade me farewell, told

us where he kept some books that did not belong to him, and stopped speaking. Only he kept his head; the rest of us had lost ours.[27]

But even after this perfectly executed performance of a stoic passing, the moment of death did not arrive. Diderot recovered and regained his appetite—perhaps even too much, as his daughter stated. Only his legs remained "very swollen."[28] This was when his friends and doctors formed the project of asking Catherine the Great to finance a move from the building where Diderot and his family had lived for thirty years, on the fourth floor (with the library one floor higher), to a first-floor location. Her Majesty, in a note from May 19, showed concern, mildly scolded Grimm for not having informed her earlier, and gave instructions to the Russian embassy to look for a new apartment with first-floor access.[29]

A luxury accommodation was found and rented at 39 Rue Richelieu, against mild protests from Grimm and Holbach who worried about the local parish priest being likely to refuse a Christian funeral—the only decent funeral available—for their friend. Diderot, by contrast, surprised everybody when he eagerly returned from Sèvres, moved into the new apartment, and greatly enjoyed it—although he by no means expected to live there for more than just a few days. He gave the impression of having recuperated some energy and grace in the immediate presence of death:

> He desired to leave the countryside and to come live here. He enjoyed his new lodgings for twelve days. Having always lived in a hovel, he now thought himself in a palace. But his body grew weaker by the day. He was sure that the end was imminent; it was impossible to convince him otherwise. And yet he didn't talk about it [. . .]. The day before he died, he was brought a more comfortable bed. The workers had a very hard time setting it up. "My friends," he told them, "you're going to a lot of trouble for a piece of furniture that will only be used for four days."[30]

———————

That evening he entertained some of his friends. Angélique wanted to remember—putting potentially "famous last words" into her father's mouth—that the conversation went about the status of philosophy and that Diderot ended his intellectual life by connecting this "science" to the central premise premise of atheism:

The conversation turned to philosophy, and the different routes that might be taken to arrive at this science. "The first step towards philosophy," he said, "is disbelief." These were the last words I heard him say. It was late, and I left him; I had hoped to see him again.[31]

The next day was Saturday, July 31, 1784.[32] After getting up, Diderot had a conversation with his son-in-law and his doctor and then sat down at the family table for lunch:

> He sat at the table. He ate soup, boiled mutton and some chicory. He took an apricot. My mother wanted to prevent him from eating the fruit. "But what the devil do you think it'll do to me?" He ate it, put his elbow on the table to eat a few cherries in compote, coughed lightly. My mother asked him a question. He kept silent, so she looked up at him: he had ceased to be.[33]

This final moment was vintage Diderot. Long and impatiently awaited, death ended up coming suddenly indeed, as he had hoped. His truly last words began with the straightforwardly secular curse (*que diable!*) he had so frequently used during his life.[34] He also profited from the very last opportunity not to follow the advice of his wife, who was probably speaking from the eighteenth-century belief that sugary fruit was bad for persons with precarious health. Above all, Diderot died while he was eating, in the most elementary metabolic relationship with the material world.

Faithful to his Materialist principles and to his fascination with medicine, he had arranged for an autopsy. There were no surprises:

> My father thought it wise to cut open those who had ceased to exist; he thought such operations useful for the living. More than once had he asked me for this to be done to him, and so it was. His head was as perfect, as well preserved as that of a man of twenty. One of his lungs was filled with water; his heart was two-thirds bigger than others'. His gallbladder was completely dry: it had no more bilious matter, but contained twenty-one stones the smallest of which was as big as a hazelnut.[35]

Diderot seems to have been less obsessed than most of his friends, both fellow atheists and non-orthodox Christian believers in some divine being, with the question of a funeral. But he was well aware how much this mattered to Angélique and to his wife. Things went quite smoothly:

His burial went ahead with only minor difficulties. The *curé* of Saint-Roch sent a priest to keep vigil over his body; he conducted this dreadful ceremony with more pomp than simplicity.[36]

The "pomp" that his daughter refers to consisted in the presence of fifty priests during the religious ceremony on the evening of August 31. Angélique and her husband received and paid a large bill for the service.[37] This may have been the unofficial but customary deal that the parish of Saint-Roch processed for the funeral of an atheist with wealthy relatives. On the other hand, the Vandeuls had more religiously conservative leanings than Diderot's daughter ever wanted her father to know. For all of her candid admiration and love, there was also a slightly hypocritical layer in Angélique's behavior and in the strangely secular tone of her *Mémoires*.

After all, education never perfectly corresponds to the values it wants to convey—and thus turns into "prose of the world." Diderot would not have been surprised to experience, once again and beyond death, the limits of his agency. But caring less about perfection and agency than about enjoying the energy of life may have been his ultimate legacy.

I am grateful

to Vittoria Borsò for being so irresponsibly generous; to Alfred Brendel for confusing me with Diderot; to Björn Buschbeck for trading early morning sleep against metabolism; to Andrea Capra for the most stylish office hours; to Vinicius de Castro for getting carried away; to Blanche Cerquiglini for a lesson on French grammar (among many other things); to Luiz Costa Lima for sharp and generous precision; to Phoebus Alexander Cotsapas for being my closest Diderot-buddy in California (and for his decisive immersion); to Marie Deer, for admirable serenity in editing the idiosyncrasies of my English prose; to Dan Edelstein for not being (unnecessarily) complicated; to Bill Eggington for elegance in agreement; to Karl Ellerbrock for trying to like an author who did not write his kind of literature; to Markus Gabriel for overlooking what I did not understand about Hegel; to Hans Martin Gauger for preferring a different Goya; to Söhnke Grothusen for telling me (too late) how wrong I was; to Anne Hamilton for not mentioning the Vernet painting; to Robert Harrison for being my gold standard for intelligence (and for recognizing a quote that I did not see); to Jochen Hieber for protecting friendship against politeness; to Alexander Honold for sharing my Diderot obsession; to Lorenz Jäger for saying he was interested; to Ivan Jaksic for engaging in contingency (the least thing he likes); to Wolfgang Kaußen for beautiful letters and angelic patience; to Roger Köppel, also for being too generous (but in a different way); to Joachim Küpper for not being picky; to Joshua Landy for exposing poor undergraduates to my suada; to Doris Lindner for being stubborn; to Sergio Missana for a great novelist's reading time; to Thomas Pavel for always remembering that battle; to Ludwig Pfeiffer for athletically argumentative tenacity (and for pushing back about Hegel); to Mareike Reisch for getting up unnecessarily early; to René for never letting things get too easy; to Ricky for not wanting to see her name here (and for reminding me that the world was surviving); to the late Ursula Schick for teaching a Proseminar and inviting me to dinner (without any reason); to Clemens Schmalhorst for knowing that I am "verrückt"; to Boris Shoshitaishvili for an underbelly; to Peter Sloterdijk for gargantuan taste; to Jan Soeffner for being a more mature than younger brother; to the late Jean Starobinski for not writing the book I could never have written; to Miguel Tamen for ultimate judgment (and for remembering Hume); to José Luis Villacanas for not letting me escape Enlightenment; to Romina Wainberg for being Argentinian-style lucid; to Erica Wetter for sharp openness; to Adam Wickberg for being patient with the *Salons*; to Christian Wollin for totally getting it;

and to several institutions and colleagues for wanting Diderot:

in Berlin, to the Wissenschaftskolleg; in Coimbra, to Manuel Portela; in Copenhagen, to Christian Benne; in Jerusalem, to the Buber Society of Fellows at the Hebrew University; in Lisbon, to Antonio Feijó, Joao Figueiredo, and Miguel Tamen; in Princeton, to Alexander Nehamas; in Rio de Janeiro, to Flora, Herculano, Luiz, Maisa, Marcelo, Otavio, and Tania; in Stanford, to my nine students; in Stockholm, to the late Sara Denius; in Weimar, to Deutsche Klassik Stiftung; in Weimar (again), to IKKM (where I finished the manuscript); and in some other places, to all those friends whom I fell short of remembering.

Notes

CHAPTER ONE: "ON FAIT DE MOI CE QU'ON VEUT"

"They can do what they want with me."

1. During the eighteenth century this word's meaning was similar to the present-day concept of the "intellectual."

2. It was my late friend Henning Ritter who first drew my attention to this particular letter.

3. *Diderot's Letters to Sophie Volland: A Selection.* Translated by Peter France. London 1972, pp. 54–55. "Je crains la cohue. J'avais résolu d'aller à Paris passer la journée [. . .]. C'étoit une foule mêlée de jeunes paysannes proprement atournées, et de grandes dames de la ville avec du rouge et des mouches, la canne de roseau à la main, le chapeau de paille sur la tête et l'écuyer sous le bras." Diderot: *Correspondance.* Paris 1963, vol. I, p. 173. Please note that because many of the quotations in this book include ellipses in the original text to indicate faltering speech or incomplete thoughts (as is common in French prose), I have bracketed my own ellipses (to indicate omissions in the quoted text) throughout for clarity.

4. "Mais Grim et Mme d'Epinai m'arrêtèrent. Lorsque je vois les yeux de mes amis se couvrir et leurs visages s'allonger, il n'y a répugnance qui tienne et l'on fait de moi ce qu'on veut." (Note that spellings of "Grim" and "Epinai" are per Diderot.)

5. "Nous étions alors dans le triste et magnifique salon, et nous y formions, diversement occupés, un tableau très-agréable."

6. Vers la fenêtre qui donne sur les jardins, Grim se faisoit peindre et Mme d'Epinai étoit appuyée sur le dos de la chaise de la personne qui le peignoit.

Un dessinateur, assis plus bas, sur un placet, faisoit son profil au crayon. Il est charmant, ce profil; il n'y a pas de femme qui ne fût tentée de voir s'il ressemble (173f.).

7. Arthur M. Wilson, *Diderot* (New York, 1972), pp. 292–94.

8. *Diderot's Letters to Sophie Volland*. L'heure du dîner vint. Au milieu de la table étoit d'un côté Mme d'Epinai, et de l'autre M. de Villeneuve; ils prirent toute la peine et de la meilleur grâce du monde. Nous dinâmes splendidement, gayement et longtems. Des glaces; ah! Mes amies, quelles glaces! C'est là qu'il fallut être pour en prendre de bonnes, vous qui les aimez. (Diderot: *Correspondance*, p. 175)

9. La personne dont je vous ai déjà parlé qui touche si légèrement et si savamment du clavecin nous étonna tous, eux par la rareté de son talent, moi par le charme de sa jeunesse, de sa douceur, de sa modestie, de ses grâces et de son innocence.

10. Je disois à M. de Villeneuve: "Qui est-ce qui oseroit changer quelque chose à cet ouvrage-là? Il est si bien." Mais nous n'avons pas, M. de Villeneuve et moi, les mêmes principes. S'il rencontroit des innocents, lui, il aimeroit assez à les instruire; il dit que c'est un autre genre de beauté (175).

11. Mme de Volland . . . est une femme d'un mérite rare.—Et sa fille aînée . . . Elle a de l'esprit comme un démon.—Elle a beaucoup d'esprit. Mais c'est sa franchise surtout qui me plaît. Je gagerois presque qu'elle n'a pas fait mensonge volontaire depuis qu'elle a l'âge de la raison (176).

12. On fit entrer les violons et l'on dansa jusqu'à dix; on sortit de la table à minuit; à deux heures au plus tard nous étions tous retirés; et la journée se passa sans l'ennui que je redoutois.

13. See Wilson, *Diderot*, pp. 714–17.

CHAPTER TWO: "PROSE OF THE WORLD"

1. Jean Starobinski, *Diderot, un diable de ramage*. Paris 2012.

2. See the first pages of chapter 6 for a more detailed discussion of Diderot's obsession.

3. Among other analyses of this constellation in the history of philosophy, see chapter 2 ("The Honest Soul and the Disintegrated Consciousness") of Lionel Trilling, "Sincerity and Authenticity," Cambridge, MA (Harvard University Press), 1972; James Hulbert, "Diderot in the Text of Hegel: A Question of Intertextuality," *Studies in Romanticism* 22 (1983): 267–91; and James Schmidt, "The Fool's Truth: Diderot, Goethe, and Hegel," *Journal of the History of Ideas* 57 (1996): 625–44. Also important for me has been an excellent seminar paper by Nicholas Fenech, a Stanford graduate student in comparative literature, entitled "The Road Not Taken: Hegel's Diderot and the Powers of Prose."

4. I quote Hegel's original text from G. W. F. Hegel, *Werke in zwanzig Bänden*, Theorie Werkausgabe (Suhrkamp Verlag / auf der Grundlage der "Werke" von 1832–1845 neu edierte Ausgabe): Frankfurt 1971—. My English translation of this passage: "Aristocrats are friendly ("family-like") with their servants; French aristocrats are even friends with them; when they are by themselves, the latter (i.e. the servant) does the talking, as you can see in Diderot's *Jacques et son maître*; the aristocrat does nothing but take pinches of tobacco and look at his watch; everything else he leaves to the servant."

5. "In poetry, common domestic life, which has the honesty, worldly wisdom, and morality of its day as its substance, is portrayed in the complications of ordinary civil life, in scenes and figures drawn from the middle and lower classes. In the case of the French, it is Diderot especially who has insisted in this sense on naturalness and the imitation of the present" (G. W. F. Hegel: The Oxford University Press Translations. Electronic Edition. *Hegel's Aesthetics*, pp. 597–98).

6. "In this connection Diderot says in the Essay on Painting translated by Goethe: The man who has got the feel of flesh has already gone far. Everything else is nothing in comparison. Thousands of painters have died without having had this feeling, and thousands more will die without having had it'" (848).

7. "The human organism in its bodily existence is still subject, even if not to the same extent, to a similar dependence on the external powers of nature. It is exposed to the same chance, unsatisfied natural needs, destructive illnesses, and to every kind of want and misery.

If we go higher up, i.e. to the immediate actuality of spiritual interests, we find that this dependence really only appears here in the most complete relativity. Here is revealed the whole breadth of prose in human existence. This is the sort of thing already present in the contrast between the purely physical vital aims and the higher aims of spirit, in that both of these can reciprocally hinder, disturb, and extinguish one another. Consequently, the individual man, in order to preserve his individuality, must frequently make himself a means to others, must subserve their limited aims, and must likewise reduce others to mere means in order to satisfy his own interests. Therefore the individual as he appears in this world of prose and everyday is not active out of the entirety of his own self and his resources, and he is intelligible not from himself, but from something else" (149–50).

8. "This is the prose of the world, as it appears to the consciousness both of the individual himself and of others:—a world of finitude and mutability, of entanglement in the relative, of the pressure of necessity from which the individual is in no position to withdraw. For every isolated living thing remains caught in the contradiction of being itself in its own eyes this shut-in unit and yet of being nevertheless dependent on something else, and the struggle to resolve this contradiction does not get beyond an attempt and the continuation of this eternal war" (151).

9. "In the first place, externality as such, i.e. objects in nature, can at once be excluded, relatively at least, from the subject-matter suitable for poetical conception. The proper subject-matter of poetry is spiritual interests, not the sun, mountains, woods, landscapes, or constituents of the human body like nerves, blood, muscles, etc. For however far poetry also involves an element of vision and illustration, it still remains even in this respect a spiritual activity and it works for *inner* intuition to which the spirit is nearer and more appropriate than *external* objects in their concrete visible and external appearance" (973).

10. "On the other hand, *ordinary* thinking has nothing to do with an inner connection, with the essence of things, with reasons, causes, aims, etc., but is content to take what is and happens as just this bare individual thing or event, i.e. as something accidental and meaningless. In this case there is none of the Understanding's dissection of that living unity in which the poetic vision keeps together the indwelling reason of things and their expression and existence; but what is missing is insight into this rationality and significance of things which therefore are without substance for this ordinary thinking and can make no further claim on a rational interest. In that event the Understanding's view of the world and its relations as connected by certain categories is exchanged for a mere view of a world of successive or juxtaposed accidents which may have a great range of external life but which is totally unable to satisfy the deeper need of reason" (976).

11. "The world of this Spirit breaks up into two. The first is the world of reality or of its self-alienation; but the other is that which Spirit, rising above the first, constructs for itself in the Aether of pure consciousness. This second world, standing in antithesis to that alienation, is for that very reason not free from it; on the contrary, it is really only the other form of that alienation which consists precisely in being conscious of two different worlds, and which embraces both" (G. W. F. Hegel, The Oxford University Press Translations. Electronic Edition. *Phenomenology of Spirit*, pp. 297–98).

12. "The content of what Spirit says about itself is thus the perversion of every Notion and reality, the universal deception of itself and others; and the shamelessness which gives utterance to this deception is just for that reason the greatest truth. This kind of talk is the madness of the musician 'who heaped up and mixed together thirty arias, Italian, French, tragic, comic, of every sort; now with a deep bass he descended into hell, then, contracting his throat, he rent the vaults of heaven with a falsetto tone, frantic and soothed, imperious and mocking, by turns.' To the tranquil consciousness which, in its honest way, takes the melody of the Good and the True to consist in the evenness of the notes, i.e. in unison, this talk appears as a 'rigmarole of wisdom and folly, as a medley of as much skill as baseness, of as many correct as false ideas, a mixture compounded of a complete perversion of sentiment, of absolute shamefulness, and of perfect frankness and truth'" (318–19).

13. Starting with the second chapter of my 2004 book *Production of Presence— What Meaning Cannot Convey,* I have described this process several times (with, I hope, increasing precision and complexity): see *After 1945—Latency as Origin of the Present* (Stanford: Stanford University Press, 2013), *Our Broad Present* (New York: Columbia University Press, 2014), and *Zum Zeitbegriff in den Geisteswissenschaften* (Wien: Akademie im Dialog [10], 2018).

14. The clarification of this point goes back to a discussion with Alexander Nehamas after a lecture on Diderot that I gave at Princeton University in April 2015.

15. In a Stanford seminar on "Diderot and the Explosions of Enlightenment," Boris Shoshitaishvili came up with the concept of an "epistemological underbelly" for this status of an intellectual matrix without a definitive institutional form.

CHAPTER THREE: "JE SUIS DANS CE MONDE ET J'Y RESTE"

"I'm in this world and I'm staying in it." Denis Diderot, *Rameau's Nephew / Le neveu de Rameau*: A Bilingual Edition, translated by Kate E. Tunstall and

Caroline Warman (Cambridge, 2016), p. 91. "Je suis dans ce monde et j'y reste."
Denis Diderot, *Le neveu de Rameau*, in *Oeuvres Romanesques*. Texte établi avec
une présentation et des notes par Henri Bénac (Paris, 1951), p. 485.

1. This is unusual both within Diderot's time and in discussions in our present.

2. For this contextualization, I have greatly profited from the detailed commentary by Henri Bénac, whose edition I am using.

3. "Qu'il fasse beau, qu'il fasse laid, c'est mon habitude d'aller sur les cinq heures du soir me promener au Palais Royal. C'est moi qu'on voit toujours seul, rèvant
sur le banc d'Argenson. Je m'entretiens avec moi mème de politique, d'amour, de
goût ou de philosophie. J'abandonne mon esprit à tout son libertinage [. . .]. Si
le temps est trop froid ou trop pluvieux, je me réfugie au café de la Régence; là,
je m'amuse à voir jouer aux échecs. Paris est l'endroit du monde, et le café de la
Régence est l'endroit de Paris où l'on joue le mieux à ce jeu" (395).

4. Dieter Henrich and Alexandru Bulucz, *Sterbliche Gedanken* (Munich:
Edition Faust, 2015), p. XX. I owe this reference to my friend Lorenz Jäger.

5. Roger Laufer, "Structure et signification du 'Neveu de Rameau' de Diderot,"
in *Denis Diderot*, ed. Jochen Schlobach, Wege der Forschung, vol. 655 (Darmstadt, 1992), analyzes the textual structure along similar lines.

6. "C'est un composé de hauteur et de bassesse, de bon sens et de déraison.
Il faut que les notions de l'honnête et du déshonnête soient bien étrangement
brouillées dans sa tête, car il montre ce que la nature lui a donné de bonnes
qualités sans ostentation, et ce qu'il a reçu de mauvaises, sans pudeur. [. . .] On
dirait qu'il a passé plusieurs jours sans manger, et qu'il sort de la Trappe. Le mois
suivant, il est gras et replète, comme s'il n'avait pas quitté la table d'un financier,
ou qu'il eût été renfermé dans un couvent de Bernardins. Aujourd'hui en linge
sale, en culotte déchirée, couvert de lambeaux, presque sans souliers, il va de
tête basse, il se dérobe, on serait tenté de l'appeler pour lui donner l'aumône.
Demain, poudré, chaussé, bien vêtu, il marche la tête haute, il se montre, et vous
le prendriez à peu près pour un honnête homme: il vit au jour la journée" (396).

7. "Adieu, monsieur le philosophe, n'est-il pas que je suis toujours le mème?"
(492).

8. "Que j'aie ce malheur-là seulement encore une quarantaine d'années: Rira
bien qui rira le dernier" (492).

9. "Mais ne voyez-vous pas qu'avec un pareil raisonnement vous renversez
l'ordre general?" (405).

10. "Comment se fait-il qu'avec un tact si fin, une si grande sensibilité pour les beautés de l'art musical, vous soyez aussi aveugle sur les belles choses en morale, aussi insensible aux charmes de la vertu?" (473).

11. "L'habit du cynique était, autrefois, notre habit monastique avec la même vertu. Les cyniques étaient les carmes et les cordeliers d'Athènes" (489).

12. "Il est dur d'être gueux, tandis qu'il y a tant de sots opulents aux dépens desquels on peut vivre. Et puis le mépris de soi; il est insupportable" (411).

13. "Quoi qu'il en soit, voilà le texte de mes fréquents soliloques, que vous pouvez paraphraser à votre fantaisie, pourvu que vous en concluiez que je connais le mépris de soi-même, ou ce tourment de la conscience qui naît de l'inutilité des dons que le ciel nous a départis; c'est le plus cruel de tous. Il vaudrait presque autant que l'homme ne fût pas né" (413).

14. "Vous savez que je suis un ignorant, un sot, un fou, un impertinent, un paresseux, ce que nos Bourguignons appellant un fieffé truand, un escroc, un gourmand . . ." (408).

15. "Je veux bien être abject, mais je veux que ce soit sans contrainte. Je veux bien descendre de ma dignité . . ." (435).

16. "Le point important est que vous et moi nous soyons, et que nous soyons vous et moi. Que tout aille d'ailleurs comme il pourra. Le meilleur ordre des choses, à mon avis, est celui où j'en devais être, et loin du plus parfait des mondes, si je n'en suis pas. J'aime mieux être, et même être impertinent raisonneur, que de n'être pas" (405).

17. "Quand je lis l'Avare, je me dis: Sois avare si tu veux, mais garde-toi de parler comme l'avare" (448).

18. "Qu'est-ce qu'une bonne éducation, sinon celle qui conduit à toutes sortes de jouissances sans peril et sans inconvénient?" (479).

19. "De la main droite, il s'était saisi les dogts et le poignet de la main gauche et il les renversait en dessus, en dessous; l'extrémité des doigts touchait au bras; les jointures craquaient; je craignais que les os n'en demeurassent disloqués" (415).

20. "Et la méthode, d'où naît-elle? Tenez, mon philosophe, j'ai dans la tête que la physique toujours sera une pauvre science, une goutte d'eau prise avec la pointe d'une aiguille dans le vaste océan, un grain détaché de la chaîne des Alpes! Et les raisons des phénomènes? En vérité, il vaudrait autant ignorer que de savoir si peu et si mal" (422).

21. The form of these lists can be described as "recursive negation," i.e. as a negation (or an "undoing") of the negation of differences that is a condiiton for subsuming specific phenomena under general concepts. See my essay "Literarische Gegenwelten, Karneval und die Epochenschwelle zwischen Spätmittelalter und Renaissance," in *Literatur in der Gesellschaft des Spätmittelalters*, ed. Hans Ulrich Gumbrecht (Heidelberg: Winter, 1980). It is also possible to explain the "frankness" of speech that is typical for Rameau—and praised using the ancient Greek word *parresia*—as an effect of recursive negation.

22. "Moi, je suis sans conséquence. On fait de moi, avec moi, devant moi tout ce qu'on veut sans que je m'en formalise" (409).

23. "Que le diable m'emporte si je sais au fond ce que je suis. En général, j'ai l'esprit rond comme une boule, et le caractère franc comme l'osier; jamais faux, pour peu que j'aie d'intérêt d'être vrai, jamais vrai, pour peu que j'aie d'intérêt d'être faux. Je dis les choses comme elles me viennent; sensées, tant mieux; impertinentes, on n'y prend pas garde. J'use en plein de mon franc parler. Je n'ai pensé de ma vie, ni avant que de dire, ni en disant, ni après avoir dit" (444).

24. "Il est attentif à tout" (486).

25. "Je ne me fatigue jamais" (416).

26. "l'atrocité de l'action" (462).

27. "Vous croyez que le même bonheur est fait pour tous. Quelle étrange vision! Le vôtre suppose un certain tour d'esprit romanesque que nous n'avons pas, une âme singulière, un goût particulier. Vous décorez cette bizarrerie du nom de virtue, vous l'appelez philosophie. Mais la virtue, la philosophie sont-elles faites pour tout le monde? En a qui peut, en conserve qui peut. Imaginez l'univers sage et philosophe; convenez qu'il serait diablement triste. Tenez, vive la philosophie, vive la sagesse de Salomon: boire de bon vin, se gorger de mets délicats, se rouler sur de jolies femmes, se reposer dans les lits bien mollets. Excepté cela, le reste n'est que vanité" (428–29).

28. MOI: Quoi, défendre sa patrie?

LUI: Vanité. Il n'y a plus de patrie; je n'y vois d'un pôle à l'autre que des tyrans et des esclaves.

MOI: Servir ses amis?

LUI: Vanité. Est-ce qu'on a des amis? Quand on en aurait, faudrait-il en faire des ingrats? Regardez-y bien, et vous verrez que c'est presque toujours là ce qu'on recueille des services rendus. La reconnaissance est un fardeau; et tout fardeau est fait pour être secoué (429).

29. "Le besoin est toujours une peine" (431).

30. "Mais il ne faut pas toujours approuver de la même manière; on serait monotone, on aurait l'air faux, on deviendrait insipide. On ne se sauve de là que par du jugement, de la fécondité; il faut savoir préparer et placer ces tons majeurs et péremptoires, saisir l'occasion et le moment. Lors, par example, s'il y a partage entre les sentiments, que la dispute s'est élevée à son dernier degré de violence, qu'on ne s'entend plus, que tous parlent à la fois, il faut être placé à l'écart, dans l'angle de l'appartement le plus éloigné du champ de bataille, avoir préparé son explosion par un long silence, et tomber subitement, comme un comminge, au milieu des contendants. Personne n'a eu cet art comme moi. Mais où je suis surprenant, c'est dans l'opposé: j'ai des petits tons que j'accompagne d'un sourire, une variété infinie de mines approbatives" (438).

31. "MOI: Quelque sublime que vous soyez, un autre peut vous remplacer. LUI: Difficilement" (410).

32. "J'ai plus de cent façons d'entamer la séduction d'une jeune fille, à côté de sa mère, sans que celle-ci s'aperçoive, et même de la rendre complice. A peine entrais-je dans la carrière, que je dédaignai toutes les manières vulgaires de glisser un billet doux; j'ai dix moyens de me le faire arracher, et parmi ces moyens j'ose me flatter qu'il y a eu de nouveaux. [. . .] Si cela était écrit, je crois qu'on m'accorderait quelque genie" (441).

33. "Je suis rare dans mon espèce, oui, très rare" (452).

34. "Je suis pourtant bien subalterne en musique, et bien supérieur en morale" (477).

35. "Au demeurant de ces mauvais contes, moi, je n'en invente aucun; je m'en tiens au rôle de colporteur" (456).

36. "En même temps il se met dans l'attitude d'un joueur de violon; il fredonne de la voix un allegro de Locatelli; son bras droit imite le movement de l'archet, sa main gauche et ses doigts semblent se promener sur la longueur du manche; s'il fait un ton faux, il s'arrête, il remonte ou baisse la corde; il la pince de l'ongle pour s'assurer qu'elle est juste; il reprend le morceau où il l'a laissé; il bat la mesure du pied, il se démène de sa tète, des pieds, des mains, des bras, du corps. [. . .] Au milieu de ses agitations et de ses cris, s'il se présentait une tenue, un de ces endroits harmonieux ou l'archet se meut lentement sur plusieures cordes à

la fois, son visage prenait l'air de l'extase, sa voix s'adoucissait, il s'écoutait avec ravissement. Il est sûr que les accords résonnaient dans ses oreilles et dans les miennes. Puis remettant son instrument sous son bras gauche de la même main dont il le tenait, et laissant tomber sa main droite avec son archet: Eh bien, me disait-il, qu'en pensez vous?" (415–16).

37. "Mais vous vous seriez échappé en éclats de rire à la manière dont il contrefaisait les différents instruments. Avec des joues renflées et bouffies, et un son rauque et sombre, il rendait les cors et les bassons; il prenait un son éclatant et nasillard pour les hautbois; précipitant sa voix avec une rapidité incroyable pour les instruments à corde dont il cherchait les sons les plus approchés; il sifflait les petites flûtes, il recoulait les traversières; criant, chantant, se démenant comme un forcené, faisant lui seul les danseurs, les danseuses, les chanteurs, les chanteuses, tout un orchestre, tout un théâtre lyrique, et se divisant en vingt rôles divers" (469).

38. "Après cette historiette, mon homme se mit à marcher la tête baissée, l'air pensif et abattu; il soupirait, pleurait, se désolait, levait les mains et les yeux, se frappait la tête du poing à se briser le front ou les doigts, et il ajoutait: 'Il me semble qu'il y a pourtant là quelque chose; mais j'ai beau frapper, secouer, il ne sort rien.' Puis il recommençait à secouer sa tête et à se frapper le front de plus belle et il disait: 'Ou il n'y a personne, ou l'on ne veut pas répondre'" (481).

39. The text was written in 1961. See Schlobach, *Denis Diderot*, pp. 214–31.

40. I owe this insight to a letter from my philosopher friend José Luis Villacañas.

41. According to his daughter Angélique, the last sentence that he uttered in his life began with the words "que diable" (see chapter 8).

42. Translation my own.

43. Edith Helman, *Trasmundo de Goya* (Madrid: Revista de Occidente, 1963). The quotations here and in the following are from pp. 219–41. Translations my own.

44. Hans Martin Gauger, a leading specialist in the history of Iberian languages, has given me many arguments to prove that, both from a grammatical and from a historical perspective, the first—enlightened—meaning of the caption is the more probable reading of this sentence. I agree, but do not believe that the opposite meaning can be ultimately eliminated.

45. Translation my own. Quoted from G. C. Lichtenberg, *Sudelbücher*, ed Franz H. Mautner (Frankfurt am Main, 1984). "Die Geschichte eines Jahrhunderts ist aus den Geschichten der einzelnen Jahre zusammengesetzt. Den Geist eines Jahrhunderts zu schildern, kann man nicht die Geister der einzelnen Jahre

zusammenflicken, unterdessen ist es dem, der ihn entwerfen will, allemal nützlich auch die letzteren zu kennen, sie können ihm immer neue Punkte darbieten, seine steten Linien dadurch zu ziehen" (B 18, 35).

46. Translation my own. "Es gibt keine Synonyma, die Wörter die wir dafür halten haben ihren Erfindern gewiss nicht Einerlei sondern vermutlich Species ausgedruckt" (A 30, 15).

47. Translation my own. "Es ist ein ganz unvermeidlicher Fehler aller Sprachen, dass sie nur genera von Begriffen ausdrücken, und selten hinlänglich das sagen, was sie sagen wollen. Denn wenn wir unsere Wörter mit den Sachen vergleichen, so werden wir finden, dass die letzteren in einer ganz anderen Reihe fortgehen als die ersteren" (A 109, 24).

48. Translations my own. "Er hatte zu nichts Appetit und ass doch von Allem" (B 3, 34). "Ein Gesichtchen nicht zum Küssen, sondern zum Hineinbeissen" (L 16, 475).

49. Translation my own. "Auch ich habe meine Empfindung beschreibende Prosa oft mit einem Entzücken gelesen, das meine sterbliche Hülle mit einer wollüstigen Gänsehaut überzog: ich habe [. . .] bei heiliger Musik und unter dem Donner der Pauken die Tritte des Allmächtigen zu hören geglaubt und Tränen der Andacht geweint. Mit unaussprechlicher Wollust denke ich noch an den Tag zurück, da ich in Westminster Abbey, über den Staub der Könige wandelnd, bei mir selber die Worte betete, Ehe denn die Berge worden und die Erde und die Welt geschaffen worden bist du Gott von Ewigkeit zu Ewigkeit." (E 191, 207).

50. The German original of this stage instruction is not available in the bilingual edition that I am using (see following note).

51. Burton D. Fisher, *Mozart's the Magic Flute*, Opera Classics Library Series (Opera Journeys Publishing, 2001) (bilingual edition), pp. 43–44.

52. "Because . . . because I doubt whether you're a real human being."

53. Until a few decades ago, the second meaning of the German diminutive *Weibchen* (the first meaning being "little wife") was "female" in the strictly zoological sense.

CHAPTER FOUR: "CHOSES BIZARRES ÉCRITES SUR LE GRAND ROULEAU"

Diderot, *Jacques the Fatalist and His Master*, translated by J. Robert Loy (New York, 1959), p. 111. "Choses bizarres écrites sur le grand rouleau": Jacques, 610.

Denis Diderot: Oeuvres romanesques. Edition par Henri Bénac. Paris: Editions Garnier Frères, 1962, pp. 493–780.

Thanks to my friend Blanche Cerquiglini for helping me with the formulation of this chapter title.

1. Contingent (*Encyclopédie*): "Le mot de contingent est très-équivoque dans les écrits de la plupart des philosophes." (M. Formey) "The word *contingent* is highly equivocal in the writings of most philosophers." (Translation my own)

2. "Vous croyez que le même bonheur est fait pour tous. Quelle étrange vision! Le vôtre suppose un certain tour d'esprit romanesque que nous n'avons pas, une âme singulière, un goût particulier. Vous décorez votre bizarrerie du nom de vertue, vous l'appelez philosophie. Mais la vertu, la philosophie sont-elles faites pour tout le monde? En a qui peut, en conserve qui peut. Imaginez l'univers sage et philosophe: admettez qu'il serait diablement triste" (428–29).

3. "Grand rouleau écrit là-haut" (543, 569, 572, etc.).

4. In *Denis Diderot*, ed. Jochen Schlobach, Wege der Forschung, vol. 655 (Darmstadt, 1992), 223.

5. In Schlobach, ed., *Denis Diderot*, 245–73.

6. G. W. F. Hegel: The Oxford University Press Translations, Vol. II, p. 280.

7. Hegel, Vol. III, p. 120.

8. Starobinski, *Diderot—un diable de ramage*: "Chaque balle a son billet" and "L'art de la démonstration." The translations in the following are my own.

9. Rainer Warning, *Illusion und Wirklichkeit in Tristram Shandy und Jacques le Fataliste* (Munich, 1965).

10. "Comment s'étaient-ils rencontrés? Par hasard, comme tout le monde. Comment s'appelaient-ils? Que vous importe? D'où venaient-ils? Du lieu le plus prochain. Où allaient-ils ? Est-ce qu'on sait où l'on va? Que disaient-ils? Le maître ne disait rien; et Jacques disait que son capitaine disait que tout ce qui nous arrive de bien et de mal ici-bas était écrit là haut" (493).

11. "Que cette aventure ne deviendrait-elle pas entre mes mains, s'il me prenait en fantaisie de vous désespérer? Je donnerais importance à cette femme; j'en ferais la nièce d'un curé de village voisin; j'ameuterais les paysans de ce village; je me préparerais des combats et des amours; car enfin cette paysanne était belle sous le linge. [. . .] Une bonne fois pour toutes, expliquez-vous; cela vous fera-t-il, cela ne vous fera-t-il pas plaisir?" (496–97).

12. "Il est évident que je ne fais pas un roman, puisque je néglige ce qu'un

romancier ne manquerait pas d'employer. Celui qui prendrait ce que j'écris pour la vérité, serait peut-être moins dans l'erreur que celui qui le prendrait pour une fable" (505).

13. "Vous allez dire que je m'amuse, et que, ne sachant plus que faire de mes voyageurs, je me jette dans l'allégorie, la ressource ordinaire des esprits stériles. Je vous sacrifierai mon allégorie et toutes les richesses que j'en pouvais tirer; je conviendrai de tout ce qu'il vous plaira, mais à condition que vous ne me tracasserez point sur le dernier gîte de Jacques et son maître" (514).

14. "Vous concevez, lecteur, jusqu'où je pourrais pousser cette conversation sur un sujet dont on a tant parlé, tant écrit depuis deux mille ans, sans en être d'un pas plus avancé. Si vous me savez peu de gré de ce que je vous dis, sachez-m'en beaucoup de ce que je ne vous dis pas" (499).

15. "Tout ce que je vous débite là, lecteur, je le tiens de Jacques, je vous l'avoue, parce que je n'aime pas à me faire honneur au nom d'autrui" (671).

16. "Vous allez prendre l'histoire du capitaine de Jacques pour un conte, et vous aurez tort. Je vous proteste que telle qu'il l'a racontée à son maître, tel fut le récit que j'en avais entendu faire aux Invalides, je ne sais en quelle année, le jour de Saint Louis, à table chez un monsieur de Saint Etienne, major d'hôtel; et l'historien qui parlait en presence de plusieurs autres officiers de la maison, qui avaient connaissance du fait, était un personage grave qui n'avait point du tout l'air d'un badin. Je vous le répète donc pour le moment et pour la suite: soyez circonspect si vous ne voulez pas prendre dans cet entretien de Jacques et de son maître le vrai pour le faux, le faux pour le vrai. Vous voilà bien averti, et je m'en lave les mains" (553).

17. "JACQUES: J'ai pris le parti d'être comme je suis; et j'ai vu, en y pensant un peu, que cela revenait presqu'au même, en ajoutant: Qu'importe comme on soit? C'est une autre resignation plus facile et plus commode.

LE MAITRE: Pour plus commode, cela est sûr" (574).

18. "Jacques, la meilleure pâte d'homme qu'on puisse imaginer, était tendrement attaché à son maître" (508).

19. "LE MAITRE: Je te veille. Tu es mon serviteur, quand je suis malade ou bien portant; mais je suis le tien quand tu te portes mal.

JACQUES: Je suis bien aisé de savoir que vous êtes humain; ce n'est pas trop la qualité des maîtres envers leur valets" (559).

20. "Tu ne sais pas la singulière idée qui me passe par la tête. Je te marie avec

notre hôtesse; et je cherche comme un mari aurait fait, lorsqu'il aime à parler, avec une femme qui ne déparle pas" (605).

21. "Le maître se mit à bailer; en baillant il frappait sur sa tabatière, et en frappant sur sa tabatière, il regardait au loin" (537, with the same words appearing in passages on pages 615, 619, 730, and 769).

22. "LE MAITRE: Pour moi, je me regarde comme en chrysalide; et j'aime à me persuader que le papillon, ou mon âme, venant un jour à percer sa coque, s'envolera à la justice divine.

JACQUES: Votre image est charmante.

LE MAITRE: Elle n'est pas de moi; je l'ai lue, je crois, dans un poète italien appelé Dante, qui a fait un ouvrage intitulé: *La Comédie de l'Enfer, du Purgatoire et du Paradis.*

JACQUES: Voilà un singulier sujet de comédie" (685).

23. "MAITRE: Je te dis, Jacques, que vous descendrez, et que vous descendrez sur-le-champ, parce que je vous l'ordonne.

JACQUES: Monsieur, commandez-moi toute autre chose, si vous voulez que je vous obéisse.

Ici le maître de Jacques se leva, le prit par la boutonnière, et lui dit gravement: 'Descendez.'

Jacques lui répondit froidement:

'Je ne descends pas.'

Le maître, le secouant fortement, lui dit:

'Descendez, maroufle, obéissez-moi'" (661).

24. "Lecteur, à quoi tient-il que je n'élève point une violente querelle entre les trois personnages? Que l'hôtesse ne soit prise par les épaules, et jetée hors de la chambre par Jacques [. . .]?" (594–95).

25. "La voilà remontée, et je vous préviens, lecteur, qu'il n'est plus dans mon pouvoir de la renvoyer.—Pourquoi donc?—C'est qu'elle se présente avec deux bouteilles de champagne, une dans chaque main, et qu'il est écrit là-haut que tout orateur qui s'adressera à Jacques avec cet exorde s'en fera nécessairement écouter" (610–11).

26. "'Le premier serment que se firent deux êtres de chair, ce fut au pied d'un rocher qui tombait en poussière; ils attestèrent de leur constance un ciel qui n'est pas un instant le même; tout passait en eux et autour d'eux, et ils croyaient leurs coeurs affranchis de vicissitudes. Oh enfants! Toujours enfants! . . .' Je ne sais de

qui sont ces réflexions, de Jacques, de son maître ou de moi; il est certain qu'elles sont de l'un des trois, et qu'elles furent précédées et suivies de beaucoup d'autres qui nous auraient menés, Jacques, son maître et moi, jusqu'au souper, jusqu'après le souper, jusqu'au retour de l'hôtesse, si Jacques n'eût dit à son maître: Tenez, monsieur, toutes ces grandes sentences que vous venez de débiter à propos de botte, ne valent pas une vieille fable des écraignes de mon village" (604–5).

27. As an example of this—very plausible—interpretative helplessness, I quote the commentary by Henri Bénac, editor of the text version that I am using: "Cette méditation, célèbre, inspirée par l'évolutionnisme de Diderot, et paraphrasée par Musset dans son *Souvenir*, est tout simplement la conclusion lyrique d'une discussion que Diderot ne nous rapporte pas en detail, entre Jacques et son maître, à propos de l'inconstance des amours humains" (898). "This famous meditation, inspired by Diderot's evolutionism and paraphrased by Musset in his *Souvenir*, is simply the lyrical conclusion of a conversation—which Diderot does not report in detail—between Jacques and his master on the subject of the inconstancy of human love" (translation my own). It is telling that Bénac writes about Jacques and his Master as if they were real human beings, with the ability to hide part of their interaction from the curious eye of an observer and author.

28. My brief plot summaries of the different stories told will rely on Warning's much more detailed renditions and their convincing analyses in his *Illusion und Wirklichkeit*, pp. 87–112.

29. "Tu parles trop" (659).

30. "'S'il est écrit là-haut que tu seras cocu, Jacques, tu auras beau faire, tu le seras; s'il est écrit là-haut que tu ne le seras pas, ils auront beau faire, tu ne le seras pas; dors donc, mon ami . . .' et qu'il s'endormait" (780).

31. "La nature est si variée surtout dans les instincts et les caractères" (553).

32. "Voici son entretien avec ma femme" (554).

33. "En vérité je crois que je ne me repens de rien; et que cette Pommeraye, au lieu de se venger, m'aura rendu un grand service" (648).

34. "Quel diable de femme! L'enfer n'est pas pire! J'en tremble: et il faut que je boive un coup pour me rassurer" (633).

35. "Vous pouvez haïr; vous pouvez redouter Mme de La Pommeraye: mais vous ne la mépriserez pas. Sa vengeance est atroce; mais elle n'est souillèe d'aucun motif d'intérêt [. . .] vous vous révoltez contre'elle au lieu de voir que son ressentiment seulement vous indigne parce que vous êtes incapable d'en

éprouver un aussi profond, ou que vous ne faites presqu'aucun cas de la vertu des femmes" (651).

36. "J'aurais une petite question à vous proposer à discuter sur votre oreiller: c'est ce qu'aurait été l'enfant né de l'abbé Hudson et de la dame de La Pommeraye?—Peut-être un honnête homme.—Peut-être un sublime coquin?" (684).

37. I. H. Smith, "The Mme de la Pommeraye Tale and Its Commentaries," *Journal of the Australasian Universities Language and Literature Association* 17 (1; 1962): 18–30, here: 29.

38. "Est-ce que tu as oublié ton refrain; et le grand rouleau et l'écriture d'en haut?" (736).

39. "Deux vraies machines vivantes et pensantes" (757).

40. "Après ces balivernes et quelques autres propos de la même importance, ils se turent; et Jacques, relevant son énorme chapeau, parapluie dans les mauvais temps, parasol dans les temps clairs, couvre-chef en tout temps, le ténébreux sanctuaire sous lequel une des meilleures cervelles qui ait encore existé consultait le destin dans les grandes occasions [. . .] aperçut un laboureur qui rouait inutilement de coups un de ses deux chevaux" (759).

41. "Voilà l'histoire Desglands. Jacques est-il satisfait: et puis-je espérer qu'il écoutera l'histoire de mes amours, ou qu'il reprendra l'histoire des siennes?" (754).

42. "Croyez-vous que je n'en sois aussi curieux que vous? [. . .] Tout ce que je débite là, lecteur, je le tiens de Jacques, je vous l'avoue, parce que je n'aime pas à me faire honneur de l'esprit d'autrui. Jacques ne connaissait ni le nom de vice, ni le nom de vertu; il prétendait qu'on était heureusement ou malheureusement né" (669–70).

43. "Et moi, j'arrête, parce ce que je vous ai dit de ces deux personnages tout ce que j'en sais.—Et les amours de Jacques? Jacques a dit cent fois que c'était écrit là-haut qu'il n'en finirait pas l'histoire, et je vois que Jacques avait raison. Je vois, lecteur, que cela vous fâche; eh ben, reprenez son récit où il l'a laissé, et continuez à votre fantaisie" (777).

44. "Des mémoires que j'ai de bonnes raisons de tenir pour suspects" (777).

45. "L'éditeur ajoute: La huitaine est passée. J'ai lu les mémoires en question; des trois paragraphes que j'y trouve de plus que dans le manuscrit dont je suis possesseur, le premier et le dernier me paraissent originaux, et celui du milieu évidemment interpolé" (777).

46. This particular passage of inconsistency in *Jacques le fataliste* did not provoke any commentary by the editor of the text version that I am using—which seems appropriate, as the text does not contain any connotations or more direct instructions for the readers to process.

47. See Hans Ulrich Gumbrecht, "Our Broad Present" (New York: Columbia University Press, 2014), and Gumbrecht, "Three Notes on Contingency Today," in *Contingency*, ed. Thomas Claviez (Bern, forthcoming).

48. See Francisco de Goya, *Caprichos—Desastres—Tauromaquia—Disparates*, textes de Alfonso E. Pérez Sánchez (Madrid: Fundación Juan March, 1979), p. 86. The explanations below the captions in bold are not historical—and I disagree with most of them.

49. Ibid., p.100.

50. Ibid., p. 87.

51. Ibid., pp. 128–30.

52. Agnes Selby, "Mozart's Gambling," in *The Classical Music Guides Forums*, August 2005 to May 31, 2006.

53. Georg Christoph Lichtenberg, *Philosophical Writings*, translated, edited, and with an introduction by Steven Tester (New York: SUNY Press, 2012), 120.

CHAPTER FIVE: "LE PRODIGE, C'EST LA VIE"

"The real wonder is life itself." Denis Diderot, *Rameau's Nephew and D'Alembert's Dream*, translated by Leonard Tancock (Harmondworth and New York, 1976), p. 176. "Le prodige, c'est la vie." Denis Diderot, *Le rêve de d'Alembert*, with introduction, notes, chronology and bibliography by Colas Duflo (Paris: Flammarion, 2002). p. 96. This is the edition used throughout this chapter.

1. Diderot, *Letters to Sophie Volland: A Selection*, p. 194. "Je vis beaucoup dans ma robe de chambre. Je lis, j'écris; j'écris d'assez bonnes choses, à propos de fort mauvaises que je lis. Je ne vois personne, parce qu'il n'y a plus personne à Paris." Letter from August 31, 1769, in Diderot, *Correspondance* IX (Janvier 1769—Décembre 1769) (Paris, 1963), p. 125.

2. "Dialogues sur le commerce des blés."

3. For the circumstances of Diderot's work on *Le rêve de d'Alembert*, see Colas Duflo's introduction, pp. 27ff.

4. "J'ai fait un dialogue entre d'Alembert et moi. Nous y causons assez gaiement et même assez clairement, malgré la sécheresse et l'obscurité du sujet. A ce

dialogue il en succède un second, beaucoup plus étendu, qui sert d'éclaircisse-
ment au premier. Celui-ci est intitule *Le Rêve de d'Alembert*. Les interlocuteurs
sont d'Alembert rêvant, mad d'Espinasse [sic], l'amie de d'Alembert, et le docteur
Bordeux [sic]" (126).

5. None of the critical interpretations or analyses of *Le rêve de d'Alembert*
seems to point to this omission, probably presupposing that Sophie Volland was
fully aware of the text's topic from the beginning.

6. "Si j'avois voulu sacrifier la richesse du fond à la noblesse du ton, Démo-
crite, Hippocrate et Leucippe auraient été mes personnages; mais la vraisem-
blance m'auroit renfermé dans des bornes étroites de la philosophie ancienne
et j'y aurois trop perdu. Cela est de la plus haute extravagance et tout à la fois
de la philosophie la plus profonde. Il y a quelqu'adresse à avoir mis mes idées
dans la bouche d'un homme qui rêve. Il faut souvent donner à la sagesse l'air de
la folie afin de lui procurer ses entrées. J'aime mieux qu'on dise: Mais cela n'est
pas si insensé qu'on croirait bien, que de dire: Ecoutez-moi, voici des choses
très sages" (126–27).

7. "Je crois vous avoir dit que j'avois fait un dialogue entre d'Alembert et moi."

8. "Il n'est pas possible d'`ètre plus profond et plus fou."

9. "J'y ai ajouté après coup cinq ou six pages capable de dresser les cheveux
à mon amoureuse, aussi ne les verra-t'elle jamais. Mais ce qui va bien vous sur-
prendre, c'est qu'il n'y a pas un mot de religion, et pas un seul mot déshonnête;
après cela, je vous défie de deviner ce que ce peut être" (140).

10. What precisely Sophie Volland had been asking for we will never know,
as none of her letters to Diderot has been preserved.

11. Translation my own. "Ce dialogue entre d'Alembert et moi, eh, comment
diable voulez-vous que je vous le fasse copier? C'est presque un livre. Et puis je
vous l'ai dit, il faut un commentateur" (167).

12. Wilson, *Diderot*, p. 559.

13. Duflo, introduction to *Le rêve de d'Alembert*, p. 46.

14. See Virgil W. Topazio, "Diderot's Supposed Contribution to D'Holbach's
Works," *Publications of the Modern Language Association* 69 (1954): 173–88.

15. Denis Diderot, *Letter on the Blind for the Use of Those Who Can See*,
translated by Kate E. Tunstall, in Tunstall, *Blindness and Enlightenment* (New
York: Continuum, 2011), p. 171; Denis Diderot, *"L'aveugle-né du Puisieux" Lettre
sur les aveugles à l'usage de ceux qui voient*, in *Oeuvres philosophiques*, edited

and with introductions, bibliography, and notes by Paul Vernière (Paris: Garnier, 1964), pp. 73–164 (quote on p. 82).

16. "L'aveugle du Puiseaux estime la proximité du feu aux dégrés de la chaleur; la plénitude des vaisseaux, au bruit que font en tombant les liqueurs qu'il transvase; et le voisinage des corps, à l'action de l'air sur son visage" (90).

17. "Comme je n'ai jamais douté que l'état de nos organes et de nos sens n'ait beaucoup d'influence sur notre métaphysique et sur notre morale, et que nos idées les plus purement intellectuelles, si je puis parler ainsi, ne tiennent de fort près à la confirmation de notre corps, je me mis à questionner notre aveugle sur les vices et sur les vertus" (92).

18. The late Stephen Hawking was one of the holders of the Lucasian Chair of Mathematics at the University of Cambridge, the highly prestigious chair that Saunderson held. Saunderson's predecessors in the chair included Isaac Newton.

19. "Saunderson voyait donc par la peau; cette enveloppe était en lui d'une sensibilité si exquise, qu'on peut assurer, qu'avec un peu d'habitude, il serait parvenu à reconnaître un de ses amis dont un dessinateur lui aurait tracé le portrait sur la main" (117).

20. The passage about portraits of his friends drawn into Saunderson's hand is preceded by a sentence that shows how Diderot's generosity easily got carried away: "The example of this illustrious blind man proves that, with practice, touch can develop and become more sensitive than sight, since by running his hands over a series of medals, he could tell real from fake ones" (197). ("L'exemple de cet illustre aveugle prouve que le tact peut devenir plus délicat que la vue, lorsqu'il est perfectionné par l'exercice; car, en parcourant des mains une suite de medailles, il discernait les vraies d'avec les fausses" [115–16].)

21. "Un phénomène est-il, à notre avis, au-dessus de l'homme? Nous disons aussitôt: *c'est l'ouvrage d'un Dieu*; notre vanité ne se contente pas à moins. Ne pourrions-nous pas mettre dans un discours un peu moins d'orgueil, et un peu plus de philosophie? Si la nature nous offre un noeud difficile a delier, laissons-le pour ce qu'il est; et n'employons pas à le couper la main d'un être qui devient ensuite pour nous un nouveau noeud plus indissoluble que le premier" (119).

22. "*O Dieu de Clarke et de Newton, prends pitié de moi!*" (124).

23. "Les derniers adieux qu'il fit à sa famille sont fort touchants. 'Je vais, leur dit-il, où nous irons tous; épargnez-moi des plaintes qui m'attendrissent. Les témoignages de douleur que vous me donnez me rendent plus sensible à ceux

qui m'échappent. Je renonce sans peine à une vie qui n'a été pour moi qu'un long désir et qu'une privation continuelle. Vivez aussi vertueux et plus heureux, et apprenez à mourir aussi tranquilles.' Il prit ensuite la main de sa femme qu'il tint un moment serrée entre les siennes: il se tourna le visage de son côté, comme s'il eût cherché à la voir; il bénit ses enfants, les embrassa tous, et les pria de se retirer, parce qu'ils portaient à son âme des atteintes plus cruelles que les approches de la mort" (125–26).

24. "Je conjecture donc que, dans le commencement où la matière en fermentation faisait éclore l'univers, mes semblables étaient fort communs. Mais pourquoi n'assurerais-je pas des mondes, ce que je croix des animaux? Comment de mondes estropiés, manqués, se sont dissipés, se reforment et se dissipent peut-être à chaque instant dans les espaces éloignés, où je ne touche point, et où vous ne voyez pas, mais où le mouvement continue et continuera de combiner des amas de matière, jusqu'à ce qu'ils aient obtenu quelque arrangement dans lequel ils puissent persévérer?" (123).

25. "La suite d'un entretien entre M. d'Alembert et M. Diderot."

26. See Wilson, *Diderot*, p. 495.

27. Wilson, *Diderot*, p. 495.

28. "D'Alembert était allé dîner dehors" (169).

29. "Le passage de l'état d'inertie à l'état de sensibilité; et les générations spontanées" (97).

30. "J'avoue qu'[. . .]un être d'une nature aussi contradictoire est difficile à admettre" (53).

31. "Il faut que la pierre sente" (53).

32. "En mangeant, que faites-vous? Vous levez les obstacles qui s'opposaient à la sensibilité active de l'aliment; vous l'assimilez avec vous-même; vous en faites de la chair; vous l'animalisez, vous le rendez sensible; et ce que vous éxecutez sur un aliment, je l'éxécuterai, quand il me plaira, sur le marbre" (57).

33. "Ecoutez-vous et vous aurez pitié avec vous-même, vous sentirez que, pour n'admettre une supposition simple qui explique tout, la sensibilité propriété générale de la matière ou produit de l'organisation, vous renoncez au sens commun, et vous précipitez dans un abîme de mystères, de contradictions et d'absurdités" (69).

34. "Qu'est-ce que cet oeuf? une masse insensible avant que le germe y soit introduit; et après que le germe y est introduit, qu'est-ce encore? Une masse

insensible, car le germe n'est lui-même qu'un fluide inerte et grossier. Comment cette masse passera-t-elle à une autre organisation, à la sensibilité, à la vie? par la chaleur. Qu'y produira la chaleur? le mouvement. Quels seront les effets successifs du mouvement?

Au lieu de me répondre, asseyez-vous, et suivons-les de l'oeil, de moment en moment. D'abord c'est un point qui oscille; un filet qui s'étend et qui se colore; de la chair qui se forme; un bec, des bouts d'ailes, des yeux, des pattes qui paraissent, une matière jaunâtre qui se dévide et produit des intestins; c'est un animal" (68).

35. "Remarquez qu'il n'y a dans le commerce des hommes que des bruits et des actions" (71).

36. "La cause subit trop de vicissitudes particulières qui nous échappent pour que nous puissions compter infailliblement sur l'effet qui s'ensuivra. La certitude que nous avons qu'un homme violent s'irritera d'une injure n'est pas la même que celle qu'un corps qui frappe un plus petit le mettra en movement" (72–73).

37. Wilson, *Diderot*, p. 46, indeed mentions "tactlessness" as a recurrent feature of Diderot's character, implying that, rather than being the product of malicious intentions, it emerged from his confidence and his openness to the world: "Diderot was big-hearted, well meaning, rather grandly negligent, brash, and tactless. Although he deemed himself shy, he was in reality endowed with an over-brimming measure of self-confidence."

38. "DIDEROT: Permettez-moi de vous faire l'histoire d'un des plus grands géomètres de l'Europe. Qu'était-ce d'abord que cet être merveilleux? Rien.

D'ALEMBERT: Comment rien? On ne fait rien de rien.

DIDEROT: Vous prenez les mots trop à la lettre. Je veux dire qu'avant que sa mère, la belle et scélérate chanoinesse Tencin, eût atteint l'âge de la puberté; avant que le militaire La Touche fût adolescent, les molecules qui devraient former les premiers rudiments de mon géomètre étaient éparses dans les jeunes et frêles machines de l'une et de l'autre, se filtrèrent avec la lymphe, circulèrent avec le sang, jusqu'à ce qu'enfin elles se rendissent dans les réservoirs destinés à leur coalition, les testicules de sa mère et de son père. Voilà ce germe rare formé. Le voilà, comme c'est l'opinion commune, amené par les trompes de Fallope dans la matrice; le voilà attaché à la matrice par un long pédicule; le voilà s'accroissant successivement et s'avançant à l'état de foetus; voilà le moment de sa sortie de l'obscure prison arrive; le voilà né, exposé sur les degrés de Saint-Jean-le-Rond qui lui donna son nom; tiré des Enfants-Trouvés; attaché à la mamelle de la bonne vitrière madame Rousseau; allaité, devenu grand de corps et d'esprit, littérateur, mécanicien, géomètre; comment cela s'est fait? En mangeant, et par d'autres opérations purement mécaniques" (59–60).

39. "C'est un petit mouvement fébril qui n'aura point de suite" (80).

40. Wilson, *Diderot*, p. 562.

41. "Et la formation de cette continuité? Elle ne l'embarrassera guère . . . Comme une goutte de mercure se fond dans une autre goutte de mercure, une molécule sensible et vivante se fond dans une molécule sensible et vivante . . . D'abord il y avait deux gouttes; après le contact il n'y en a plus qu'une . . . Avant l'assimilation il y avait deux molécules; après l'assimilation il n'y en a plus qu'une . . . La sensibilité devient commune à la masse commune. En effet pourquoi non?" (83–84).

42. "Avez-vous quelquefois vu un essaim d'abeilles s'échapper de leur ruche? . . . Le monde ou la masse générale de la matière est la grande ruche . . . Les avez-vous vues s'en aller former à l'extrémité de la branche d'un arbre, une longue grappe de petits animaux ailés, tous accrochés les uns aux autres par les pattes? [. . .]

Si l'une de ces abeilles s'avise de pincer d'une façon quelconque l'abeille à laquelle elle s'est accrochée, que croyez-vous qu'il en arrive? [. . .]

Il s'excitera dans toute la grappe autant de sensations qu'il y a de petits animaux; le tout s'agitera, se remuera, changera de situation et de forme; il s'élèvera du bruit, de petits cris; et celui qui n'aurait jamais vu une pareille grappe s'arranger, serait tenté de la prendre pour un animal à cinq ou six cents têtes et à mille ou douze cents ailes . . ." (85).

43. "Le vase où il apercevait tant de générations momentanées, il le comparait à l'univers. Il voyait dans une goutte d'eau l'histoire du monde" (93).

44. "Qu'est-ce que notre durée en comparaison de l'éternité des temps? Moins que la goutte que j'ai prise avec la pointe d'une aiguille en comparaison de l'espace illimité qui m'environne. Suite indéfinie d'animalcules dans l'atome qui fermente. Même suite indéfinie d'animalcules dans l'autre atome qu'on appelle la terre. Qui sait les races d'animaux qui nous sont précédés? qui sait les races d'animaux que succèderont aux nôtres? Tout change. Tout passe. Il n'y a que le tout qui reste. Le monde commence et finit sans cesse" (93–94).

45. "Laissez agir le grand sediment inerte quelques millions de siècles. Peut-être faut-il pour renouveler les espèces dix fois plus de temps qu'il n'est accordé à leur durée" (96).

46. "Tout est en un flux perpétuel . . . Tout animal est plus ou moins homme; tout minéral est plus ou moins plante, toute plante est plus ou moins animal. Il n'y a rien de précis en nature . . . [. . .]

Et la vie? Une suite d'actions et de réactions . . . Vivant, j'agis et je réagis en masse . . . mort, j'agis et je réagis en molécules. Je ne meurs donc point . . . Non, sans doute, je ne meurs point en ce sens, ni moi, ni quoi que soit . . . Naître, vivre et passer, c'est changer de formes. Et qu'importe une forme ou une autre?" (103–4).

47. "MADEMOISELLE DE LESPINASSE: Mais si un atome fait osciller un des files de la toile de l'araignée, alors elle prend l'arme, elle s'inquiète; elle fuit ou elle accourt. Au centre, elle est instruite de ce qui se passe en quelque endroit que ce soit de l'appartement immense qu'elle a tapissé. Pourquoi est-ce que je ne sais pas ce qui se passe dans le mien, ou le monde, puisque je suis un peloton de points sensibles, que tout presse sur moi et que je presse sur tout?

BORDEU: C'est que les impressions s'affaiblissent en raison de la distance d'où elles partent" (107–8).

48. "Puis il ajoutait en soupirant, O vanité de nos pensées! ô pauvreté de la gloire de nos travaux! ô misère, ô petitesse de nos vues! Il n'y a rien de solide, que de boire, manger, vivre, aimer, et dormir . . . Mademoiselle de Lespinasse, où êtes-vous?—Me voilà.—Alors son visage s'est coloré. J'ai voulu lui tater le pouls; mais je ne savais pas où il avait caché sa main. Il parassait éprouver une convulsion. Sa bouche s'était entr'ouverte. Son haleine était pressée. Il a poussé un profond soupir; et puis un soupir plus faible et plus profond encore. Il a re-tourné sa tête sur son oreiller et s'est endormi. Je le regardais avec attention, et j'étais tout émue sans savoir pourquoi. Le coeur me battait, et ce n'était pas de peur. Au bout de quelques moments, j'ai vu un léger sourire errer sur ses lèvres. Il disait tout bas . . . dans une planète où les hommes se multiplieraient à la manière des poissons, où le frai d'un homme pressé sur le frai d'une femme . . . j'y aurais moins de regret" (94).

49. "*Sur les deux heures le docteur revint. D'Alembert était allé dîner dehors, et le docteur se trouva en tête-à-tête avec mademoiselle de Lespinasse. On servit. Ils parlèrent de choses assez indifférentes jusqu'au dessert; mais lorsque les domes-tiques furent éloignés, mademoiselle de Lespinasse dit au docteur:*

MADEMOISELLE DE LESPINASSE: Allons, docteur, buvez un verre de Malaga, et vous me répondrez ensuite à une question qui m'est passé cent fois par la tête et que je n'oserais faire qu'à vous.

BORDEU: Il est excellent ce malaga—Et votre question?

MADEMOISELLE DE LESPINASSE: Que pensez-vous du mélange des espèces?" (169).

50. Jean Starobinski, "Le philosophe, le géomètre, l'hybride," in *Diderot, un diable de ramage*, pp. 247–73, associates the motif with the discursive hybridity of *Le rêve de d'Alembert*. While I will come back to this important essay, I do not share its intuition about the passages on "le mélange des espèces" being an allegorical self-commentary on the text.

51. "Ces questions-là sont trop sublimes pour moi" (177).

52. "De physique, de physique" (178).

53. "BORDEU: C'est que nous en tirerions une race vigoureuse, intelligente, infatigable et véloce dont nous ferions d'excellents domestiques.

MADEMOISELLE DE LESPINASSE: Fort bien, docteur. Il me semble déjà que je vois derrière la voiture de nos duchesses cinq à six grands insolents chèvre-pieds, et cela me réjouit" (180).

54. "Vos chèvres-pieds seraient d'effrénés dissolus" (181).

55. "D'abord vous n'étiez rien. Vous fûtes en commençant un point imperceptible, formé de molécules plus petites éparses dans le sang, la lymphe de votre père et de votre mère; ce point devint un fil délié; puis un faisceau de fils. Jusque là, pas le moindre vestige de cette forme agréable que vous avez. Vos yeux, ces beaux yeux, ne ressemblaient non plus à des yeux, que l'extrémité d'une griffe d'anémone ne ressemble à une anémone" (112).

56. "Il y a plaisir à causer avec vous. Vous ne saisissez pas seulement ce qu'on vous dit; vous en tirez encore des conséquences d'une justesse qui m'étonne" (112).

57. "C'est cela. Venez que je vous embrasse" (115).

58. "Ainsi faites de moi tout ce qu'il vous plaira, pourvu que je m'instruise" (117).

59. "Après avoir été un homme pendant quatre minutes, voilà vous reprenez votre cornette et vos cotillions et que vous redevenez femme" (177).

60. "Adieu donc, docteur. Ne nous délaissez pas des siècles, comme vous le faites. Et pensez quelquefois que je vous aime à la folie" (183).

61. Translations my own. "Elle avait un grand fonds de raison, une douceur charmante, une finesse peu commune dans les idées, et de la naïveté" (155).

"De toutes les qualités, c'étaient le jugement sain, la douceur et la gaieté qu'elle prisait les plus. Elle parlait peu et écoutait beaucoup: *Je ressemble aux oiseaux, disait-elle, j'apprends à chanter dans les ténèbres"* (159).

62. Leo Spitzer, "Der Stil Diderots" (1948), in *Denis Diderot*, ed. Jochen Schlobach (Darmstadt, 1992), pp. 59–74.

63. "Passons, passons . . . On pourrait peut-être vous chicaner; mais je ne me soucie pas. Je n'épilogue jamais . . . Cependant reprenons . . . Un fil d'or très pur. Je m'en souviens; c'est une comparaison qu'il m'a faite. Un réseau homogène, entre les molécules duquel d'autres s'interposent et forment peut-être un autre réseau homogène; un tissu de matière sensible; un contact qui assimile; de la sensibilité active ici, inerte là" (84).

64. Translation my own. "c'est le procédé dynamique gràce auquel la systematisation peut être remise à plus tard" (247).

65. "Qu'était-ce d'abord que cet être marvelleux? Rien" (59).

66. "Le voilà attaché à la matrice par un long pédicule; le voilà s'accroissant et s'avançant à l'état de foetus [. . .]; le voilà né, exposé sur les degrés de Saint-Jean-le-Rond" (60).

67. "Allaité, devenu grand de corps et d'esprit, littérateur, mécanicien, géomètre; comment cela s'est fait? [. . .]

Celui qui exposerait à l'Académie le progrès de la formation d'un homme ou d'un animal n'emploierait que des agents matériels dont les effets successifs seraient un être inerte, un être sentant, un être pensant, un être résolvant le problème de la précession des équinoxes, un être sublime, un être merveilleux, un être viellissant, dépérissant, mourant, dissous et rendu à la terre végétale" (60).

68. Translation my own. "Pour avoir posé avec tant d'impudente certitude la notion d'un 'océan de matière,' pour s'être affranchi si vigoureusement de la tutelle spiritualiste, il fallait [. . .] que la parole, qui se déclare issue de la matière, affirme et exerce avec non moins d'impudence tout le pouvoir dont elle se sent détentrice: pouvoir d'imiter, de parodier, de romper, puis d'enchaîner, de varier son régime, d'engendrer par déplacement lateral d'autres voix semblables et différentes, de provoquer autour d'elle la présence d'auditeurs réels et imaginaires" (273).

69. See my essay about "Rhythm and Meaning" in Hans Ulrich Gumbrecht and Karl Ludwig Pfeiffer, ed., *Materialities of Communication* (Stanford, 1994).

70. Translation my own. "Monsieur Diderot, d'après l'expérience qu'il en a, devrait, ce me semble, s'interdire de parler ou de faire parler des femmes qu'il

ne connaît point." Diderot, *Correspondance* IX, p. 156. See the following pages regarding the context of this quote, as well as Diderot's "Lettre d'envoi" from "Fin Septembre 1769," which he dedicated to d'Alembert.

71. Wilson, *Diderot*, p. 570.

72. Translation my own. "J'ai satisfait à votre désir autant que la difficulté du travail et le peu d'intervalle que vous m'avez accordé me le permettaient. J'espère que l'historique de ces dialogues en excusera les défauts. Le plaisir de se rendre compte à soi-même de ses opinions les avoit produits; l'indiscrétion de quelques personnes les tira de l'obscurité, l'amour allarmé en désira le sacrifice, l'amitié tyrannique l'exigea, l'amitié trop facile y consentit; ils furent lacérés. Vous avez voulu que j'en raprochasse les morceaux; je l'ai fait [. . .].

Je vous rappellerai la parole sacrée qui vous engage à ne les communiquer à personne. Je n'en excepte que votre ami [sic]" (157).

73. In his epilogue to an Insel Taschenbuch edition of Lichtenberg's *Sudel-bücher* (Frankfurt am Main and Leipzig, 1984), p. 594, Franz H. Mautner names Diderot as one of three thinkers from outside Germany who had the greatest similarity to Lichtenberg (the two others being Joubert and Valéry).

74. "Unsere Psychologie wird endlich bei einem subtilen Materialismus stille stehn, indem wir immer von der einen Seite (Materie) mehr lernen und von der andern über alles hinausgegriffen haben."

75. "Wenn die Seele einfach ist, wozu der Bau des Gehirns so fein? Der Körper ist eine Maschine und muß also aus Maschinen-Materialien bestehen. Es ist ein Beweis daß sich das Mechanische in uns sehr weit erstreckt, da selber noch die innern Teile des Gehirns mit einer Kunst geformt sind, wovon wir wahrschein-licher Weise nicht den hundertsten Teil verstehen."

76. "Die Vorstellung, die wir uns von einer Seele machen, hat viel Ähnliches mit der von einem Magneten in der Erde. Es ist bloß Bild. Es ist ein dem Men-schen angeborenes Erfindungsmittel sich alles unter diesen Formen zu denken."

77. "Wenn die Physiognomik das wird, was Lavater von ihr erwartet, so wird man die Kinder aufhängen ehe sie den Taten getan haben die den Galgen verdienen."

78. Karol Berger, *Bach's Cycle, Mozart's Arrow. An Essay on the Origins of Musical Modernity* (Berkeley, 2007), pp. 293ff.

79. See Wolfgang Hildesheimer, *Mozart* (Frankfurt, 1993), p. 59: "Seine wirkliche Sprache, die Musik, nährt sich aus uns unkenntlichen Quellen, sie

lebt von einer suggestiven Kraft, die sich über den Gegenstand ihrer Suggestion so weit erhebt, dass er sich uns entzieht. Ihr Schöpfer bleibt uns unzugänglich."

80. Hildesheimer, *Mozart*, pp. 127–28.

81. I think above all of my friend Robert Harrison's works on "Forests," "The Dominion of the Dead," "Gardens," and "Juvenescence" (all published at the University of Chicago Press).

CHAPTER SIX: "QUELS TABLEAUX!"

"What paintings!" "Quels tableaux!" Diderot used this exclamation quite frequently and always as an expression of positive judgment, when, in his discussions of the biannual Salons in Paris, he referred either to groups of paintings or to individual works, for example in the first sentence of a reflection on landscape and sea paintings by Claude Joseph Vernet in the Salon of 1767 (*Oeuvres esthétiques de Diderot*, ed. Paul Vernière [Paris, 1966], p. 568).

1. "Tableau de Van Loo exposé au Salon de 1767, actuellement au Musée de Coutances": "Diderot's highly precise description leaves no doubt: it is the *Diderot* of the Louvre, the subject facing forward, the writer at his desk, and not the copy at the museum of Langres, in three-quarter profile, his hands joined." (My translation) "La très précise description de Diderot ne permet aucun doute: c'est le *Diderot* du Louvre, de face, écrivain à son bureau, et non la réplique du musée de Langres, de trois quarts et les mains jointes" (quoted from a footnote in *Oeuvres esthétiques*, p. 509). I already wrote about this portrait in chapter 2.

2. This change does not become visible in the text selection of the *Oeuvres esthétiques* (from which I am partly quoting here and which does not include the earlier years of Diderot's *Salons*). For a comprehensive picture, see the complete edition of Diderot, *Salons*, ed. Jean Seznec (Oxford, 1975ff.) (where Diderot's reaction to van Loo's portrait appears in volume III, pp. 66ff.).

3. Diderot, *Selected Writings on Art and Literature*, trans. Geoffrey Bremner (London: Penguin, 1994), p. 288. "MOI. J'aime Michel; mais j'aime encore mieux la vérité" (509).

4. "Assez ressemblant; il peut dire à ceux qui ne le reconnaissent pas, comme le jardinier de l'opéra comique; 'C'est qu'il ne m'a jamais vu sans perruque.' Très vivant; c'est sa douceur, avec sa vivacité; mais trop jeune, tête trop petite, joli comme une femme, lorgnant, souriant, mignard, faisant le petit bec, la bouche en coeur; rien de la sagesse de couleur du *Cardinal de Choiseul*."

5. The two editions of the *Salons* offer no explanation as to why Diderot attributed this potential misjudgment to the "gardener of the comic opera." Besides the possibility of referring to a long-forgotten anecdote from the year 1767, the gesture may be generic, in the sense of mentioning somebody who would only see Diderot in the public sphere, where it was impossible not to wear a wig.

6. "et puis un luxe de vêtement à ruiner le pauvre littérateur, si le receveur de la capitation vient à l'imposer sur sa robe de chambre."

7. "L'écritoire, les livres, les accessoires aussi bien qu'il est possible."

8. "Du reste, de belle mains bien modelées, exceptée la gauche qui n'est pas dessinée."

9. "C'est cette folle madame Van Loo qui venait jaser avec lui, tandis qu'on le peignait, qui lui a donné cet air-là, et qui a tout gâté" (510).

10. "Il fallait le laisser seul, et l'abandonner à sa rêverie. Alors sa bouche se serait entre-ouverte, ses regards distraits se seraient portés au loin, le travail de sa tête, fortement occupée, se serait peint sur son visage; et Michel eût fait une belle chose."

11. "J'avais en une journée cent physionomies diverses, selon la chose dont j'étais affecté. J'étais sérain, triste, rêveur, tendre, violent, passionné, enthousiaste; mais je ne fus jamais tel que vous me voyez là. J'avais un grand front, des yeux très vifs, d'assez grand traits, la tête tout à fait du caractère d'un ancien orateur, une bonhomie qui touchait de bien près à la bêtise, à la rusticité des anciens temps."

12. "Je n'ai jamais été bien fait que par un pauvre diable appelé Garand, qui m'attrapa, comme il arrive à un sot qui dit un bon mot. Celui qui voit mon portrait par Garand, me voit" (512).

13. Diderot, *Letters to Sophie Volland*, p. 148. "C'est certainement la meilleure chose que j'ai faite depuis que je cultive les lettres, de quelque manière qu'on la considère, soit par la diversité des tons, la variété des objets, et l'abondance des idées qui n'ont jamais, j'imagine, passé par aucune tête que la mienne. C'est une mine de plaisanteries tantôt légères, tantôt fortes. Quelquefois c'est la conversation toute pure comme on la fait au coin du feu. D'autres fois, c'est tout ce que je puis imaginer ou d'éloquent ou de profond." Lettre à Sophie Volland (10 novembre 1765), in Diderot, *Correspondance*, vol. V, p. 167.

14. Michel Delon, *Album Diderot. Iconographie choisie et commentée par Michel Delon* (Paris, 2004), p. 92. See also Jean Seznec in the introduction to the

first volume of his edition of the *Salons*, pp. 16ff., and Paul Vernière in *Oeuvres esthétiques*, p. 439.

15. Jean Starobinski, "L'espace des peintres," in *Diderot, un diable de ramage*, pp. 335–373, here quoting pp. 336–37.

16. The most complete example of such a description without conceptual contours is Jean Seznec's essay "Diderot critique d'art" (1967), in Schlobach, *Denis Diderot*, pp. 111–25.

17. See Seznec, "Diderot critique d'art," p. 115 (also in the preface to vol. 1 of the complete edition of the *Salons*, p. 17); Wilson, *Diderot*, p. 524.

18. See Wilson, *Diderot*, pp. 526ff. Chapter 58 of his biography (pp. 522–41) is dedicated to "Diderot as Critic and Philosopher of Art."

19. See for example Wilson, *Diderot*, p. 531: "But his method of articulating conflicting propositions makes it possible, indeed even unavoidable, to find numerous contradictory statements in his works. Perhaps the greatest virtue of this way of seeking truth is that it presupposes a tentative and non-dogmatic approach."

20. Michael Fried, *Absorption and Theatricality. Painting and Beholder in the Age of Diderot* (Chicago, 1980).

21. The online edition of the *Encyclopédie* mentions Louis de Cahusac as the author, a libretto writer who died in 1759. While the year of his death would not necessarily exclude the possibility of Cahusac's authorship (the publication of the *Encyclopédie* was interrupted in 1757, after the first seven volumes, and resumed only in 1765, with the simultaneous appearance of volumes VIII–XVII), there is no evidence that he would have qualified for an article with philosophical ("metaphysical") content. In referring to the Chevalier de Jaucourt as the likely author of the entry on "Jugement," I follow the advice of my Stanford colleague Dan Edelstein, an eminent specialist in eighteenth-century French intellectual history.

22. Translation my own. "S'il y a des choses exposées à nos yeux dans une entière évidence, il y en a un beaucoup plus grand nombre, sur lesquelles nous n'avons qu'une lumière obscure, & si je puis ainsi m'exprimer, un crépuscule de probabilité. Voilà pourquoi l'usage & l'excellence du *jugement* se bornent ordinairement à pouvoir observer la force ou le poids des probabilités; ensuite à en faire une juste estimation; enfin, après les avoir pour ainsi dire toutes sommées exactement, à se determiner pour le côté qui emporte la balance."

23. Translation my own. "Le *jugement* [...] travaille à approfondir les choses,

à distinguer soigneusement une idée d'avec une autre, à éviter qu'une infinité ne lui donne le change. [. . .] Il suffit de remarquer ici, que c'èst à se représenter nettement les idées, & à pouvoir les distinguer exactement les unes des autres, lorsqu'il règne entre elles quelque différence, que consiste en grande partie la justesse du *jugement.* Si l'esprit unit ou sépare les idées, selon qu'elles le sont dans la réalité, c'est un *jugement* droit."

24. Translation my own. "Heureux ceux qui réussissent à former (un *jugement* droit). Plus heureux encore ceux que la nature a gratifiés de cette rare prérogative."

25. Lichtenberg, *Philosophical Writings,* p. 72 (from Scrapbook E, 418).

26. Translation my own. "Mais que signifient tous ces principes, si le goût est une chose de caprice, et s'il n'y a aucune règle éternelle, immutable du beau? Si le goût est une chose de caprice, s'il n'y a aucune règle du beau, d'où viennent donc ces émotions délicieuses qui s'élèvent si subitement, si involontairement, si tumultueusement au fond de nos âmes?" *Oeuvres esthétiques,* p. 736.

27. Translation my own. "ce n'est rien, c'est une vérité purement spéculative."

28. Translation my own. "Qu'est-ce donc que le goût? Une facilité acquise, par des expériences réitérées, à saisir le vrai ou le bon, avec la circonstance qui le rend beau, et d'en être promptement et vivement touché. Si les expériences qui déterminent le jugement sont présents à la mémoire, on aura le goût éclairé; si la mémoire en est passée, et qu'il n'en reste que l'impression, on aura le tact, l'instinct" (758).

29. Translation my own. "De là l'incertitude du succès de tout ouvrage de génie. Il est seul. On ne l'apprécie qu'en le rapprochant immédiatement à la nature. Et qui est-ce qui sait remonter jusque-là? Un autre homme de génie" (740).

30. Florian Klinger, *Urteilen* (Berlin, 2011).

31. It is very possible that in my summary I will not do justice to the degree of philosophical differentiation reached by Klinger's analysis. But even on a comparatively superficial level of intellectual appropriation, his description of seven different dimensions relevant to the act of judgment has provided the decisive clarification for my own thinking about the topic.

32. There is no exact English equivalent for the concept of *Richtigkeit,* with its strong practical and pragmatic connotations. Despite its lack of verbal elegance, I have chosen "rightness" as the predominant translation, due to its semantic closeness to *Richtigkeit*—"appropriateness" and "accuracy" would be idiomatically more convincing but semantically less precise alternatives.

33. *Setzung* highlights the act in and through which forms become part of a reality, while "positivity" accentuates the reality status of a form as a consequence of the act that produced it.

34. The prefix *an-* in *An-messung* suggests a reference to a specific object of measuring that the English word "measurement" does not yield.

35. In my historical description of the Salons I mainly rely on Jean Seznec's introduction to the first volume of Diderot, *Salons*, pp. 8–33.

36. Seznec's three-volume edition of the *Salons* has an appendix that presents reproductions of a great number of the works shown in 1759, 1761, 1763, 1765, and 1767. The documentation for each year is preceded by documents from the planning process for the Salons, providing a good impression of how the paintings were hung and how the sculptures were distributed within the different spaces reserved in the Louvre.

37. Translation my own. "Les grands seigneurs se plaignent d'y rencontrer des laquais [. . .]. Les bourgeois y sont très nombreux, et semblent fort heureux de trouver un guide bénévole, quelque garçon beau parleur, qui a étudié de près le 'Livret.' Les beaux ésprits, les intellectuels d'alors, sont aussi assidus, certains prétendent venir tous les jours" (Seznec, introduction, in Diderot, *Salons*, p. 12).

38. Translation my own. "[Nos] simples littérateurs [. . .] ne s'entendent ni au dessin, ni aux lumières, ni au coloris, ni à l'harmonie du tout, ni à la touche, etc. A tout moment ils sont exposés à élever aux nues une production médiocre et à passer dédaigneusement devant un chef-d'oeuvre de l'art" (Diderot, *Salons*,16).

39. Translation my own. "Pour décrire un Salon à mon gré et au vôtre, savez-vous, mon ami, ce qu'il faudrait avoir? Toutes les sortes de goût, un coeur sensible à tous les charmes, une âme susceptible d'une infinité d'enthousiasmes différents, une variété de styles qui répondit à la variété des pinceaux" (18).

40. Translation my own. "Je me trouve parfois tiraillé par des sentiments opposés. Il y a des moments où je voudrais que cette besogne tombât du ciel tout imprimé au mileu de la capitale; plus souvent, lorsque je réfléchis à la douleur profonde qu'elle causerait à une infinité d'artistes [. . .] je serais désolé qu'elle parût" (19).

41. Translation my own. "Voici, mon ami, des idées qui m'ont passé par la tête à la vue des tableaux qu'on a exposé cette année au Salon. Je les jette sur le papier, sans me soucier ni de les trier ni de les écrire. Il y en aura des vraies, il y aura des fausses. Tantôt vous me trouverez trop sévère, tantôt trop indulgent. Je con-

damnerai peut-être où vous approuveriez; je ferai grâce où vous condamneriez; vous exigerez encore où je serai content. Peu m'importe. La seule chose que j'ai au coeur, c'est de vous épargner quelques instants que vous emploieriez mieux" (108).

42. For example, at the end of Diderot's second *Salon*, following a particularly favorable judgment on a painting by Greuze: "Monsieur Diderot is right. It would be hard to react too ecstatically to this charming painting. I have never seen anything more pleasing, more interesting, more tender in its effect. Oh! how beautiful and touching simple, honest ways of life can be! Wit and subtlety are nothing compared to them!" Translation my own. "M. Diderot a raison, on ne saurait trop s'extasier sur ce charmant tableau. Je n'en ai pas vu de plus agréable, de plus intéressant, et dont l'effet soit plus doux. O que les moeurs simples sont belles et touchantes, et que l'esprit et la finesse sont peu de chose auprès d'elles!" (144–46).

43. Translation my own. "Je ne serois pas fâché d'avoir ce tableau. Toutes les fois que vous viendriez chez moi, vous en diriez du mal, mais vous le regarderiez" (69). In a similar trope, Diderot always implied a positive judgment when he imagined that a work could be in Grimm's possession: "I would much rather these paintings were in your study than in the home of that odious Trublet, to whom they belong." "J'aimerois bien mieux que ces derniers [tableaux] fussent dans votre cabinet que chez ce villain Trublet à qui ils appartiennent" (66).

44. Translation my own. "Cet homme deviendra un grand artiste ou rien. Il faut attendre" (68). Diderot is referring here to Gabriel François Doyen, who was thirty-three years old in 1759.

45. Translation my own. "Nous avons beaucoup d'artistes; peu de bons, pas un excellent; ils choisissent de beaux sujets; mais la force leur manque; ils n'ont ni esprit, ni chaleur, ni imagination. Presque tous pèchent par le coloris. Beaucoup de dessein, point d'idées" (69).

46. Translation my own. "Jamais nous n'avons eu un plus beau Salon. Presque aucun tableau absolument mauvais; plus de bons que de médiocres, et un grand nombre d'excellents [. . .]. On ne peint plus en Flandre. S'il y a des peintres en Italie et en Allemagne, ils sont moins réunis; ils ont moins d'émulation et moins d'encouragement. La France est donc la seule contrée où cet art se soutienne, et même avec quelque éclat" (140).

47. Translation my own. "Il y a de Colin de Vermont une mauvaise Adoration des Rois. De Jeurat, des Chartreux en méditation; c'est pire encore, point de

silence; rien de sauvage; rien qui rappelle la Justice divine, nulle idée, nulle adoration profonde; nul receuilment intérieur; point d'extase; point de terreur" (64).

48. Translation my own. "Je n'ai pas mémoire d'avoir vu [. . .] les autres
tableaux de Challe. Vous sçavez avec quelle dédaigneuse inadvertence on passe
sur les compositions médiocres" (66).

49. Translation my own. "Vous savez que je n'ai jamais approuvé le mélange
entre des êtres réels et des êtres allégoriques, et le tableau qui a pour sujet la
Publication de la Paix en 1749 ne m'a pas fait changer d'avis. Les êtres réels
perdent de leur vérité à côté des êtres allégoriques, et ceux-ci jettent toujours
quelque obscurité dans la composition. Le morceau dont il s'agit n'est pas sans
effet. Il est peint avec hardiesse et force. C'est certainement l'ouvrage d'un
maître" (108–9).

50. Translation my own. "Dites-moi comment un coussin de couleur a pu se
trouver dans une étable où la misère réfugiait la mère et l'enfant, et où l'haleine
de deux animaux réchauffait un nouveau-né contre la rigueur de la saison? Ap-
paramment qu'un des rois avait envoyé un coussin d'avance par son écuyer pour
pouvoir se prosterner avec plus de commodité" (134).

51. Translation my own. "Ce n'est pas assez de me montrer dans Psyché la
curiosité de voir l'Amour; il faut que j'y aperçoive encore la crainte de s'éveiller.
Elle devrait avoir la bouche entr'ouverte et craindre de respirer. C'est son amant
qu'elle voit, qu'elle voit pour la première fois, au hasard de le perdre. Quelle joie
de le voir et de le voir si beau!" (119).

52. Translation my own. "Enfin il y a d'un M. Briand un *Passage des âmes
du purgatoire au ciel*. Ce peintre a relégué son purgatoire dans un coin de son
tableau. Il ne s'en échappe que quelques figures perdues sur une toile d'une étendue immense [. . .]. Pour se tirer d'un pareil sujet, il eût fallu la force d'idées,
de couleurs et d'imagination de Rubens, et tenter une de ces machines que les
Italiens appellant *opera da stupire*. Une tête féconde et hardie aurait ouvert le
gouffre de feu au bas de son tableau; il eût occupé toute l'étendue et toute la
profondeur" (136).

53. Translation my own. "Je me rappelle que l'Annonciation est traitée d'une
manière sèche, raide et froide; qu'elle est sans effet" (63).

54. Translation my own. "Peut-être y a-t-il de belles choses parmi les tableaux
dont je ne vous ai point parlé, et parmi les sculptures dont je ne vous parle pas:
c'est qu'ils ont été muets, et qu'ils ne m'ont rien dit" (138).

55. Translation my own. "Il y a de la volupté dans ce tableau, des pieds nus, des cuisses, des tétons, des fesses; et c'est moins peut-être le talent de l'artiste qui nous arrête que notre vice. La couleur a bien de l'éclat. Les femmes occupées à servir les figures principales sont éteintes avec jugement; vraies, naturelles et belles, sans causer de distraction" (64).

56. Translation my own. "Beaucoup de tableaux, mon ami; beaucoup de mauvais tableaux. J'aime à louer. Je suis heureux quand j'admire. Je ne demandois pas mieux que d'être heureux et admirer" (63).

57. Translation my own. "La tête [de la nymphe] a de la jeunesse, des grâces, de la vérité, de la noblesse. Il y a partout une grande molesse de chair; et par ci par là des vérités de detail qui font croire que l'artiste ne s'épargne pas les modèles. Mais comment fait-il pour en trouver des beaux?" (69).

58. Translation my own. "Et ce jugement de Pâris? Que vous en dirai-je? Il semble que le lieu de la scène devoit être un paysage écarté, silencieux, désert, mais riche; que la beauté des déesses devoit tenir le spectateur et le juge incertain; qu'on ne pouvoit rencontrer le vrai caractère de Pâris que par un coup de génie. Mr de la Grenée n'y a pas vu tant de difficultés. Il étoit bien loin de soupçonner l'effet sublime du lieu de la scène. Son jeune Satyre qui s'amuse du sifflet de Pan a plus de gorge qu'une jeune fille. Le reste, c'est de la couleur, de la toile et du temps perdu" (66).

59. See, among others, Wilson, *Diderot*, p. 527; Fried, *Absorption and Theatricality*, p. 109; Seznec, introduction, in Diderot, *Salons*, p. 16.

60. The portrait in question belongs to those works for which the supplement of Seznec's *Salons* does not provide any pictorial documentation. This means that in the reading of Diderot's text, we find ourselves in a situation similar to that of the readers of the *Correspondance littéraire* in 1763.

61. Translation my own. "Je jure que ce portrait est un chef-d'oeuvre qui, un jour à venir, n'aura point de prix. Comme elle est coiffée! Que ces cheveux châtains sont vrais! Que ce ruban qui serre la tête fait bien! Que cette longue tresse qu'elle relève d'une main sur les épaules et qui tourne plusieurs fois autour de son bras, est belle! Voilà des cheveux, pour le coup!" (530). I quote the texts written for the Salons between 1773 and 1781 from Diderot, *Oeuvres esthétiques*, ed. Paul Vernière.

62. Translation my own. "Il faut voir le soin et la vérité dont le dedans de cette main et les plis de ses doigts sont peints. Quelle finesse et quelle variété de teintes sur le front."

63. Translation my own. "On reproche à ce visage son sérieux et sa gravité; mais n'est-ce pas là le caractère d'une femme grosse qui sent la dignité, le péril et l'importance de son état? [. . .]

Que ne lui reproche-t-on pas aussi ce teint jaunâtre sur les tempes et vers le front, cette gorge qui s'appesantit, ces membres qui s'affaissent et ce ventre qui commence à se relever?"

64. Translation my own. "Ce portrait tue tous ceux qui l'environnent."

65. Translation my own. "La délicatesse avec laquelle le bas de ce visage est touché et l'ombre du menton portée sur le cou est inconcevable. On serait tenté de passer sa main sur ce menton, si l'austérité de la personne n'arrêtait et l'éloge et la main" (530–31).

66. Translation my own "Mettez l'escalier entre ce portrait et vous, regardez-le avec une lunette, et vous verrez la nature même; je vous défie de me nier que cette figure ne vous regarde et ne vive."

67. Translation my own. "Ah! Monsieur Greuze, que vous êtes différent de vous même lorsque c'est la tendresse ou l'intérêt qui guide votre pinceau!"

68. Diderot, *Selected Writings on Art and Literature*, p. 242. "Ce peintre est certainement amoureux de sa femme; et il n'a pas tort" (540). Like the portrait of 1763, this later one does not appear in Seznec's documentation.

After the sentence about Greuze's attachment to his wife, Diderot again "entered" the scene of the painting, this time through memories of his encounters with Mme de Greuze during an earlier stage of her life: "I loved her myself, when I was young and she was called Mademoiselle Babuty. She worked in a little bookshop on the Quai des Augustins; she was all dolled up, her skin was white and she was straight as a lily, red as a rose." "Je l'ai bien aimée, moi, quand j'étais jeune, et qu'elle s'appelait Mlle Babuty. Elle occupait une petite boutique de libraire sur le quai des Augustins; poupine, blanche et droite comme le lis, vermeille comme la rose." The scene continues with a dialogue between the young author and Mlle Babuty.

69. "Il y avait, au Salon dernier, un *Portrait de Mme Greuze enceinte*; l'intérêt de son état arrêtait; la vérité des détails vous faisait ensuite tomber les bras. Celui-ci n'est pas aussi beau; cependant l'ensemble en est gracieux; il est bien posé; l'attitude en est de volupté; ses deux mains montrent des finesses de ton qui enchantent. La gauche seulement n'est pas ensemble; elle a même un doigt cassé; cela fait peine" (540–41).

70. "Les passages du front sont trop jaunes: on sait bien qu'il reste aux femmes qui ont eu des enfants de ces taches-là; mais si l'on pousse l'imitation de la nature jusqu'à vouloir les rendre, il faut les affaiblir; c'est là le cas d'embellir un peu, puisqu'on le peut sans que la ressemblance en souffre."

71. "Au reste, le tour de la bouche, les yeux, tous les autres details sont à ravir."

72. "C'est toujours le dernier ouvrage de ce grand maître qu'on appelle le plus beau" (576).

73. Of the seven works that Vernet exposed in the Salon of 1767, Seznec shows only three in his documentation—and none of them seems to correspond to the one Diderot is describing.

74. "Je ne sais pas ce que je louerai de préférence dans ce morceau. Est-ce le reflet de la lune sur les eaux ondulantes? Sont-ce ces nuées sombres et chargées de leur mouvement? Est-ce ce vaisseau qui passe au-devant de l'astre de la nuit, et qui le renvoie et attache à son immense éloignement? Est-ce la réflexion dans le fluide de la petite torche que ce marin tient à l'extrémité de la nacelle? Sont-ce les deux figures adossées à la fontaine? Est-ce le brasier dont la lueur rougeâtre se propage sur tous les objets environnants, sans détruire l'harmonie? Est-ce l'effet total de cette nuit?"

75. See number 113 in Seznec's documentary supplement in Diderot, *Salons*.

76. Translation my own. "D'abord le genre me plaît; c'est de la peinture morale. Quoi donc! Le pinceau n'a-t-il pas été assez et trop longtemps consacré à la débauche et au vice? Ne devons-nous pas être satisfaits de le voir concourir enfin avec la poésie dramatique à nous toucher, à nous instruire, à nous corriger et à nous inviter à la vertu?" (524).

77. Translation my own. "Le principal personnage, celui qui occupe le milieu de la scène et qui fixe l'attention, est un vieillard paralytique étendu dans son fauteuil, la tête appuyée sur un traversin et les pieds sur un tabouret. Il est habillé; ses jambes malades son enveloppées d'une couverture. Il est entouré de ses enfants et de ses petits-enfants, la plupart empressés à le servir. Sa belle tête est d'un caractère si touchant, il paraît si sensible aux services qu'on lui rend, il a tant de peine à parler, sa voix est si faible, ses regards si tendres, son teint si pâle, qu'il faut être sans entrailles pour ne pas les sentir remuer" (525).

78. Translation my own. "Chacun ici a précisément le degré d'intérêt qui convient à l'âge et au caractère" (526).

79. Translation my own. "Ce tableau est beau et très beau, et malheur à celui qui peut le considérer un moment de sang-froid! Le caractère du vieillard est unique;

le caractère du gendre est unique; l'enfant qui apporte à boire, unique; la vieille femme, unique. De quelque côté qu'on porte ses yeux, on est enchanté" (528).

80. Translation my own. "il est brusque, doux, insinuant, caustique, gallant, triste, gai, froid, chaud, sérieux ou fou, selon la chose qu'il projette" (529).

81. Number 54 in the documentation of the Salon of 1765.

82. Salomon Gessner (1730–1788) was a Swiss poet and painter proverbially famous in Diderot's time for his idyllic texts and artworks.

83. "La jolie élégie! le joli poème! la belle idylle que Gessner en ferait! C'est la vignette d'un morceau de ce poète. Tableau délicieux!" (533).

84. With the words "strongest emotional impact" I try to render the eighteenth-century meaning of the adjective "intéressant" that Diderot uses here.

85. "Comme elle est naturellement placée! que sa tête est belle! qu'elle est élégamment coiffée! que son visage a d'expression! Sa douleur est profonde; elle est à son malheur, elle y est tout entière. Le joli catafalque que cette cage! Que cette guirlande de verdure qui serpente autour a de grâces! O la belle main! la belle main! le beau bras! Voyez la vérité des détails de ces doigts; et ces fossettes, et cette mollesse, et cette teinte de rougeur dont la pression de la tête a coloré le bout de ses doigts délicats, et le charme de tout cela."

86. "On s'approcherait de cette main pour la baiser, si on ne respectait cette enfant et sa douleur."

87. "Mais, petite, votre douleur est bien profonde, bien réfléchie! Que signifie cet air rêveur et mélancholique! Quoi! pour un oiseau! Vous ne pleurez pas, vous êtes affligée; et la pensée accompagne votre affliction. Ça, petite, ouvrez-moi votre coeur: parlez-moi vrai; est-ce la mort de cet oiseau qui vous retire si fortement et si tristement en vous-même?" (533–34).

88. He indeed believed that this was also the understanding of the work intended by Greuze: "The subject of this little poem is so subtle that many people didn't understand it; they thought it was only her canary the girl was weeping for. Greuze painted the same subject once before. He placed before a broken mirror a tall girl dressed in white satin, sunk in deep melancholy. Don't you think it would be as stupid to attribute the tears of the girl in this Salon to the loss of a bird, as the melancholy of the girl in the Salon before it to her broken mirror?" (238–39). "Le sujet de ce petit poème est si fin, que beaucoup de personnes ne l'ont pas entendu; ils ont cru que cette jeune fille ne pleurait que son serin. Greuze a déjà peint une fois le même sujet: il a placé devant une glace fêlée une grande

fille en satin blanc, pénétrée d'une profonde mélancolie. Ne pensez-vous pas qu'il y aurait autant de bêtise à attribuer les pleurs de la jeune fille de ce Salon à la perte d'un oiseau que la mélancolie de la jeune fille du précédent Salon à son miroir cassé?" (536).

89. "'Et mon oiseau? . . .—Vous souriez.' (Ah! mon ami, qu'elle était belle! ah! si vous l'aviez vu sourire et pleurer!) Je continuai. 'Eh bien, votre oiseau! Quand on s'oublie soi-mème, se souvient-on de son oiseau? Lorsque l'heure du retour de votre mère approcha, celui que vous aimez s'en alla. Qu'il était heureux, content, transporté! qu'il eût de peine à s'arracher d'auprès de vous! . . . Comme vous me regardez! Je sais tout cela'" (535–36).

90. "Mais quel âge a-t-elle donc? . . . Que vous répondrai-je? et quelle question m'avez-vous faite? Sa tête est de quinze à seize ans, et son bras et sa main sont de dix-huit à dix-neuf. C'est un défaut de cette composition qui devient autant plus sensible, que la tête étant appuyée contre la main, une des parties donne tout contre la mesure de l'autre. Placez la main autrement, et l'on ne s'apercevra plus qu'elle est un peu trop forte et trop caractérisée. C'est, mon ami, que la tête a été prise d'après un modèle, et la main d'après un autre" (536–37).

91. "Ce peintre peut avoir fait aussi bien, mais pas mieux."

92. "Que ferai-je? que deviendrai-je? S'il était ingrat? . . .—Quelle folie! Ne craignez rien: cela ne se peut, cela ne sera pas!" (536).

93. Herbert Dieckmann, "Das Problem der Ausdrucksform des Denkens bei Diderot," in Schlobach, *Denis Diderot*, p. 87.

94. "Le cou soutient la tête à merveille. Il est beau de dessin et de couleur, et va, comme il doit, s'attacher aux épaules; mais pour cette gorge, je ne saurais la regarder; et si, même à cinquante ans, je ne hais pas les gorges. Le peintre a penché sa figure en devant, et par cette attitude il semble dire au spectateur: 'Voyez la gorge de ma femme.' Je la vois, monsieur Greuze. Eh bien, votre femme a la gorge molle et jaune. Si elle ressemble, tant pis encore pour vous, pour elle et pour le tableau" (541).

95. "Toujours petits tableaux, petites idées, compositions frivoles, propres au boudoir d'une petite maîtresse, à la petite maison d'un petit maître; faites pour de petits abbés, de petits robins, de gros financiers ou autres personnages sans moeurs et d'un petit goût" (469).

96. Unlike Vernet, Jean-Baptiste Greuze, clearly Diderot's favorite contemporary artist in France, had a reputation for being particularly difficult and un-

pleasant (see Starobinski, *Diderot, un diable de ramage*, 360). While in Greuze's confrontation with the Académie over the "moralist" genre of painting, Diderot supported him, he was openly critical of Greuze's public behavior, as shown for example in a remark about Vernet's reaction to his colleague in personal conversation: "Vernet replied, 'The fact is that you have a swarm of enemies, and among them there's someone who appears to love you madly, but who'll lead you to ruin.'—'And who is that someone?' Greuze asked him.—'It's you,' Vernet replied." (Translation my own) "C'est, lui répondit Vernet, que vous avez une nuée d'ennemis, et parmi ces ennemis un quidam qui a l'air de vous aimer à la folie, et qui vous perdra.—Et qui est ce quidam? lui demanda Greuze.—C'est vous, lui répondit Vernet" (537).

97. Translation my own. "Il semble que tous nos artistes se soient cette année donné le mot pour dégénérer. Les excellents ne sont que bons, les bons sont médiocres et les mauvais sont détestables. Vous aurez de la peine à deviner à propos de qui je fais cette observation; c'est à propos de Vernet, oui, de ce Vernet que j'aime, à qui je dois de la reconnaissance et que je me plais tant à louer" (580).

98. Translation my own. "L'éruption de l'incendie de l'Opéra fait de l'effet; mais cet effet est dur et sec; il n'y a pas assez d'air, et les figures n'en sont pas très bien dessinées.

L'intérieur de la salle incendiée me plaît davantage; je le trouve mieux d'accord, mais je n'en aime pas les figures. Du reste, ces figures sont bien groupées.

(LES RUINES DU COLYSEE DE ROME) Me paraissent égales de ton; les masses y sont, et produisent de l'effet; j'y voudrais seulement une variété qui ne détruisit pas cet effet; cela donnerait de l'harmonie et ajouterait à la magie pittoresque" (653–55).

99. Translation my own. "moins ignorant d'un Salon à l'autre, je suis plus réservé et plus timide." Quoted via Starobinski, *Diderot, un diable de ramage*, p. 341.

100. Translation adapted from Diderot, *On Art and Artists: An Anthology of Diderot's Aesthetic Thought*, ed. Jean Seznec, trans. John S. D. Glaus (Dordrecht: Springer, 2011), pp. 59–60. "Au reste, n'oubliez pas que je ne garantis ni mes descriptions, ni mon jugement sur rien; mes descriptions, parce qu'il n'y a aucune mémoire sous le ciel qui puisse emporter fidèlement autant de compositions diverses; mon jugement parce que je ne suis ni artiste, ni même amateur. Je vous dis seulement ce que je pense et je vous le dis avec toute ma franchise. S'il m'ar-

rive d'un moment à l'autre de me contredire, c'est que d'un moment à l'autre j'ai été diversement affecté, également impartial quand je loue et je me dédis d'un éloge, quand je blâme et que je me dépars de ma critique" (Starobinski, *Diderot, un diable de ramage*, pp. 340–41).

101. Diderot, *Selected Writings on Art and Literature*, p. 235. "Je ne hais pas les grands crimes, premièrement parce qu'on en fait des beaux tableaux et de belles tragédies; et puis, c'est que les grandes et sublimes actions et les grands crimes portent le même caractère d'énergie. Si un homme n'était pas capable d'incendier une ville, un autre homme ne serait pas capable de se précipiter dans un gouffre pour la sauver" (Starobinski, *Diderot, un diable de ramage*, p. 360).

102. Klinger, *Urteilen*, pp. 606–11.

103. Lichtenberg, *Philosophical Writings*, pp. 97–98 (from Scrapbook H, 15).

104. Lichtenberg, *Philosophical Writings*, pp. 102–3 (Scrapbook H, 150, 151).

105. Wolfgang Hildesheimer, *Mozart* (Frankfurt am Main, 1993), p. 93.

106. "Everywhere Mozart's hand shows that the writing of the scores was something purely technical for him, something like half an hour of focused and yet relaxed concentration where only clarity and readability mattered. Masterpieces of calligraphy—with not a single note corrected." Translation my own (adapted). "Überall ergibt die Handschrift den Beweis, dass der Akt der Niederschrift ein rein technischer war, der Vollzug von vielleicht nicht mehr als einer halben Stunde scharfer, doch entspannter Konzentration, in der es vor allem auf Klarheit und Leserlichkeit ankam: ein wunderbar aufrechtes und dabei bewegtes Notenbild, ohne auch nur eine winzigste Korrektur, auch dies ein kalligraphisches Meisterwerk. Auch hier also: Nichts verraten." Hildesheimer, *Mozart*, pp. 93–94.

107. "He *always* composed *against* his own texts—against the texts of his letters, his notes, even against his appearance and against his style of behavior. Music, as his true language, came from sources unknown, it lived from a suggestive power beyond all comprehension and access." Translation my own (adapted). "Gegen die eigenen Texte hat er *immer* komponiert—gegen die Texte seiner Briefe, der Aufzeichnungen, und damit gegen den Anschein, sein Auftreten und Gebaren. Oder umgekehrt: Seine wirkliche Sprache, die Musik, nährt sich aus uns unkenntlichen Quellen, sie lebt von einer suggestiven Kraft, die sich über den Gegenstand ihrer Suggestion so weit erhebt, dass er sich uns entzieht. Ihr Schöpfer bleibt uns unzugänglich." Hildesheimer, *Mozart*, p. 59.

108. "Mozart never made an effort to project himself into the world around him. [. . .] Instead, until very late in his life, he considered himself a normal member of the social world, one among many, a member, however, with a specific competence, somebody who could do more than the others. Unlike Beethoven or Goethe, Mozart would never have made the effort to consciously transmit anything specific from his own world to these others." Translation my own. "Mozart hat sich niemals in seine Mitwelt projiziert. [. . .] (Er) meinte vielmehr bis spät in seinem Leben, zu seiner Mitwelt zu gehören, einer unter anderen zu sein, freilich einer, der mehr konnte als die anderen. Niemals hätte er versucht, diesen anderen etwas aus seiner Welt bewusst zu vermitteln, wie Beethoven oder Goethe." Hildesheimer, *Mozart*, p. 64.

CHAPTER SEVEN: "PROSE OF THE WORLD"

1. Adapted from Diderot, *Selected Writings on Art and Literature*, p. 290. "J'avais en une journée cent physiognomies diverses, selon la chose dont j'étais affecté. J'étais sérain, triste, rêveur, tendre, violent, passionné, enthousiaste." *Oeuvres esthétiques*, p. 510.

2. As we have already seen, Jean Starobinski chose this self-reference as the title for the collection of his essays on Diderot: *Diderot, un diable de ramage*. (See especially the introductory text, "Le ramage et le cri.")

3. Translation my own. "Je vais rentrer dans la volière dont je me suis échappé depuis quinze mois. Mon ramage, qui n'était pas déjà trop mélodieux, n'aura-t-il point souffert des ramages durs et barbares des oiseaux moraves, helvétiens, belges, prussiens, polonais, esclavons et russes avec lesquels j'ai vécu?" Quoted in Starobinski, *Diderot, un diable de ramage,* p. 11 (the addressee of Diderot's letter was the mother of the author of *De l'Allemagne*).

4. In a review of two Diderot monographs published in the *New York Review of Books* (March 7, 2019), Lynn Hunt describes both Diderot's personality and his texts as "mercurial."

5. I take most intuitions developed in the following paragraph from an intense (and very early morning) conversation with Mareike Reisch and Björn Buschbeck at Stanford in March 2019.

6. Translation my own. "De combien de "Neveux," de "Fatalistes," de "Est-il bon? est-il méchant?" la postérité n'a-t-elle pas été privée à cause de ce quart de siècle occupé à des tâches sommes toutes mercenaires? On dirait une longue

parenthèse, triste et grise. Alors on sauve Diderot comme on peut: un exemple d'abnégation, dit-on. De courage surtout, car il en fallait tout de même pour maintenir l'entreprise comme il l'a fait, quelques fois seul contre tous et au péril de sa liberté. La réalité n'est pas si simple." Jacques Proust, "L'Encyclopédie dans la pensée et dans la vie de Diderot" (1963), in *Denis Diderot*, ed. Schlobach, p. 100.

7. Translation my own. "Cet arbre de la connaissance humaine pouvait être formé de plusieurs manières, soit en rapportant aux diverses facultés de notre âme nos differentes connaissances, soit en les rapportant aux êtres qu'elles ont pour objets. Mais l'embarras était d'autant plus grand, qu'il avait plus d'arbitraire. Et combien ne devait-il pas y avoir? La nature ne nous offre que des choses particulières, infinies en nombre, et sans aucune division fixe et determinée. Tout s'y succède par des nuances insensibles. Et sur cette mer d'objets qui nous environnent, s'il en paraît quelques-uns, comme des pointes de rochers qui semblent percer la surface et dominer les autres, ils ne doivent cet avantage qu'à des systèmes particuliers, qu'à des conventions vagues, et qu'à certains événements étrangers à l'arrangement physique des choses, et aux vraies institutions de la philosophie." "Prospectus," Wikisource edition, p. 4.

8. The one—rhetorically motivated—exception is the first sentence of the final paragraph in the "Prospectus," where Diderot refers to a "system that exists in the divine understanding / système qui existe dans l'entendement divin" as a counterpoint to the infinity of possible (and always arbitrary) systems of knowledge based on human understanding: "But one consideration, to which we can never draw enough attention, is that there are as many possible systems of human knowledge as there are minds, and that only the system that exists in the divine understanding is sure to be free from all arbitrariness. / Mais une considération que nous ne pouvons trop rappeler, c'est que le nombre des systèmes possibles de la connaissance humaine est aussi grand que le nombre des esprits, et qu'il n'y a certainement que le système qui existe dans l'entendement divin d'où l'arbitraire soit exclu." Translation my own.

9. Denis Diderot, "Encyclopedia," in *The Encyclopedia of Diderot & d'Alembert Collaborative Translation Project,* trans. Philip Stewart (Ann Arbor: Michigan Publishing, University of Michigan Library, 2002). Web. 26 May 2020. http://hdl.handle.net/2027/spo.did2222.0000.004. Translation of "Encyclopédie," *Encyclopédie ou dictionnaire raisonné des sciences, des arts et des métiers,* vol. 5. (Paris, 1755). "Encyclopédie," Wikisource edition, p. 9.

10. NB: This translation is taken from d'Alembert's *Preliminary Discourse* in the University of Michigan's *Encyclopédie* translation project. D'Alembert incorporated a lot of the text of Diderot's "Prospectus" in his *Preliminary Discourse*. "Voilà ce que nous avions à exposer au public sur les sciences et les beaux arts. La partie des arts mécaniques ne demandait ni moins de details, ni moins de soins. Jamais peut-être il ne s'est trouvé tant de difficultés rassemblées, et si peu de secours pour les vaincre. On a trop écrit sur les sciences, on n'a pas assez bien écrit sur la plupart des arts libéraux, on n'a presque rien écrit sur les arts mécaniques; car qu'est-ce que le peu qu'on rencontre dans les auteurs, en comparaison de l'étendue et de la fécondité du sujet?" (8).

11. Ibid. "Les opérations des artistes et la description de leurs machines."

12. Ibid. "Tout nous déterminait donc à recourir aux ouvriers. On s'est adressé aux plus habiles de Paris et du royaume. On s'est donné la peine d'aller dans leurs ateliers, de les intérroger, d'écrire sous leur dictée, de développer leurs pensées, d'en tirer les termes propres à leur profession, d'en dresser les tables, de les définer, de converser avec ceux dont on avait obtenu des mémoires . . ." (9).

13. Ibid. "Nous avons vu des ouvriers qui travaillaient depuis quarante années sans rien connaître à leurs machines. Il nous a fallu exercer avec eux la fonction dont se glorifiait Socrate, la fonction pénible et délicate de faire accoucher les esprits: *obstetrix animorum*."

14. It would be a complex philosophical task to distinguish different degrees of "singularity," and not only in Diderot's work. The word is always used as a critique of generally assumed levels of abstraction and as a change of focus from them. In the following quote, the expression "métiers singuliers" insists on analyzing different crafts individually, instead of talking about them on a general level. In the *Salons*, by contrast, the movements of "singularization" through judgment specify individual paintings and sculptures within the work of different individual artists (for example, those paintings by Greuze that Diderot particularly appreciated as opposed to those that he disliked).

15. Ibid. "Il est des métiers si singuliers, et des manoeuvres si déliées, qu'à moins de travailler soi-même, de mouvoir une machine de ses propres mains, et de voir l'ouvrage se former sous les propres yeux, il est difficile d'en parler avec précision. Il a donc fallu plusieurs fois se procurer les machines, les construire, mettre la main à l'oeuvre, se rendre, pour ainsi dire, apprenti, et de faire soi-même de mauvais ouvrages pour apprendre aux autres comment on

en fait de bons. C'est ainsi que nous nous sommes convaincus de l'ignorance dans laquelle on est sur la plupart des objets de la vie, et de la nécessité de sortir de cette ignorance."

16. "Finally, in the *Encyclopédie*, Diderot sketched out the broad lines of an approach to politics. Indeed, is there anything apolitical about a project that presents itself as an assessment of the conquests of the human mind, an assessment undertaken at a specific historical juncture with the goal of giving more illustrative power to the demand for necessary and revolutionary changes?" Translation my own. "Enfin Diderot a tracé dans l'*Encyclopédie* les grandes lignes d'une politique. Et d'ailleurs tout n'est-il pas politique dans une entreprise qui se présente comme un bilan des acquisitions de l'esprit humain dans une conjoncture historique précise pour donner une force plus démonstrative à l'exigence des changements nécessaires et révolutionnaires à faire?" Proust, "L'Encyclopédie dans la pensée et dans la vie de Diderot," p. 107.

17. "The politically 'revolutionary' articles in the *Encyclopédie* are not by Diderot, as was long thought." Translation my own. "Les articles 'révolutionnaires' de l'*Encyclopédie*, en matière politique, ne sont pas de Diderot comme l'on a cru longtemps." Ibid.

18. For more elaborate symptomatologies of this present, see my collection of essays *Brüchige Gegenwart. Reflexionen und Reaktionen* (Stuttgart, 2019); my book *Our Broad Present* (New York, 2014); and my essays "Humanism," in *The Bloomsbury Handbook of Posthumanism*, ed. Mads Rosendahl Thomsen and Jacob Wamberg (New York, 2020), and "Konservativ, utopisch, melancholisch: 'Nabelschnur zum Kosmos,'" in *konservativ?!: Miniaturen aus Kultur, Politik und Wissenschaft*, ed. Michael Kühnlein (Berlin, 2019).

19. I use "global" to refer to all humans capable of participating in (and with easy access to) electronic communication.

20. Quoted, again, from G. W. F. Hegel: The Oxford University Press Translations. Electronic Edition. *Hegel's Aesthetics*, p. 151.

21. Ibid., p. 976.

CHAPTER EIGHT: "JE NE FAIS RIEN"

"I'm not doing anything." Translation my own. Letter to Mme de Vandeul dated July 28, 1781, in Diderot, *Correspondance*, Vol. 15 (1970), p. 256.

1. Three previously born children of Denis and Anne-Toinette Diderot had

died prematurely. Anne-Toinette was forty-three years old when she was pregnant with Angélique.

2. *Correspondance*, Vol. 15, p. 259.

3. See Diderot's letter to Sophie Volland dated November 22, 1768, when
Angélique was fifteen: "She seemed so advanced to me that last Sunday, when
her mother sent me out for a walk with her, I decided to tell her all that it means
to be a woman, beginning with the question: 'Do you know what the difference
is between the sexes?' […] I have asked a few sensible people what they thought
of this talk and they all approved of it. Could it be that it is no use condemn-
ing something when there is no cure for it? […] If I were to lose this child, I
think I should die of grief. I love her more than I can say" (*Diderot's Letters to
Sophie Volland: A Selection,* trans. *Peter France*, pp. 187–88). "Je l'ai trouvée si
avancée, que dimanche passé, chargé par sa mère de la promener, je pris mon
parti et lui révélai tout ce qui tient à l'état de femme, débutant par cette question:
Sçavez-vous quelle est la différence des deux sexes? […] J'ai consulté sur cet
entretien quelques gens sensés. Ils m'ont tous dit que j'avois bien fait. Seroit-ce
qu'il ne faut pas blâmer une chose à laquelle il n'y a plus de remède? […] Si je
perdois cet enfant, je crois que j'en périroit de douleur. Je l'aime plus que je ne
sçaurois vous dire" (*Correspondance*, Vol. 15, pp. 231–33). Angélique's feelings
for her father seem to have corresponded to this strong attachment: "I am quite
enchanted of my daughter. She says that her mama prays to God and her papa
does good." / "Je suis fou à lier de ma fille. Elle dit que maman prie Dieu, et que
son papa fait le bien."

4. See Wilson, *Diderot*, pp. 676–77.

5. Translation my own. "Je ne sçais, mon enfant, si tu as grand plaisir à me
lire, mais tu n'ignores pas que c'est un supplice pour moi que d'écrire; et cela
ne t'empêche pas d'exiger encore une de mes lettres; voilà ce qui s'appelle de la
personnalité toute pure, et se donner à soi-même bien décidément la preference
sur un autre" (252–53).

6. Translation my own. "Je vois avec une certaine satisfaction toutes mes
liaisons se découdre" (255).

7. Translation my own. "Si je travaille modérément? Je ne fais rien" (25).

8. Translation my own. "Je lui administre trois prises de *Gilblas* tous les
jours; une le matin; une l'après dîner; une le soir. Quand nous avons vu la fin
de *Gilblas*, nous prendrons le *Diable boîteux*, le *Bachelier de Salamanque*; et les

autres ouvrages gais de cette nature. Quelques centaines et quelques années de ces lectures finiront la guérison. Si j'etois bien sûr du success, la corvée me sembleroit point dure. Ce qu'il y a de plaisant, c'est qu'elle régale tous ceux qui la visitent de ce qu'elle a retenu, et que la conversation redouble l'efficacité du remède. J'avois toujours traité les romans comme des productions assez frivoles; j'ai enfin découvert qu'ils étoient bons pour les vapeurs" (253–54).

9. Translation my own. "Votre mère vous fait des confitures de groseilles et d'abricots. On lui a donné le fruit, et elle me fait payer le sucre. Pour un homme dont le désespoir est de faire des réponses, en voilà une suffisamment longue" (257).

10. See Wilson, *Diderot*, p. 575.

11. Translation my own. "Votre absence a attristé la ville et embelli la campagne, surtout lorsque le ciel fondoit en eau, et que la prairie étoit sur le point de disparoître entre les deux bras de la Seine, au-dessous de notre terrasse. J'enrageois comme vous contre la pérennité de ce beau temps. La nuit, il me sembloit que j'entendois les feuilles des arbres frémir sous les gouttes de pluie. Je me levois en chemise, et ne voyant qu'un ciel bien étoilé, ou l'horizon coloré d'un beau pourpre, j'allois m'attrister entre mes draps, de ce qui enchantoit les autres à leur lever. D'où je concluois qu'un bon père est souvent très méchant homme; et je portois secrètement au fond de mon coeur, ce sentiment, honnête, doux et humain: périssent tous les autres, pourvu que mes enfants prospèrent, et je me persuade que c'est là pourtant un de ces cas où l'on estime moins et l'on n'en aime que davantage" (147–48.). Letter dated May 31, 1779. *Correspondance*, vol. 15.

12. Translation my own. "Apropos, j'oubliois de vous parler des deux grands malheurs arrivés à Madame Diderot. L'ingrat Bibi s'est envolé; et le perfide Collet, c'est un chat mari d'une chatte appellée Colette, a estropié un de ses serins et dépouillé le dos de sa serine d'un coup de griffe. Il n'y a point de bonheur parfait dans ce monde."

13. Translation my own. "Embrassez Caroillon pour moi; j'aime vos petits enfants à la folie, quoiqu'ils me trouvent mal élevé, depuis que je n'ai pu leur dire où Charlemagne étoit mort. Ménagez leur petite cervelle et leur poitrine délicate, ne bourrez ni leur tête ni leur estomac."

14. See Wilson, *Diderot*, p. 698, and *Correspondance* XV, p. 259, where the editors state that Diderot died of a "syndrome cardio-rénal" and add Angélique de Vandeul's description of his situation during the summer of 1781: "It was then that he started to complain about his health. He found that his brain was spent,

he said he had no new ideas. He was always weary, and getting dressed was an ordeal. His teeth didn't hurt, but he would gently pull them out as one might a pin. He ate less, read less. For three or four years he felt himself being destroyed, although those who did not know him well could not perceive this, for he always maintained his liveliness and tenderness in conversation." Translation my own. "Il commença alors à se plaindre tout à fait de sa santé; il trouvait sa tête usée. Il disait qu'il n'avait plus d'idées; il était toujours las; c'était pour lui un travail de s'habiller; ses dents ne le faisaient point souffrir, mais il les ôtait doucement comme on détache une épingle; il mangeait moins, il lisait moins: pendant trois ou quatre ans il a senti une destruction dont les étrangers ne pouvaient s'apercevoir, ayant toujours le même feu dans la conversation et la même douceur" (260).

15. See Wilson, *Diderot*, pp. 698–99.

16. See *Correspondance*, vol. 15: "Because of his knowledge in the field of physiology, Diderot knew how long he had left to live." Translation my own. "Grâce à ses connaissances physiologiques, Diderot savait quel temps il lui restait à vivre" (322).

17. Wilson, by contrast, took it seriously enough to finish his biography with a chapter entitled "The Appeal to Posterity."

18. *D'Alembert's Dream*, p. 182. "Vivant, j'agis et je réagis en masse . . . mort, j'agis et je réagis en molecules . . . je ne meurs donc point . . . Non, sans doute, je ne meurs point en se sens, ni moi, ni quoi qu'il soit . . . Naître, vivre et passer, c'est changer de forme. Et qu'importe une forme ou une autre?" *Rêve de d'Alembert*, pp. 103–4.

19. See the appendix to Starobinski, *Diderot, un diable de ramage*, entitled "Note sur l'angine de poitrine et la mort subite," pp. 410–13.

20. See *Correspondance*, Vol. 15, p. 322, with detailed documentation of Sophie's life circumstances during her final years.

21. See *Correspondance*, Vol. 15, p. 283 (as was normal and tacitly tolerated by the state censorship system, a city outside the kingdom of France [in this case London] was mentioned as the place of publication).

22. See Wilson, *Diderot*, pp. 704ff.

23. That generosity was most enthusiastically and beautifully described by his daughter Angélique in *Mémoires pour servir à l'histoire de la vie et des ouvrages de M. Diderot, par Mme de Vandeul, sa fille*, in Diderot, *Oeuvres completes*, ed. and with notes by Arthur M. Wilson et al. Vol. 1. (Paris, 1975): "He worked a

great deal; however, three quarters of his life were spent coming to the aid of those who were in need of his wallet, his talents, and his intercessions." Translation my own. "Il a beaucoup travaillé; cependant les trois quarts de sa vie ont été employés à secourir tous ceux qui avaient besoin de sa bourse, de ses talents et de ses demarches" (25).

24. Translation my own. "Ecoutez, mon ami; je travaille à une edition complète de mes ouvrages. J'ai quatre copistes qui me coûtent près de 120 l. par mois. Je suis épuisé, et je vous supplie de venir à mon secours. Vous me devez 349 l. Si vous pouvez me les rendre, sans vous gêner, tant mieux; s'il faut que vous vous gêniez, gênez vous." Letter to Sédaine (secretary of the Academy of Architecture), October 11, 1781.

25. Wilson, *Diderot*, pp. 700–701.

26. October 7, 1781, *Correspondance*, Vol. 15, pp. 272–73.

27. Translation my own. "Le 19 février 1784, il fut attaqué d'un violent crachement de sang. 'Voilà qui est fini, me dit-il, il faut nous séparer: je suis fort, ce sera peut-être pas dans deux jours, mais deux semaines, deux mois, un an . . .' J'étais si accoutumé à le croire, que je n'ai pas douté un instant la vérité; et pendant tout le temps de sa maladie, je n'arrivai pas chez lui qu'en tremblant, et je n'en sortais qu'avec l'idée que je ne le reverrais plus. [. . .] Le huitième jour de sa maladie, il causait: sa tête se troubla; il fit une phrase à contresens; il s'en aperçut, la recommença et se trompa encore. Alors il se leva: "Une apoplexie," me dit-il en se regardant dans une glace, en me faisant voir sa bouche qui tournait un peu et une main froide et sans mouvement. Il passe dans sa chambre, se met sur son lit, embrasse ma mère, lui dit adieu, m'embrasse, me dit adieu, explique l'endroit où l'on trouverait quelques livres qui ne lui appartenaient pas, et cesse de parler. Lui seul avait sa tête; tout le monde l'avait perdue" (Angélique's *Mémoires*, 32).

28. See the description of the February 1784 crisis and the recovery in Wilson, *Diderot*, pp. 709–10, ending with the sentence: "The flow of his energy had come to almost a complete halt."

29. See *Correspondance*, Vol. 15: "I am very upset to learn that Diderot is so ill, and to hear of his granddaughter's extraordinary misfortune." Translation my own. "Je suis bien fâchée de ce que Diderot est si mal et du malheur inoui arrivé à sa petite-fille" (pp. 334–35).

30. Translation my own. "Il désira quitter la campagne et venir y habiter; il en a joui douze jours; il en était enchanté. Ayant toujours logé dans un taudis,

il se trouvait dans un palais. Mais le corps s'affaiblissait chaque jour. La tête ne s'altérait pas: il était bien persuadé de sa fin prochaine, mais il n'en parlait pas [. . .]. La veille de sa mort, on lui apporta un lit plus commode; les ouvriers se tourmentaient pour le placer. 'Mes amis, leur dit-il, vous prenez là bien de la peine pour un meuble qui ne servira que quatre jours'" (Angélique's *Mémoires*, 32).

31. Translation my own. "La conversation s'engagea sur la philosophie et les différentes routes pour arriver à cette science: 'Le premier pas, dit-il, vers la philosophie, c'est l'incrédulité.' Ce mot est le dernier qu'il ait proféré devant moi: il était tard, je le quittai; j'espérai le revoir encore" (34).

32. Angélique erroneously wrote "samedi, 30 juillet" (see Wilson, *Diderot*, p. 883).

33. Translation my own. "Il se mit à table. Mangea une soupe, du mouton bouilli et de la chicorée. Il prit un abricot; ma mère voulut l'empêcher de manger ce fruit. 'Mais que diable veux-tu que cela me fasse?' Il le mangea, appuya son coude sur la table pour manger quelques cerises en compote, toussa légèrement. Ma mère lui fit une question; comme il gardait le silence, elle leva la tète, le regarda: il n'était plus (35).

34. See Starobinski, *Diderot, un diable de ramage*, p. 10.

35. Translation my own. "Mon père croyait qu'il était sage d'ouvrir ceux qui n'existaient plus; il croyait cette opération utile aux vivants. Il me l'avait plus d'une fois demandé; il l'a donc été. La tête était aussi parfaite, aussi bien conservée que celle d'un homme de vingt ans. Un des poumons était plein d'eau; son coeur, les deux tiers plus gros que celui des autres personnes. Il avait la vésicule du fiel entièrement sèche: il n'y avait plus de la matière bilieuse, mais elle contenait vingt et une pierres dont la moindre était grosse comme une noisette."

36. Translation my own. "Son enterrement n'a pas prouvé que de légères difficultés. Le curé de Saint-Roch lui envoya un prêtre pour le veiller; il mit plus de pompe que de la simplicité dans cette affreuse cérémonie."

37. Wilson, *Diderot*, pp. 712f.

Lightning Source UK Ltd.
Milton Keynes UK
UKHW010121200321
380655UK00001BA/21/J